DILETTANTE

DILETTANTE

**True Tales
of Excess, Triumph,
and Disaster**

DANA BROWN

BALLANTINE BOOKS·NEW YORK

Published in the United States by Ballantine Books,
an imprint of Random House, a division of
Penguin Random House LLC, New York.

BALLANTINE and the HOUSE colophon
are registered trademarks of Penguin Random House LLC.

Grateful acknowledgment is made to Hal Leonard LLC for permission to reprint an
excerpt from "Can I Kick It" words and music by Lou Reed, copyright © 1990
by Oakfield Avenue Music Ltd. All rights administered by Sony Music Publishing
(US) LLC, 424 Church Street, Suite 1200, Nashville, TN 37219. International
copyright secured. All rights reserved. Reprinted by permission of Hal Leonard LLC.

Hardback ISBN 978-0-593-15848-7
Ebook ISBN 978-0-593-15849-4

Printed in the United States of America on acid-free paper

randomhousebooks.com

1 2 3 4 5 6 7 8 9

First Edition

Book design by Diane Hobbing

For Aimee, Izzy, and Ollie, who taught me to love,
Graydon, who taught me everything else,
and Adrian, who I miss

If you can dream—and not make dreams your master;
If you can think—and not make thoughts your aim;
If you can meet with Triumph and Disaster
And treat those two impostors just the same

—RUDYARD KIPLING

Can I kick it? (*Yes, you can!*)
Can I kick it? (*Yes, you can!*)
Can I kick it? (*Yes, you can!*)
Well, I'm gone (*Go on then!*)

—A TRIBE CALLED QUEST

Introduction

There's a tradition that originated in medieval times. When you turned twenty-one, you were given a key to the home. You were now considered old enough to take on the responsibility of being an adult and a senior member of the family. In some cultures, this tradition lives on. Nowadays, it's mostly symbolic, a metaphoric key to your future, a key charm on a necklace or bracelet, maybe an antique key to carry around in a pocket or to sit on your desk. While I didn't recognize it at the time, on April 25, 1994, when I was twenty-one years old, I was given a key.

The key I received wasn't from a family member. It wasn't an actual key nor was it a symbolic key—it was a job. An entry-level job at a magazine. Not just any magazine, but one of the most popular, high-profile, successful, and culturally relevant magazines around, *Vanity Fair*, as an assistant to its editor, Graydon Carter. For the next twenty-five years, that key would unlock doors that would define my life, and the person I became.

At the time I was fairly aimless, a college dropout living in a fourth-floor walk-up railroad apartment in Manhattan's grubby East Village: two bedrooms; lumpy futons on rickety loft beds, one for me and one for my twenty-five-year-old brother; $550 a month; mice; roaches; walls thinner than the junkies passed out in the building's vestibule. There was a bodega on the ground floor that sold nothing but cocaine, its storefront window covered with faded yellow-and-red cans of Café Bustelo. The coffee wasn't for sale, the cans simply there to obstruct the view of the store's interior, which was nothing more than barren shelves and a Dominican guy behind two-inch-thick bulletproof glass. The cocaine was low-grade stuff, cut with who knows what, but it worked in a pinch, if it was late and the decent stuff had run out.

The Hells Angels were my neighbors, just a few buildings east. The Angels had moved into the neighborhood in 1969, bought an old tenement building, and turned it into a clubhouse, making East Third Street between First and Second Avenues the "safest block in Manhattan." Fifty years later they'd sell that building at 77 East Third Street for $10 million to a developer, the aging Angels having finally met a foe they couldn't vanquish with pipes, chains, and tire irons. "We're being harassed by the yuppies down here," one Angel told the *New York Post* about the imminent sale. "When the neighborhood was shit, nobody minded us." Gentrification is no victimless crime.

At the time, I had no future plans. I hadn't given a second of thought to a career. Working at a magazine was not something I aspired to or was equipped to do. But what began as an opportunity I couldn't refuse, something that I thought I might do for a year or two—*if* I made it that far—eventually became my life, the halls of Condé Nast's building on Madison Avenue the beginning of my journey into adulthood and the start of a career that would continue for a quarter of a century. I learned a lot during that time—about writing, journalism, culture, media, glamour, nostalgia, and maybe most important, the power of words and the importance of narrative.

I learned a lot about myself, too. *Vanity Fair* was the first institution I felt connected to, that accepted me for who I was. It provided me both an education and a surrogate family, with Graydon at the center of it all, as both my mentor and my guardian angel.

I bore witness to the power, vitality, and culture-shaping abilities of journalism and monthly magazines in what would turn out to be a golden age for the medium. We didn't just tell the story of our time, we played a part in driving the narrative for contemporary culture, celebrated its highs and shuddered at its lows. Some of what we did was frivolous. But a lot of it was important. Journalism was always considered a highly respected and vaunted industry, critical to society and democracy.

Language, and writing, is what separates us from our monkey ancestors. It's what makes us human, for better or worse. Stories, and narratives, have a way of taking hold and not letting go.* Which is why the truth is so important. But narratives take hold whether they're true or not. Journalism is our guardrail. It's our story, the official record of humanity. When it's called into question, attacked, or practiced in bad faith, then the truth becomes subjective, and as a result, everything falls apart.

At *Vanity Fair,* we worked hard and took our role as a major responsibility. And when the hard work was done, we had fun. I might have had more fun than most. Who am I kidding. . . . I was a fucking dilettante, a role I assumed and perfected. Ultimately, my identity and my career became intertwined into one tight weave, to the point that I couldn't tell where one began and the other ended. And if your job is creating a fantasy, a luxury item— and that's what we did—it's understandable why that would be appealing.

The story of the magazine business in the waning days of the twentieth century and the dawning of the twenty-first is also the story of New York, a place I have called home for most of my life and have developed a grumpy middle-aged revulsion to (while I'm simultaneously willing to admit to a begrudging acceptance of its strange new traditions and culture). It's a city that's always attracted dreamers and misfits, artists and musicians, writers and weirdos, rich and poor, the aimless and ambitious alike, bound by the lore and lure of this place and the endless opportunities it presented. They were the fuel that made this place burn brightly for so many years. Inspired by the city, they gave us all that great art and poetry and journalism and literature and music, each generation's work inspiring a younger crop of creative immigrants and natives alike, passed down like an older sibling's book or record collection, who would take it, twist it into something new, something wonderful, from abstract expressionism to graffiti, from Rothko to Basquiat, from the beats to punk, from punk to

* Religion is the most obvious example to reach for here.

hip-hop, which might just be the last great art form to emerge from New York's cultural cauldron, the end of the line.

As I sat in a SoHo café eating vegan sugarless date-sweetened chocolate cashew pudding and drinking an oat milk cortado after a particularly *brutal* Barry's Bootcamp (see: *begrudging acceptance*), staring at my iPhone, A Tribe Called Quest's 1990 song "Can I Kick It" came on the café's speakers, with its sample of Lou Reed's 1972 New York anthem "Walk on the Wild Side," inspired by all that New York poetry from the fifties and Warhol's band of Factory misfits in the sixties (and produced by beloved New Yorker and immigrant David Bowie!)—more than half a century of New York's towering cultural influence and achievements in one sublime track, linking the poetry of the past to the beat of the present. There may be no song quite as quintessentially New York as "Can I Kick It," a not-so-missing link from then to now and everything in between. I lost focus for a moment as my mind wandered, thinking back to the first time I heard it all those years ago, a different time, the same place but a very different place, my foot tapping and my lips moving involuntarily. (Proust can have his madeleines. I've got Tribe.)

As I sat there, I feared we'd witnessed the end of that mythological place that gave us so much important culture and so many important people over the years, a place that could produce a song like "Walk on the Wild Side" and then reimagine and repackage it as "Can I Kick It" a generation later, the end of New York as the cultural capital of the world, and the end of the naked ambition, unabashed reinvention, and propulsive forward cultural progress that made it so. The end of the creative mecca that I'd aspired to be a part of and managed to navigate somewhat successfully, and then, in middle age, was forced to watch go through such profound and disappointing changes. As an old friend and early-nineties partner in crime Marc Spitz—the writer, not the swimmer—once wrote, "When your own Manhattan starts to vanish, you feel compelled to tell the story of what used to be there." Marc never got the chance. He died in 2017 at the age of forty-seven, my age as I write these words.

This book is perhaps a paean to *Vanity Fair,* Condé Nast, the magazine business; the nineties and the aughts; the end of the millennium and the American Century; the highs and lows of culture, journalism, media, and technology; disruption and change; the zeitgeist; baby boomers, Gen X, millennials, and Gen Z; New York the place, New York the *idea;* generational shifts and rifts; a country attempting to pivot to whatever's next, struggling with an identity crisis and what the hell we are— individually and collectively.

This is a book about success and failure and a generation caught in the middle, with one foot firmly planted in the past and one on shaky ground in the present while staring over the precipice into an unknown future. My generation hit middle age at a time of immense cultural and technological disruption; we're a tiny generation *squeezed* on either side by giants—the one in front of us unwilling to cede control, the ones behind us slowly taking over—who couldn't be further apart culturally or emotionally, Gen X caught in the middle of a conversation between strangers who don't speak the same language but desperately *need* to understand each other. We're interpreters on a cultural battlefield; not quite the colonizers and not quite the natives, we're something in between, nothing if not expendable. I can't think of another time and place where the dynamic has shifted so drastically within just a few generations. This is a book about the rise and fall of a great civilization. A universal account of change. And my own personal journey through this fertile tableau and morass. Part memoir, part social history, part journalistic exploration and cultural criticism. A lament, celebration, and elegy. The biography, obituary, and capstone of an era.

I've written much of this book in New York City, my home and co-conspirator for most of my life. I lost my virginity here, fell in love, had my heart broken more than a few times, got married, had my two children on its soil. I wrote bits and pieces of these pages elsewhere, too. I wrote on planes, on trains, and in airports. Movement and travel and a change of location can be creatively inspiring. Occasionally they have the opposite effect. But what never fails to inspire is that view of Manhattan from the Long Island Expressway as you come over that final ridge heading toward the Midtown Tunnel after landing at JFK, that warm embrace of stone and steel, the comfort of home.

It's fascinating to look back and see so clearly just how much a place can shape you, become not only inextricably linked with your identity but a character in the story of your life. It's also fascinating to write about yourself. You become an archaeologist, or anthropologist, of your own psyche. It's an experience that can change your opinions of your own narrative and the past, which has a profound effect on the present and future. What can also warp your view of the past, present, and future is a once-in-a-century worldwide catastrophe. Like, say, a global pandemic. Because out of nowhere, that fucking thing came along, at first softly, but then it hit like a Mack truck one day, right smack in the middle of March 2020. (Beware the Ides of March.)

Twenty twenty had a profound effect on me, as it did for many. But somehow, at a time when everything seemed hopeless, apocalyptic even, I felt a sense of optimism for the first time in years. Maybe this was the beginning of some great realignment and cleansing that we had all been secretly yearning for, *the flood* ("the wickedness of man was great in the earth"). Perhaps it's naïve of me, but it gave me some hope for the future of America, whatever comes next, for the world and the generations behind mine who will have to pick up the pieces and rebuild, form something new out of a lump of neglected and misshapen clay. It gave me newfound optimism for my children and future grandchildren, who will be part of what I hope is a rebuilding process. And maybe the biggest surprise was it gave me hope for New York, which is as much mine as it is everybody's. The city may suffer in the short term, and be fundamentally changed, but will somehow be okay because it's New York. And New York never turns its back on you.

I can't wait to see what these kids do with the place.

—*Dana Brown, New York City, 2021*

DILETTANTE

Chapter 1

We all have a moment or chance encounter that defines us, sets the narrative of our life in motion. Newton and that apple; John meeting Paul at St. Peter's Church in Liverpool; Mick running into Keith on that Dartford train platform; Justin meeting Britney, I'm guessing in Orlando, both head to toe in denim of some era-specific wash. My origin story may not be as significant as those, but it was to me, and it began behind the bar of a restaurant in midtown Manhattan in April 1994.

At the time, I was toiling away behind that bar, living off tips, residing in that roach-infested dump with my older brother Nathaniel in the East Village. Only twenty-one, I had a spotty record in life already, the shadow of wild and unproductive teen years chasing me into early adulthood. I had no skills, no real passions or interests. I had a vague interest in being a rock star and was playing guitar in a few bands, but in reality I wasn't a very good musician, and debilitating stage fright was a roadblock to that fantasy. Expectations for my future were low. The youngest of four, I was the one who wasn't talked about, or if I was, the topic was quickly changed to something more pleasant. I wasn't just the black sheep, I was a complete fuckup.

I was quiet and shy when I was young, sensitive to a fault. A late-in-the-year birthday meant I was always small for my age, more a follower than a leader. I wasn't a bad kid, never had any of that toxic masculinity that plagues so many boys. I was kind and friendly, but I lacked confidence, suffering from crushing insecurity and gutting self-doubt that only got worse as I moved into my teens. I began biting my fingernails obsessively, to the point that my fingertips were so swollen and disfigured that I always kept them hidden in my pockets or behind my back.

I was never good at much, especially school. And when you're never good at anything as a child, you get frustrated, and eventually stop trying, and sometimes end up rebelling. Watching others succeed and find their passions just made me feel smaller, more insignificant, and sadder. How come I couldn't have *that*?! Negative and nihilistic thoughts calcified. I retreated into the cavern of my own head, always thinking there was somewhere else I was meant to be, somewhere better, or just different from a suffocating suburb of New York City. A geographic cure.

Looking back, I didn't quite know where or how I fit into the world, and it made me uncomfortable and detached. I had two imaginary friends when I was little. They were from another planet, or dimension, and lived behind my bedroom wall. I'd spend hours alone, talking to them in some made-up language. They might have been figments of my imagination, but they were *mine*, and they understood me. In a cruel twist, I could never get to them or actually see their faces behind that wall.

I barely made it out of high school.* And not having gone to college, I missed out on an important experience—more than the academics, the formative friendships that are cemented over those years. Those core relationships that last a lifetime for many and create a support network as you begin to develop and make that passage into adulthood.

I knew a lot of people and always had an active social life. In the spring of 1994, it was co-workers and other acquaintances from the neighborhood. I frequented downtown's bars and clubs, staying out all night *every* night and managing to get into all kinds of trouble—I was a lot of fun, especially when there were drugs and drinking involved, and there always were. But I didn't have many close friends. I had difficulty connecting with people, especially those around my age. I never felt good enough, and that ended up making me feel self-conscious and, worse, desperate for

---

* *Two* high schools, actually.

approval and acceptance. I was able to move on from friendships without sentiment, like an emotional transient, always looking for something or someone that would make me feel more comfortable.

Of course, this level of introspection and self-evaluation isn't available to most twenty-one-year-old kids—it only comes with maturity and time*—but this is who I was back then, a bit of a car crash, working as a barback and occasional bartender at a restaurant called 44. For those who were in New York in the early to midnineties, especially those in media, the entertainment business, fashion, or the arts—and back then, those were the only people who mattered in New York—44 needs no explanation. It would be like describing clouds to a fighter pilot. It was a place so sublime, so awe inspiring, that it was hard to believe it had been built by human hands or conjured in the imagination of a human mind. And yet, like the pyramids, the Taj Mahal, or the Great Wall, it had been.

To those who have no idea what I'm talking about, 44 was, quite simply, a restaurant in a hotel lobby in midtown Manhattan. But calling 44 a restaurant is like calling the sun a star. It was so much more than that, and for a brief, shining period, roughly 1990 to 1995, 44 might have been the most important cultural institution in New York City. And while 44 still exists, in name and location, 44 no longer exists.

44 took its name from its address—44 West Forty-fourth Street. Between Fifth and Sixth Avenues, closer to Sixth, on the south side of the street, behind two giant, unmarked lacquered wood doors, the words ROYALTON HOTEL etched in stone above them, visible if you craned your neck just right. You could walk right by it without knowing that on the other side of those doors was a flourishing civilization you didn't know existed, a party you weren't invited to. There was always a young man or two standing in front, about six feet tall, sample size, cheekbones for days, an expensive haircut, in a minimalist Mao-like dark blue uniform,

* And some therapy.

the outfit as unmarked as the hotel's doors—no name tags or hotel branding to defile the look. The bellmen worked for the Royalton Hotel, which was owned by Ian Schrager.

If Ian Schrager's name sounds familiar, it's because of his association with Studio 54, the most storied New York nightclub ever. That is, until December 14, 1978, when federal agents raided the West Fifty-fourth Street club. What they found were cooked books showing extensive profit skimming, garbage bags full of cash stashed behind the ceiling panels of the club's office, and five ounces of cocaine (though in fairness you could have found five ounces of cocaine just about anywhere in New York in 1978). Ian Schrager and his partner, Steve Rubell, were arrested and, in 1980, pleaded guilty to tax evasion and sentenced to three and a half years in prison, spending a little over a year in jail, first in Manhattan, then in Alabama.

Once out of the clink, Schrager and Rubell turned their back on the nightclub business and got into the hotel business. This was at least partly out of necessity: They were ex-cons, so neither man could get a liquor license. Their Morgans Hotel was located on the east side of Madison Avenue between Thirty-seventh and Thirty-eighth, a block up from the Morgan Library. They imported some of that nightclub flair and high-design aesthetic to their new venture, dimming the lights, painting the walls in dark, muted tones, a fur throw pillow here, a faded leather club chair from the Paris flea markets there, Robert Mapplethorpe prints on the walls, Calvin Klein–designed uniforms on the hotel staff, who were all gorgeous. They also redefined the hotel restaurant and lobby as more than just a place to grab a quick meal or read a newspaper, but a proper scene. And that's how the boutique hotel was born, and quickly copied.

But before they could open, there was the issue of the elusive liquor license. The solution they came up with was simple in retrospect: Let's rent out the restaurant and lobby space to some restaurateur and let *them* get a liquor license and make the food and serve the drinks. After all, Schrager and Rubell were hoteliers now, and hotelier and restaurateur are two very different classes in the hospitality caste system. Who wants the headache of dealing with food and beverage, pouring drinks, slinging hash, sniffing fish—let's bring in some schmuck, collect a monthly rent check, focus on the hotel, and make *real* money. And that's exactly what they did.

In 1984, Morgans Hotel opened its doors for business to a collective gasp. It would turn out to be a trial balloon, and it floated up up up, so with proof of concept in their back pocket, Schrager and Rubell decided to expand and, like they'd done before with Studio 54, hunt bigger game in the heart of midtown Manhattan.

The two opened the Royalton Hotel on Forty-fourth Street and the Paramount Hotel across Times Square on Forty-sixth in quick succession, in 1988 and 1990, respectively.* While they were both red-hot out of the gate, it was the Royalton that really landed.

Looking back, there were a number of reasons the Royalton popped. But the biggest was French designer Philippe Starck's lobby, which was anarchic and upscale, edgy and elegant in a way that hadn't really been seen before. It was dark but thoughtfully lit. Everything was purposeful, in its right place, no detail too small to go unnoticed or unattended, not an inch of the place an afterthought. There was an endless royal-blue carpet running down the long central passageway, an artery straight through the heart of the lobby, almost a full city block long, like a fashion-show runway—it didn't matter who you were, every walk down it was dramatic and flamboyant. It made everyone feel like a star, like the main attraction. A row of thick polished columns ran alongside the carpet on the left, separating a long, recessed seating area with chunky white couches and high-backed club chairs that looked up at the runway, like it was a stage, as if you were in a theater. And it *was* theater. On the right was a long, dark-wood-paneled wall, curving slowly, subtly, with glowing horn sconces

---

* Rubell died of AIDS-related complications in 1989 at forty-five and didn't live to see the opening of the Paramount.

separating it from the high ceiling. The hotel's front desk was hidden, recessed within one of these curved panels, followed by a passageway to the elevators.

The Royalton lobby was a palace as imagined by a mad king and executed by a madman. There was something almost early twentieth century about it all, an old vision of the future, along with an *actual* vision of the future, as if Phillipe Starck had traveled back in time, then forward, had a look around at both, taken notes, come home, and created a pastiche of the two, dueling visions of the future from the past and the *actual* future, which only he had seen, interpreted for the present. I once overheard Karl Lagerfeld, fashion icon and 44 regular, say, "This lobby is so amazing that it will take people another twenty years to realize just how amazing it is."

And that's just the lobby—44, the hotel's restaurant, was in the back, and a natural extension of the lobby, one flowing seamlessly into the other, the same but different, like fraternal twins. Four big lime-green velvet banquettes lined the back left wall. Those four banquettes watched over the dining room like the gods on Mount Olympus. A few rows of white-tableclothed tables, two-tops and four-tops, filled the middle of the room, leading to a long black bar. In a devious wink and nod to form over function, the stools Starck designed had only three legs, which led to drunks' toppling over onto the floor at a rate of three or four or more an evening.

And the urinal! The Royalton lobby's men's room had the most talked about urinal since Marcel Duchamp's—a four-foot-wide, communal, stainless steel wall with a constant cascade of water flowing down it like Niagara Falls.

44 was run by Brian McNally, an East London–born restaurateur. He started as a bartender in the late seventies at One Fifth, a hot downtown restaurant whose name was also its location (there was a lot of that going around), then opened the Odeon, an ode to an imagined midcentury Parisian bistro and named after a London movie theater, in the fall of 1980, with his brother Keith and Keith's soon-to-be wife, Lynn Wagenknecht. It was on a dead cor-

ner in TriBeCa—West Broadway and Thomas—when TriBeCa was a no-man's-land, not cool, not *uncool*, just a bunch of old warehouse buildings and a smattering of artists.

The Odeon became a destination. Some of its regulars included Warhol, Basquiat, John Belushi and the rest of the *Saturday Night Live* cast, Tom Wolfe, Scorsese, De Niro, and up-and-coming literary stars like Jay McInerney and Bret Easton Ellis. The Odeon not only became a destination, it created TriBeCa as we know it today. It would become an iconic New York restaurant, endure, and help define the decade it opened in and shaped, even landing on the cover of the book that would define New York in the eighties, McInerney's *Bright Lights, Big City*. It would launch the careers of the McNallys and Wagenknecht, who went on to open some of New York's most famous restaurants, including Balthazar, Pastis, and Indochine, to name just a few.

Ian Schrager, looking for someone new to take over the lease on 44, reached out to Brian, the cool downtown restaurateur and raconteur, to see if he'd be interested in taking his show to uncool midtown. Brian thought about it, hemmed and hawed: *Midtown? What do I know about midtown? I do downtown.* Which is exactly why Schrager wanted him. He wanted to bring downtown uptown to midtown.

According to legend, Brian's friend, fellow London expat, and future 44 regular Anna Wintour convinced him to take the offer. At that time, Anna was a few years into her job as the editor of Condé Nast's *Vogue*. She was a star. Not yet a superstar and household name, not yet Nuclear Wintour and the cultural icon she'd become after being portrayed by Meryl Streep in *The Devil Wears Prada*, but a New York star, in a business that was star heavy, especially at Condé Nast, whose office building was a block and a half away, at 350 Madison Avenue. There were Tina Brown at *Vanity Fair*, then *The New Yorker*; Art Cooper at *GQ*; James Truman at *Details*, who would be named editorial director of Condé Nast in the spring of 1994; and Condé Nast's billionaire owner, Si Newhouse. It was the age of the glossy magazine and the celebrity editor—they were the arbiters of taste, the translators of culture and style to the culture-and-style-hungry masses. They decided what was cool, what was important, what was necessary, what made it onto their pages, what people would be talking about, watching, reading, wearing, *thinking*.

Brian signed the lease, shook Schrager's hand, brought some of that downtown edginess and cool, piped Leonard Cohen into the lobby, hired gorgeous waiters and waitresses of all different ethnicities and dressed them in black, and hired a young chef named Geoffrey Zakarian, who elevated the food, put a hamburger on an English muffin and charged an unheard-of $20 for it.*

Anna showed up one day for lunch, sat in one of those lime-green banquettes, ordered a burger, no bun, mashed potatoes, and a cappuccino. Then Tina Brown. Then Si Newhouse. Then, like an avalanche, *everyone*. 44 became *the* publishing and fashion power lunch spot. The buzz carried over to the evening, to the couches in the lobby and the bars, a younger publishing and fashion crowd, looking for a contact high from the power lunch scene, mingling with movie stars and rock stars and models and fashion designers, drinking late into the night, doing coke in the bathrooms, talking, flirting, hooking up, getting a room. It was hotel lobby as dinner *and* the show, a whole night rolled into one place, *a destination*. It was the convergence of nightclub, restaurant, and hotel. It was as if Studio 54, Morgans, and the Odeon all merged into one magnificent existence.

This was where you could find me most nights, in my black uniform, with a blue apron tied tightly around my waist, behind that long stone bar, quietly cleaning glasses, running around refilling ice buckets and replacing empty bottles of liquor on the glass shelves, trying to stay out of the way. Like many kids in their early twenties, I was unsure what shape my life would take. But I wasn't thinking about it. I assumed something might eventually reveal itself to me, but I had no idea when or what that might be.

---

* Geoffrey would go on to culinary-world celebrity in the next decades thanks to the recently launched Food Network.

And I was in no rush. At the time, I didn't think it would have anything to do with that glamorous, Technicolor world that was playing out in front of me on the other side of that bar. But it did, and 44 would turn out to be my entry point, the place where the narrative of the rest of my life began.

Chapter 2

How did I end up walking into the Royalton Hotel looking for a job a year earlier? By providence. By design. I'd heard about it from a friend of a friend who knew someone who had a sister whose boyfriend worked there, a place full of big-tipping stars—of the movie and rock and fashion variety—who said he walked out of work every night with three hundred bucks cash. That didn't just *sound* like a lot of money, that *was* a lot of money—a far cry from the slightly above minimum wage I was making at my current job.

In early 1993, I was living in what was then known as Little Italy, although thanks to the rules of gentrification it would soon be dubbed the cute and posh-sounding Nolita. Fifty-five Spring Street, between Lafayette and Mulberry, was a beat-up old tenement building. I had moved in with a girl who had recently graduated from Bennington College, a friend of a friend of a friend. *You'll love her, she's great.* I didn't, she wasn't. We disliked each other immediately and wholeheartedly.

It was a ground-floor apartment in the back of the building, one big room looking north through dirty windows over a rat-infested courtyard, a dark kitchen tucked into the interior of the apartment. There were two loft beds, one in the main room and one over the kitchen, which was mine. There was a shower in the living room. It costs $500 a month and calling it a shithole would be offensive to proper shitholes everywhere.

I was working in the kitchen of Union Square Cafe, Danny Meyer's upscale bistro on Sixteenth Street, as the dinnertime pastry expediter—I looked about twelve, and everyone called me

"Pastry Child"—which meant I was in charge of plating desserts. This was before the foodie revolution of the next decade would take hold and being a cook or a chef was suddenly considered an art form and an actual career choice. Back then kitchens were rough places, full of alcoholics, drug addicts, ex-cons, and assorted characters with anger management issues who wouldn't have been able to hold down any other kind of job. The waitstaff was mostly downtown actors and actresses, singers and artists.

Working in a kitchen was high-stress, yeoman's work, *hell*, overwhelming during those post-dinner dessert rushes, followed by a night of heavy drinking until four A.M. with the other cooks and waitstaff at the Cedar Tavern on University Place. It didn't take me long to figure out that kitchen work was not my calling, but becoming an underage regular at the Cedar Tavern was almost worth the suffering—it was a fabled old bar, its heyday in the fifties and sixties, as a generation of young artists and writers and musicians were making Greenwich Village the cool cultural capital of the world, a scene that would color downtown Manhattan for generations. Pollock, de Kooning, Rothko, Kerouac, Ginsberg, O'Hara, *Dylan*—the through-line of modern popular culture able to be traced through the Cedar's walls. It was a New York landmark, the sounds of ancient fistfights and ghostly whispers of poetry and lyrics and discussions about art bouncing around its walls if you listened closely and had too much to drink.

But the Cedar Tavern would always be there, and I wanted out of the kitchen. I needed to manifest destiny. So, one afternoon that week, on my day off, I swung by my brother's East Village apartment, borrowed one of his dress shirts, combed my hair, and took the F train from the Second Avenue stop to Forty-second Street.

It was only six stops to midtown, but I might as well have been taking a journey to a different world, like those kids stepping into a wardrobe in blitzed-out England and finding themselves in Narnia. Downtown was tenements, dirty streets, the homeless everywhere, shady characters, *delis that sold nothing but cocaine, for*

God's sake, and grubby kids like me trying to scrape by while not getting murdered; midtown was skyscrapers, businessmen, commuters, wide avenues, and packed sidewalks, the New York they shot for the opening scene of *every* New York–set studio film. Everyone walked with purpose. Even the cabbies honked with purpose. Midtown was for grown-ups. Downtown was the soiled and stained kids' table.

I walked two blocks up Sixth Avenue, turned onto Forty-fourth Street, and walked right by the two big, imposing, glossy wood doors of the Royalton. I crossed the street to reconnoiter, and have a panic attack, terrified, a crippling insecurity rearing its ugly head. The doors were guarded by two sentries in dark blue, creaseless armor. They didn't protect the entrance with traditional weapons like swords and spears, but with cold stares, scowls, and really terrific hair. The implication was clear: *None shall pass.* I spied the scene from across the street, chain-smoking nervously, shaking my head, questioning my decision, talking to myself like a crazy person, thinking about turning around and going home. *What was I thinking? What would they want with some dingy kid?*

I finally got my nerve up, crossed the street, and made contact with the first sentry I encountered.

"Hey," I said, trying to sound calm, confident, and cool. "Who would I talk to about getting a job?"

He looked me over, searching for flaws, looking for a reason to tell me to beat it, but to my surprise, he didn't.

"At the hotel or the restaurant?" he said, trying to mask his midwestern accent.

"What's the difference?"

"Well, I work for the hotel—the Royalton. I'm a bellman. The restaurant, 44, is in the back. Different owners, different jobs."

"What does a bellman do?"

"I open the doors for guests, hail cabs, help them with their luggage. The restaurant has waiters, bartenders, busboys, usual restaurant stuff."

I could open doors, and hailing cabs sounded easy, but the bags part sounded like a lot of heavy lifting; this guy looked big and strong, a working animal, like a really pretty ox. That didn't sound fun, nor did I think I was suited for it. I was already working in a restaurant, and while I had been in the kitchen and didn't have any front-of-the-house experience, it was those tips I was after, so that answered that.

"I guess the restaurant."

"Head to the back. There's a podium on the left. Ask for Jonathan. He's the manager."

That's it? I waited for a catch that never arrived.

"Good luck." He opened the giant doors. No turning back now. And there it was, the Royalton lobby, shimmering like a mirage in front of me. I was like Moses, stumbling across the well of Midian, or Cortés, as the jungle thicket is parted to reveal the glory of Tenochtitlán. I moved in cautiously.

It was late afternoon, the lunch rush was over, and the hordes of post-work drinkers hadn't arrived, so it wasn't crowded, but it still had a certain buzz about it, hinting that something *had* happened here earlier and that something *would* happen later. A stunning, long-limbed cocktail waitress, with short hair and bright red lipstick, dressed in black with a dark blue apron, ambled by, elegantly carrying a tray of drinks toward a group of women having an afternoon cocktail. An attractive busboy, also in all black, polished a cocktail table until the glass reflected like perfectly still water.

I slowly made my way down the long blue carpet toward the back of the lobby and 44, nervously looking around, waiting for security to rush and tackle me, drag me out by my hair, tell me, *Go back downtown, you dingy kid.*

I finally reached the dark wood podium. There was a woman not just standing at it but towering over it, a tall redhead, leaning over a giant hardbound book that looked a thousand years old— I could make out line after line after line of names and numbers, numbers and names, like passages in the Bible. Her intensity frightened me, the way she studied that book, and I thought about turning back but instead just froze a few feet in front of her—*Maybe if I don't make a move, she won't notice I'm here.*

After a few moments my plan fell apart spectacularly, as she looked up and stared at me for a few uncomfortable seconds.

"Can I help you?"

Suddenly, I couldn't speak. Words got lost somewhere on the path from my brain to my mouth.

"Are you okay?"

"I . . . was looking for Jonathan."

"Is he expecting you?"

"No . . . I'm here for a job."

"Doing what exactly?!"

"I . . . I don't know."

"Have you ever worked in a restaurant before?"

"I work at Union Square Cafe. In the kitchen."

"So, you'll want to talk to Geoffrey. He's the chef."

"Oh, no, I don't want to work in kitchens anymore. I thought . . ."

"Do you have any front-of-the-house experience?"

"Um. No . . ."

She stepped out from behind the podium and looked me up and down, walking around me in a slow circle. She shrugged. "This could work. Maybe. A haircut, some better shoes. Let me see if Jonathan's around. Have a seat." She pointed to a table behind the podium and then walked off, disappearing behind a swinging door nearby.

A few moments later, a man emerged. He was around thirty—which to a twenty-year-old seemed quite grown-up—and dressed in a black suit with a black shirt, like a Bond villain or a general in Andy Warhol's private army, if he had one. He walked with a sense of purpose, a stern look on his face. He stopped to carefully wipe a smudge off the shiny black marble bar, staring menacingly at that smudge as if it had insulted him.

Jonathan made his way over to the table slowly, taking in the room, making sure everything was in its proper place. A handful of busboys, beginning to set up for dinner service, arranged flowers and silverware and glasses on the tables, watching him intently from the corners of their eyes, carefully reading his body language. He lowered himself into the chair across from me without saying a word. As if by magic, a cappuccino appeared in front of him, delivered by a busboy who slipped in and out like an apparition. Jonathan lifted the elegant white porcelain cup off its saucer and took a sip. He put the cup back down. He looked displeased. The busboy quickly reappeared.

"What is this?" Jonathan asked him.

"A cappuccino."

"I know what it's *supposed* to be. . . . What is *this*?"

The busboy nervously picked up the elegant little cup and saucer and walked off quickly. Jonathan looked across the table at me with a coy smile.

"What's your name?"

I told him everything: my name, where I was working, why I was now sitting in front of him. Jonathan nodded. He wrote something down and asked me for my phone number.

The busboy arrived with a fresh cappuccino and placed it on the table. He stood there motionless as Jonathan raised it to his lips, took a sip, then slowly put it back down as the busboy ran off.

"Do you know what was wrong with the first cappuccino?"

I shook my head.

"Nothing, really."

He paused dramatically and took another sip, a mischievous grin on his face.

A former tank commander in the Israel Defense Forces, Jonathan came across as a frightening taskmaster and boss, as evidenced by the fear he instilled in all the busboys, but there was something playful about him, as if he wasn't taking it nearly as seriously as he seemed to, like it was all a joke that he was in on.

"When can you start?"

This caught me off guard—it couldn't possibly be this easy—but I told him as soon as possible.

"Let me introduce you to Brian."

Jonathan got up and disappeared behind the swinging door by the bar. The busboy arrived and placed a cappuccino in front of me. I thanked him, then sat silently and waited for a few minutes. I watched as the other busboys prepared the dining room for dinner, setting tables carefully, polishing silverware and wineglasses. A tall bartender stood behind the bar, checking liquor bottles on the glass shelves lining the wall, placing matchbooks in ashtrays on the bar. In a few hours this place would be packed, the air full of smoke and the buzz of conversation.

Jonathan returned with another man, older than him, maybe in his midforties. He was elegantly dressed in a dark suit and a white shirt, no tie, and had unkempt black hair, with soft curls in the back, speckled with gray. I stood up, shook his hand.

"Brian McNally," he said with a heavy working-class, East London accent.

I introduced myself. Brian looked down at the piece of paper that Jonathan had scribbled my name and phone number on, then looked up, like a cop about to interrogate a perp.

"Your surname—English?"

"No . . . it was changed at Ellis Island a hundred years ago."

"Where were they coming from?"

"Eastern Europe, Russia . . . it's unclear."

"Jewish?"

"Yeah. On my father's side."

"What's the other side?"

"Irish and German. Queens, Brooklyn."

He looked back at the piece of paper.

"Your phone number—an old SoHo exchange. Where do you live?"

"Spring Street. Just off Lafayette."

Brian nodded in approval. But how did he know just by my phone number, and what did he mean by "an old SoHo exchange"? If you're of a certain age, or familiar with old movies, you can skip this next paragraph. For the rest of you:

In olden times, there was an actual person manning telephone switchboards. It seems like every old movie—to use an obvious

example, because it illustrates my point twofold, *B Utterfield 8*—
has a cutaway to a woman (and it's always a woman, and she always
looks and sounds the same in every film, same glasses) in front of
a switchboard and a messy tangle of wires, literally connecting
calls. This is how the phone system worked. Your call was patched
through a maze of these switchboards until it landed at its final
destination, with the person you were calling picking up the line.
As the volume of households with phones in America grew, so
did these switchboards, which were given names tied to their locations, which were then assigned as the first two letters of all the
phone numbers in that area or neighborhood, which is why eight
of the numbers on phones have corresponding letters. There were
hundreds of these exchanges in New York City alone, and they
had the side effect of announcing to the world what neighborhood you lived in. It was an unavoidable part of your biography.

So, seeing that my phone number started with three 7s
(SPring 7) told Brian that I lived somewhere in or near SoHo, and
for him, downtown was a big part of his brand, so it instantly gave
me some credibility and assured him, "He's one of us." This still
occurs in a different form, but with cell phone area codes, which
tell a story about your past, where you *came* from or were, not
where or what or who you are *now*. That, coupled with our digital
footprint, is troubling; the possibility of reinvention, once so important to the appeal and landscape of New York City and its inhabitants, has become more challenging, if it hasn't disappeared
altogether.

Brian gave me a brief smile—he wasn't big on smiling—shook
my hand, nodded to Jonathan, and walked off, my old SoHo exchange apparently sealing the deal. Jonathan looked at me.

"Saturday at seven A.M. Wear black pants and black shoes. And
get a haircut."

"Okay. And what am I going to be doing, exactly? Busboy?"

He thought for a moment.

"You're too delicate to be a busboy. We'll figure something
out."

Chapter 3

I went to work early that evening, at Union Square Cafe, and nervously gave my notice to the owner, Danny Meyer. I'd never quit a job before, and making major life changes always scared me. That said, I told him that I needed to make more money, and I wasn't sure kitchen work was my calling.

I was just a low-level pastry expediter and had no interest in a career working in a kitchen—well, I had no interest in a career in *anything*. Danny seemed personally hurt that I was leaving "the Union Square Cafe family." He probably said a version of this to everyone, but I felt like I was letting him down, and the disappointment in his face was familiar to me. I wanted to comfort him but thought better of it. Danny soon opened Gramercy Tavern, followed by a string of other celebrated restaurants in New York, eventually opening his first Shake Shack in 2004 and redefining fast food on his way to becoming one of America's most successful restaurateurs. I like to think the pain I caused him that day inspired him to do better and that he wouldn't be the man he is today without my leaving.*

It wasn't easy finding a quiet moment at 44, but breakfast on a weekend was one of those times. The hotel's clientele wasn't of the wake-up-early variety, and there was no power breakfast scene on the weekends, what with all the weekday power breakfasters off in the Hamptons or Connecticut.

As instructed, I showed up at seven A.M. at the Royalton's basement entrance on Forty-third Street, hair cut, shoes polished.

* I do like to think that.

Jonathan looked me over, nodding in approval. I was given the black button-down shirt and royal-blue apron of a 44 soldier and sent off for basic training, which was like a restaurant version of the Mr. Miyagi/Ralph Macchio scenes in *The Karate Kid* with Jonathan and me in the respective roles. Instead of catching flies with chopsticks, I was asked to balance three plates, two in my hands and one on my forearm, while navigating the stairs from the basement kitchen to the dining room; walk fast holding two cups of coffee without spilling even a *drop* on the saucers; balance six full cocktail glasses on a tray while moving through the dining room. But I was no Daniel-san.

After a few broken plates, coffee cups, and martini glasses, it was clear I wasn't cut out for carrying things, especially in a dining room full of high-profile customers. That would seem to limit what I could do, considering most front-of-the-house restaurant jobs entail bringing or retrieving various items to and from customers. I was apparently too delicate to be a busboy, and now it looked like waiter was out of the question, too. And I was too young to be a host. That said, Jonathan wouldn't give up, trying once again to think of a role for me that was somehow unfuckupable. I wasn't sure why he was making such an effort, although he would later admit that he thought I was adorable and just wanted me around in some capacity, which was both creepy and sweet.

I didn't quite know what a barback was or did, when Jonathan suggested it, but he seemed pleased with the idea. He explained that it was essentially like an assistant to the bartenders: refilling ice, washing glasses, restocking the bottles. These all sounded like things I could do. And best of all, I'd get 15 percent of the bartenders' nightly tip haul, and they were the biggest earners in the place, because they not only made all the tip money from their bar patrons, but they got a share of the waiters' and waitresses' tips from the restaurant and lobby. On a busy night—and most of them were—the bar was pulling in as much as $1,000 in tips, which meant I could be making $150 a night. Which meant around

$750 a week, which meant $3,000 a month, which meant almost $36,000 a year. In *cash*! This was more money than I ever thought I'd make in a year. I was entering an exciting new phase of my life.

I liked working behind that bar. I wasn't serving people, so I could be anonymous, moving quietly behind the bartenders, there but not there, which suited me. I liked watching the bartenders, how they became characters and interacted with patrons, charming them into leaving big tips. I threw myself into that job like it was the most important thing in the world. And at the time, it really was. I had nothing else going on in my life, but I knew I wanted to be good at something and rewarded with praise and validation. I might have been just a lowly barback, but I was going to be the best damn lowly barback that place had ever seen.

I'd arrive at four P.M. every day, a few hours before the post-work cocktail and pre-theater dinner rush, comb my hair, shine my shoes, tie my apron, and get to work. I'd go down the line of bottles on the shelves behind the bar, making notes about what was running low, bring up refills, fill up the ice tubs, make sure all the glasses were washed and none of the martini glasses were chipped or cracked. I'd check the wine cabinet, make sure it was full, the Burgundies and Bordeaux, Sancerres and Sauternes in their rightful places, having learned from the bartenders and sommeliers about wine varietals and regions. The bartenders would arrive at five, inspect my work, nod in approval. The waiters and waitresses would get there around the same time, huddle with the kitchen staff, learn about Geoffrey's specials for the night, what dishes to push, how to pronounce tricky French words.

The waitstaff at 44, along with the Royalton's doormen, might have been the best-looking group of people ever assembled under one roof outside of a fashion show. They were all models and actors and dancers, spending their days auditioning, once in a while landing a role on Broadway or in a film, a big ad campaign, an offer to join the Rockettes—that was still a thing—suddenly gone one day, never to be heard from again, replaced by a newer model, as if they never existed. Magazines would stage fashion shoots in the Royalton's lobby, but instead of hiring professionals, they would use the restaurant's staff.

I never made it into one of those shoots. I wasn't tall, didn't look like a model. I was still a boy; they were all men and women. I was a few years younger than most of them, which at that age is a pronounced difference. I was introverted and clumsy, could never have moved around the dining room with grace and elegance, as they did, balancing a tray of drinks or hot plates, all the while remaining charming and animated. I wasn't pursuing a career in *anything*, so I wasn't part of their discussions about castings and callbacks. Nor was I part of the clique of busboys, most of whom were Asian, Hispanic, Indian, or Pakistani, their job placement determined by that ugly restaurant caste system that still lingers today. As a barback, I was caught between these two worlds, not quite part of either.

A typical night would, like clockwork, go exactly like this: Around five-thirty or six, the post-work drinks crowd and the pre-theater crowd would arrive en masse. And it was instant chaos. The pre-theater crowd was mostly older, a study-the-check-to-make-sure-they-weren't-overcharged-for-something-*anything* crowd, who would all arrive at exactly the same time, filling the restaurant, ordering at exactly the same time, slamming the kitchen, all while needing to be paid up and out to catch an eight P.M. curtain. The lobby and the bar would be packed with office workers, including many young staffers from Condé Nast and other publishing companies, out for an after-work cocktail. The theatergoers would depart before eight; half of the office workers would leave to catch a train home, the other half would be so drunk they'd just keep going, order food and increasingly expensive booze. A more upscale crowd would arrive for their eight P.M. dinner reservations. Things would calm down for a few hours, become manageable, then sometime after ten, a new wave would arrive. Post-theater, post-dinner, cool downtowners and glamorous uptowners, supermodels, regular models, rock and movie stars, all deciding what fun it would be to go to the Royalton for a late-night drink. It was the crossroads of New York City. The music would be turned up a little, the lights dimmed; guests would hop from table to table, wobble around the lobby; someone would fall into the urinal in the men's room, or fall down the lobby's stairs, or tip over on a barstool. It was a clublike atmosphere, and it would go on until one or two in the morning, when we'd finally kick out the last of the lingering drunks and count our money.

When your shift was over you could go home, with those fresh bills, put the cash in your sock drawer, be responsible. Get a good night's sleep. *Or*—I mean, it's only one-thirty. The bars and lounges and clubs are open for another two and a half hours, then the after-hours clubs open up. Imagine you're in your early twenties, with very little responsibility or common sense; you have $150 in your pocket; you're in New York City; and you don't have to be at work until four o'clock the next afternoon.

"Sure, but just one . . ."

This is when I would come out of my shell, transitioning from Dr. Jekyll to Mr. Hyde. The first stop might be one of the seedy bars on the west side of Times Square, places that have all since been knocked down to make way for office towers. They were like a Charles Bukowski novel come to life, full of old drunks and nodding-out junkies and prostitutes, fading leftovers from the seventies and eighties. We'd play pool for money, against one another, against others, sometimes hustling, sometimes getting hustled. There'd be fights; hookers arguing with their pimps; drugs sold, snorted, and shot out in the open. We'd head downtown to the Tenth Street Lounge, on East Tenth in the East Village, to spend more of our money. It was in an old garage with high ceilings, low couches, and a big rectangular bar in the back. The music wasn't loud—you could have a conversation, which was important, because everyone was snorting cocaine, the continuous dialogue overlapping, like in a Robert Altman film, bouncing off the walls along with the patrons. This was one of the first of these new lounges, an alternative to the madness of the frenetic and loud nightclubs of the eighties, and a signature of New York nightlife in the nineties.

At four A.M., when the bars closed, the real party began at the after-hours clubs, where I became a regular. There was Cave Canem on First Avenue and Save the Robots on Avenue B, with its ground floor covered in sand, like a sandbox for adults. There was Marylou's on Ninth Street between Fifth and Sixth Avenues, where a slightly older and more upscale crowd would spend their late nights partaking in cocaine laid out on tables. You would emerge from these places into the sunlight, kicking yourself for having spent the previous night's haul *again*, now ready for a few hours of sleep.

I'd wake up the next afternoon and do it all over again. Which was fine with me. I liked the structure, the routine, being nocturnal. I was thriving at my job and making decent money. As far as I was concerned, this was as good as it got.

Chapter 4

After a few months of barbacking at 44, I had learned enough from the bartenders that Jonathan decided I was ready to be given some shifts on my own, beginning with the weekend brunch shifts—which nobody wanted because: low tips—and to fill in during the weekday lunches occasionally. Since I hadn't yet turned twenty-one, it was illegal for me to be serving drinks behind a bar, though I kept that to myself. But bartending during the weekdays would allow me to witness the drama of 44's lunch, up close.

As I was adjusting to my new life at 44, Anna Wintour's star had been rising steadily. In the early nineties, top-tier magazine editors were New York's movie stars. They were fawned and fussed over wherever they went, covered in the gossip columns like celebrities and in the business sections like industrialists. And Anna was the market maker. She had been the powerful editor of *Vogue* since 1988, and her ascent had been swift. Wintour was pedigreed—her father was the editor of London's *Evening Standard*. She was bred for success. If you were to create a fashion editor in a lab, you would have created Anna Wintour, down to her auburn bob, dark glasses, and disinterested demeanor. And in the ecosystem of 44, she was the center of gravity.

Anna would have lunch at 44 nearly every day, along with those whose names filled out the tops of Condé Nast's mastheads.* One of those names was the relatively new editor of *Vanity Fair.*

A year before I began at 44, there had been an earthquake in the magazine business, a reshuffling in the halls of Condé Nast,

* 44 was referred to as the Condé Canteen or the Condé Cafeteria for good reason.

palace intrigue. Tina Brown, who, like Brian and Anna before her, had come from London to reinvent herself in New York, and had turned *Vanity Fair* into a hot property, an eighties yuppie life-style bible and upscale tabloid for culture-starved and scandal-obsessed suburban women, was moved over to *The New Yorker*. To fill the vacancy at *Vanity Fair,* Si Newhouse looked outside Condé Nast and hired the editor of *The New York Observer,* a Canadian in his early forties named Graydon Carter.

Graydon was an interesting, to some confounding, out-of-left-field choice—he had launched the wonderfully satirical and beloved *Spy* in 1986, a magazine that mercilessly satirized the powerful and took pleasure in aiming its sharpened arrows at New York's elite, including—*especially*—the imperious and upscale Condé Nast. Graydon had left *Spy* with dreams of starting his own weekly newspaper but instead took over the struggling *New York Observer*—a sleepy, pink-hued broadsheet owned by a man named Arthur Carter (no relation), an investment banker playing dress-up as a newspaperman—which was published out of a town house on the Upper East Side. Graydon turned the *Observer* into a must-read among New York's cognoscenti, a small but *highly* influen-tial readership that flocked to the *Observer*'s upmarket gossip and inside jokes both skewering and delighting media insiders and wealthy Manhattanites. It was like a small-town paper for the media and moneyed elite, and in that small town, its creator got noticed.

The moment he took over *Vanity Fair,* Graydon became one of the most important and influential editors in New York and America, a kingmaker in the publishing business, which meant not only was he given a seat at the table but a whole table: one of those four lime-green banquettes at 44. Anna had table 1, the first banquette; Tina had table 5, the second; table 10 was left open for whatever big shot happened to be in that day—Jackie O, Karl Lagerfeld, Calvin Klein, to name a few—then Graydon was at table 15. If Si was in for lunch, he'd get table 1, bumping Anna to table 5, Tina to table 10. Whether a power move or accidental, this meant that table 15 was always Graydon's. This was the power lunch as scripted by Shakespeare, *Game of Thrones* as written by

Truman Capote. In New York's publishing world, these four tables were the ultimate seats of power.

For everyone else who had lunch at 44, proximity to the banquettes was tied to your professional standing and calculated by the restaurant's staff using a formula of title (yours) and *title* (your magazine's). So, if you were, say, a deputy editor or executive editor at *Vogue, The New Yorker,* or *Vanity Fair,* you had a good chance of being in the first row of tables from the banquettes. A senior editor at one of these titles might also have a chance at that first row, though this is where the math gets hazy, the science imperfect. Maybe you got bumped to the second row, which was acceptable. What if you were the editor in chief of one of the second-tier titles, say *GQ* or *Glamour,* or *Condé Nast Traveler?* Or, God forbid, a third-tier magazine like *Mademoiselle* or *Self?* Throw in senior editors from one of the big three, deputy editors or executive editors from the second tier, and so on, and the soup gets cloudy quickly.

This data was pored over for hours by Jonathan and Brian, who prepared the day's seating chart like it was a game of human chess. It got to the point where editors would call an hour before their reservation to ask what table they were at—they literally knew the table numbers used by waiters, which isn't normally interesting enough to be public information—and if its location risked public humiliation, they would cancel. Art Cooper, the longtime editor of *GQ,* once stormed out after being led to his table (fourth row from the banquettes!), which he deemed below his stature, never to return, becoming a regular at the Four Seasons, another famous power lunch spot, where he was given prime real estate.* Apparently the term *Siberia,* as in being "banished to Siberia"—meaning getting a bad table in a restaurant—was coined in a *New York Times* review of 44.

But in the 44 dining room, at lunchtime, Anna Wintour was

---

* Art Cooper had a stroke at his table at the Four Seasons in June 2003, soon after he was pushed out of *GQ.* He died four days later. He was sixty-five.

the sun that all the other planets orbited around. Her every move was studied, processed, her every want and need and whim and habit adjusted to by the restaurant's staff. They were like scientists studying a virus, trying to predict its path, its future behavior, anticipating its next move so as to stop the breakout, avert disaster. For instance, she would never take off her coat when she arrived. She preferred to walk to her table fully sheathed, taking off her coat in one quick motion right as she sat down. So instead of asking her at the hostess stand if she would like to check her coat, as would happen to a typical restaurant patron, someone—oftentimes Jonathan—would follow Anna to her table, a few steps behind, like a shadow. When she took off her coat, dramatically, like James Brown discarding one of his capes, there was always someone right there to catch it.

Anna always ordered a cappuccino the moment she sat down for lunch. This too was anticipated, so a cappuccino would be placed in front of her the second she was seated—not a second before or a second after. Between the coat catching and cappuccino lowering, it was like watching a well-choreographed dance. But the cappuccino-in-wait system was imperfect, because Anna would never arrive at her exact reservation time. The data scientists in 44's laboratory theorized that if Anna's lunch date was important, maybe a big advertiser or big-name fashion designer, she would arrive ten minutes early to greet them when they arrived. If her lunch date was *not* that important, she would make them wait, arrive ten minutes late, a gorgeous power move if true. These machinations were impossible to anticipate, as the reservation was in her name. So Jonathan devised a system in which Ahmed, the designated cappuccino maker—and he truly was one of a kind, a magician when it came to cranking out cappuccinos with alarming speed and precision—would begin making cappuccinos for Anna ten minutes before her reservation time. After a minute or two of the cappuccino's sitting there, cooling down, had Anna not arrived, he would dump it, maybe send it to another customer, or a waiter or busboy would drink it, and the process would begin again. This means that on some days, as many as ten or more cappuccinos were sacrificed to the gods of fashion.

While the dining room was packed and buzzing during those lunches, the bar was quiet. I'd make drinks for diners at a relatively slow pace, the liquid lunch beginning to fade, and you'd rarely have a customer sit at the bar. This gave me time to watch the room. I didn't quite understand what was going on in that dining room at first, but I began to study it, like Darwin observing all those plants and animals in the Galápagos, got to know all these odd species, came up with my own theories. That bar was my very own HMS *Beagle*. Everyone in that room beyond the four banquettes was fighting for attention, hoping to get noticed, get rewarded, or stave off the guillotine. None of these people were there to eat, or socialize, or do any real business. They were there to be seen. That's why table location was so important. That's why if you dared to show up, it had better be with a famous writer or celebrity or recognizable fashion designer. That was the game. But in that room, to those career-obsessed Condé Nast corporate climbers, it was more than a game; it was life and death. The late twentieth century's version of social Darwinism on the rocky island of Manhattan, this unnatural selection played out every day over duck à l'orange and a glass of Meursault.

As I watched the drama unfold, my social antennae started to develop. I began to know who was who, understand the dynamics of the room. I enjoyed watching this scene from my perch behind the bar. It was like being in a zoo—they were a different species.

So, while the power elite jockeyed for tables, the real winner here was Brian. He had stumbled on the perfect storm of business models. He had a roomful of Condé Nast editors packing the place every day, paying top dollar for their meal, while they all charged it back to the company. Of course, the guy who was footing the bill, Si Newhouse, was also sitting right there, at table 1.

But Brian wasn't making any money on the weekends during the day. And neither was I. The brunch shifts, on weekends, which I got stuck with, were dead. Hotel guests might swing by for a quick bite, but midtown on weekends was mostly a ghost town. You'd be lucky to get one customer to break up the boredom.

During one quiet weekend afternoon, toward the end of my shift, out of the corner of my eye I saw a man walk up to the bar and take a seat. He spoke with an English accent.

"Mate, can I get a cup of tea?"

I looked down the bar and instantly recognized him, his mop of brown hair almost covering his eyes, his angular features. It was Paul Weller, the front man of the Jam, the mod-punk British band from the late seventies. I had grown up with all the great punk and new wave music of the late seventies and early eighties, and he was one of my heroes, his jagged guitar riffs a major influence on my own playing and musical awakening.

We chatted for a while. He'd released his first solo album the year before and was playing that night at the Academy, a midsized performance space just off of Times Square. I'd listened to that CD so much it was etched in my brain. I told him what I thought of it, my favorite songs, quoted a few lyrics to him, and he seemed genuinely touched.

I occasionally had to pinch myself during our conversation. This was a mind-blowing experience for a kid who'd worshipped at the altar of rock and roll his whole life. And now, here I was, having a conversation with an apostle. This was someone I'd only heard on records and seen in images and music videos, who seemed so unreal and otherworldly, like a religious icon, etched in stained glass, and now here he was, in front of me, *talking to me*.

He finished his tea. As he started to get up, he shook my hand and asked me my name.

I told him, and he wrote it down.

"I'll leave you two tickets at the door."

He took out a twenty-dollar bill but I told him not to worry about it, the tea was on me. He left the bill on the bar, and I told him his money was no good there. He smiled; I thanked him for the tickets and for chatting with a fan, wished him luck that night, and told him I couldn't wait to see him perform. He thanked me as he headed off to his sound check for the gig, which was one of the most memorable performances I'd ever seen, if only because of that human connection with him earlier in the day.

Like L.A.'s Riot House before it in the sixties and seventies, the Royalton became a destination for rock stars passing through town in the early nineties, especially the Brits. Pete Townshend stayed for months, when he was working on the play *Tommy*, which premiered on Broadway in March 1993. Mick Jones, from the Clash, seemed to always be around. Duran Duran would check into the Royalton when they were in town—you could tell by all the aging groupies who would sit in the lobby waiting to catch a glimpse of Simon Le Bon or Nick Rhodes. Michael Hutchence, the INXS singer, who would be found dead in a Sydney hotel room with a belt around his neck in November 1997—in what was ruled a suicide by the Australian coroner, although rumors persist that it was a case of autoerotic asphyxiation gone wrong—was often a guest at the Royalton.

I served most of them at the bar at one time or another, and having been fanatical about music all my life, it was a thrill to be in their presence and meet some of my childhood heroes. I was so intimidated by Pete Townshend and Mick Jones I could barely look them in the eye. I told Nick Rhodes, who seemed more approachable and friendly, if a little mischievous, how important Duran Duran had been to me a decade earlier, and how I'd bring a picture of him or Simon Le Bon or John Taylor to the barber— "I want to look like *this*." Moments like that with Nick Rhodes or Paul Weller were what made bartending at 44 exciting. And if you're interested in people, and their stories, there's no better place to connect with someone than across a two-foot slab of wood or stone while pouring them a drink.

Working behind a bar was valuable to me personally. It forced me out of my shell, to interact, to be visible and less introverted. I began to learn how to have a conversation with a stranger and to stop being so self-conscious. It helped me, at twenty, begin to forge an identity as I barreled toward adulthood. And it prepared me for my next act. Which, unbeknownst to me, was about to drop in my lap.

Chapter 5

Brian had created a nice little side business for himself, regularly catering fancy dinners and parties for Condé Nast editors, many of them at their homes. Budgets appeared to be limitless, and, as I was to find out in the coming years, if you were a Condé Nast editor in chief, there was essentially no ceiling on your spending whatsoever. When Tina Brown threw a lavish seventy-fifth-anniversary party for *The New Yorker*, she enlisted Brian. Graydon, too, who began to host intimate dinners at his apartment, came to Brian. The waiters who were called on for the smaller affairs, like Graydon's, were the most polished, presentable, and professional of 44's staff. Like SEAL Team Six for cater waiters. Over the first few months of my service I'd proven myself to be a tireless worker, battle tested, a trusted grunt in the 44 Corps, and was added to this tactical unit in late 1993.

Every few months, Graydon threw what can only be described as "salons"—cocktails and dinner at his apartment in the Dakota, one of New York's most iconic buildings, usually celebrating a guest of honor who was being fêted for something or other, maybe an author with a book, or a director releasing a new film, or a visiting dignitary. One of these was thrown for James Carville and Mary Matalin, the married political consultants famous for being on opposite sides of the ideological spectrum—Carville had run Bill Clinton's winning campaign in 1992, while Matalin was on the losing side in that election. The political cognitive dissonance of their relationship made them a fascinating pair and of-the-moment media darlings—they were a *thing* for a few years in the nineties. Another was thrown for Queen Elizabeth's sister, Princess Margaret. The guest list at these gatherings was always an intriguing mix of writers and editors, actors and actresses, business and thought leaders, social and fashion figures, with perhaps forty or fifty of them seated around five or six large round tables set up in the entryway and living room of the apartment. In many ways these dinners were the real-world manifestation of an issue of *Vanity Fair*.

While I was part of this upscale cater-waiter team, I was still considered too unskilled to actually serve people *anything* aside from handing glasses across a bar one at a time, so my role at these dinners was strictly behind the scenes, backup, lugging tables and chairs through the Dakota's cavernous basement, helping set tables, pouring drinks in the back. I never once stepped foot in the living room and dining room when the dinners were in full swing, which was fine with me. I did my job without complaint or drama. I was respectful of the fact that we were in someone's home, with small children running around. I'd sneak Graydon's sons a Coca-Cola or two as they sat in the kitchen eating dinner or doing homework while their parents entertained in the living room. My interactions with Graydon and his wife, Cynthia, were brief but always friendly. I never expected more out of these gigs than a few hundred dollars cash in an envelope at the end of the night.

A week or so after the most recent of these dinners, on my day off, I woke up at about four P.M. to a message on my answering machine from Brian.

"Dana, it's Brian. Call me. I'm at the restaurant."

Brian had never called me before. I immediately assumed I was about to get fired. I'd never been fired from a job before, and I began to panic. I really needed that job. A few months earlier I had managed to escape that dump in Little Italy and move into the second bedroom of my brother's East Village walk-up. It was also a dump, but at least the shower was in the bathroom. It was pricier, though now that I was making significantly more money, I was able to afford it. Without my 44 job, that would no longer be true. Failure was not an option. I figured I'd wait a few hours before calling him back. Maybe he'd cool off, change his mind, realize whatever it was I'd done was a minor infraction after all, or a misunderstanding that had been cleared up.

Just then my phone began to ring. I stared at it, too frozen to move. It rang for what felt like hours, but was seconds, before the answering machine picked up. The outgoing message played. Then: *beep.*

It was a woman's voice, with a pronounced yet soft English accent. "Hello, Dana. It's Pat Kinder calling from Graydon Carter's office." She left a number and asked me to call her back.

What the fuck had I done? First Brian, now Graydon Carter? Had I somehow offended Graydon? Had I done something terrible at dinner the week before? Did one of his kids rat me out for the soda? My mind raced. Pissing off Brian was one thing. But pissing off Graydon Carter, one of the most powerful men in New York's media world, didn't seem like something you could come back from. I'd have to change my name, move out of the city, start over in some dinky midwestern town like some mobster turned rat.

I swallowed hard and called 44. One of the hostesses picked up and grabbed Brian for me. He got on the line.

"You're going to get a call from Graydon Carter's office."

"I know—I *did*. Look, Brian, did I do something wrong? Am I in trouble?"

"No. Graydon's looking for a new assistant. He wants to interview you."

"Me? That's absurd!"

Brian laughed. "That's what I said. But give it a shot. An opportunity like this doesn't come around that often. What's the worst that can happen?"

I hung up, relieved that I wasn't in trouble, or getting fired, but also confused. *Why me?* Why the hell would Graydon Carter want to interview me for a job? I'd barely made it out of high school and I'd never worked in an office, nor did I know anything about the magazine business. This must have been some sort of mistake, or an elaborate prank of Brian and Graydon's.

I paced for a few minutes, then took a deep breath and called Pat Kinder.

"Graydon Carter's office."

"Uhh . . . hi. Pat. It's Dana. Dana Brown."

"Yes, hello. Thank you for calling me back."

"So, Brian told me something about coming in to see Mr. Carter?"

"Yes. He's looking for a new second assistant. He's keen to discuss the role with you."

I didn't know what to say. I stood there in silence, deeply confused.

"Are you still there?"

"Yeah, yeah, sorry, I'm . . . I'm keen to discuss the role with him. I guess."

Pat scheduled time for me to come in a week later. After hanging up I sat down, not sure what had just happened. Did I imagine it? Was it a dream?

I went into the Royalton the next afternoon for my usual night shift. Word had spread throughout the ranks about my being approached, and I was offered encouragement and discouragement in equal measure. Brian called me over.

"When's the interview?"

"In a week. Next Monday."

"Do you have a suit?"

"*No!* I've got *nothing*! I don't even know how to tie a tie!"

Brian thought for a moment. He motioned for me to come with him.

I followed him to the long coat closet behind the bar, where he looked through some suit jackets hanging in the back. He grabbed a dark gray Agnès B jacket that I recognized as part of his daily uniform.

"The lining's ripped, but you can get it mended."

I put it on, and Brian inspected it. It was gigantic on my small frame. I looked like David Byrne from Talking Heads during his *Stop Making Sense* phase.

Brian reached into his pocket and took out a few hundred-dollar bills.

"Go to Agnès B in SoHo. Buy the suit pants. Then take the suit to a tailor."

I thanked him and told him how much it meant to me.

"This is a great opportunity," he said.

I did as Brian instructed. I went to Agnès B and paid for the suit pants and a white shirt with crisp hundred-dollar bills, feeling like Julia Roberts in *Pretty Woman*. I took the pants and suit jacket to a cheap Polish tailor on Second Avenue, tried it on, and made sure they could have it ready before my interview.

I stopped by a newsstand and bought the latest issue of *Vanity Fair*, which had Jack Nicholson on the cover dressed as a werewolf (he was promoting the Mike Nichols film *Wolf*—terrible film; even worse magazine cover). I had seen the issue at Graydon's apartment when I worked at one of his recent dinner parties, sitting on the desk of his home office with a blue FIRST BOUND sticker affixed to its bottom right corner. There was something exciting about seeing that issue with the sticker on it, before it was released publicly, like I was being let in on some great secret.

I read that issue from cover to cover, all two hundred pages, half of which were ads. I stared at the black and white picture of Graydon on his Editor's Letter page, in a double-breasted suit, holding a pencil and grinning widely behind his desk, which I would be sitting across from in a week. There were the Contributors pages, with glamorous photographs and short bios of that issue's writers and photographers, who were presented like the movie stars in the issue. There was a two-page spread on Salvador Dalí, a piece on choreographer Merce Cunningham, six pages of pouty young starlets—"It Girls" (high, low)—including a young Liv Tyler. Christopher Hitchens had a column on the chaos in the newsroom at the *Los Angeles Times*, Bret Easton Ellis reviewed Caleb Carr's *The Alienist*, Bill Clinton's embattled attorney general Janet Reno was profiled, Dominick Dunne had written a postmortem on the trial of the Menendez brothers—Lyle and Erik—who were accused of killing their parents in the family's

Beverly Hills mansion in 1989. The issue had a number of stories about Hollywood, including a story on Swifty Lazar, one of Hollywood's most powerful agents for half a century, who had died six months earlier.

I wasn't a complete stranger to *Vanity Fair*, or magazines. Growing up in the seventies and eighties, magazines were ubiquitous, strewn around everywhere you went, on coffee tables, in doctor's offices, discarded on empty train seats. Everyone read magazines. *Time, New York, Sports Illustrated, The New Yorker, Reader's Digest, Highlights*. What Gen X kid didn't love *Mad* magazine? They were one of the most popular and powerful mediums in media, as culturally relevant as newspapers and books. As a kid I had some friends whose parents were in the magazine business and it seemed so impressive. Magazines even had their own buildings: There was the massive Time & Life Building on Sixth Avenue; in the early eighties my father's office was in the *Newsweek* building, on Madison Avenue, which had a giant red *Newsweek* logo atop it, a beacon that you could see from twenty blocks away.

My mother had been a subscriber to *Vanity Fair* in the 1980s. I remembered seeing issues around the house, with glamorous movie stars bathed in golden light on their covers.

Over the course of the next week, in preparation for my interview, I'd occasionally flip through that April issue, spend time with it, stare at its pages, waiting for it to tell me something. I didn't want to make a complete fool of myself. I tried to break it down as simply as possible, in an attempt to make it less intimidating. *Magazines are just pictures and words*, I told myself. *A magazine editor's job is choosing the right combinations of pictures and words*. That sounds simplistic, and of course it is, but I was a hard worker—maybe that could get me through until I eventually figured it out? As I stared at that issue, I began to fantasize about a future in magazines, regardless of how unlikely it really was.

I picked up the tailored Agnès B suit the Saturday before my interview. It was April 9, the day after Kurt Cobain's body was found at his Seattle home, with a self-inflicted shotgun blast to his head and a suicide note next to him quoting Neil Young ("It's better to burn out than to fade away"). It had just hit the news that day. Makeshift shrines were erected on the East Village's streets in Cobain's memory. There were teary crowds gathered, impromptu memorial services, Nirvana's music playing from open apartment windows. I waded through the emotional crowds, holding my new suit, in that moment feeling like I was somehow turning my back on my generation, trading in my rock T-shirts and flannel and freedom for a white button-down and a shot at that brass ring of corporate America, which had never been part of the plan. Not that there was a plan.

I borrowed a tie from my brother Nathaniel, which he had to tie, standing behind me like a proud parent. I tried the whole ensemble on, admiring myself in the mirror, practicing my handshake and greeting and talking points to my reflection. "Hello, Mr. Carter, very nice to see you. Thank you for this opportunity. Let me tell you a little something about magazines—they're just pictures and words. . . ." As ridiculous as I must have looked, standing there talking to myself, I knew I had one shot to make an impression.

As Monday rolled around, preceded by two tossing-and-turning sleepless nights, my nerves were getting the better of me. I was terrified, pacing around the apartment, convincing myself that this must have been some elaborate practical joke. And right on cue, the phone rang. I picked up.

"Hello, Dana, it's Pat from Graydon Carter's office. I'm afraid something's come up—"

There we go. I should have known. This was all some sort of mistake. Some elaborate mix-up on Graydon's part, or he'd already hired someone else, someone more qualified, smarter, better connected. As I waited for Pat to finish her sentence, I should have been disappointed but instead felt a sense of relief. I didn't have to go through with this charade, didn't have to humiliate myself. But then—

"Can we push this to next Tuesday, at twelve o'clock?"

Oh. Okay. Of course I could. I thanked her and hung up. I'd have to sweat it out for another week.

The week passed, punctuated with bursts of self-doubt, until there I found myself again, putting on the suit, combing my hair, having my brother tie my tie. I took a few deep breaths and headed out, toward Astor Place, to catch the 6 train to Grand Central. As I walked outside, I was hit with a blast of hot air—it was an unseasonably hot and humid day for April, in the low eighties. After walking a couple of blocks, something that had seemed unremarkable a few days earlier was suddenly an issue: The Agnès B suit was wool and had a silk lining, as did the pants, which might have added an extra layer of warmth on a chilly day, but in the heat it was like a sweat accelerator. I started sweating. The subway car held no respite from the heat, as it was too early in the year for the air-conditioning to be turned on. By the time I got out at Grand Central, I looked like I had showered fully dressed, my hair matted to my head, sweat stinging my eyes.

Vanity Fair's offices were at 350 Madison Avenue on the corner of Forty-fifth Street, in an unspectacular but elegant brick-and-stone, twenty-five-story pre-war office building from the 1920s. There was an endless line of Lincoln Town Cars in front, with elegant bright young things coming and going through the building's revolving doors. I paced back and forth on the sidewalk, more nervous than I'd ever been in my life. Eventually I took a deep breath, walked in, and gave my name to one of the security guards, who sent me up to the fourth floor.

The elevator opened, and I stepped out into the lobby. I looked around, and to my left saw an older woman, with gray hair, sitting behind a reception desk. She was on the phone, looking exasperated. As I approached slowly, she looked at me and rolled her eyes and shook her head, holding the phone a foot away from her ear for a moment. I could hear a raised voice coming out of the receiver. She put the phone back to her ear when the shouting stopped.

"Ma'am . . . ma'am . . . ma'am, please, you'll have to call our subscriptions department. If you stop yelling, I can give you the number."

She gave the woman the 800 number and hung up, still shaking her head.

The receptionist, Bernice Ellis, had a friendly, raspy outer-borough accent that had no doubt come from years of smoking, as I noticed the pack of Parliaments on her desk. She hung up the phone and told me that this was something she had been dealing with for months. Roseanne Barr (then Arnold) had been on the February cover, in lingerie, in what was meant as a well-intentioned spoof of a sexy glamour shot, the comedian in on the joke. Apparently many readers were up in arms, finding the sight of her on the cover in lingerie tacky, low-rent, and beneath *Vanity Fair*, although the underlying issue was that Roseanne was a bigger woman, and this was nothing short of fat shaming in the pre-body-consciousness age, though neither of those terms existed yet. (Because Twitter didn't, either.) Readers were calling to cancel their subscriptions nonstop, and poor Bernice had been fielding these calls for months.

"What can I help you with, dear?"

"I'm here to see Graydon Carter."

"What's your name?"

"Dana Brown."

She looked at me. "That's a girl's name. And my, you're sweaty."

Yes. It is. And I was.

She picked up the phone and dialed.

"There's a Dana Brown here to see Mr. Carter."

She hung up and told me to have a seat. I slunk over to the couch and sat down, mopping my brow with my sleeve.

The new issue, May, was lying on the table. I picked it up and started thumbing through it. Jodie Foster was on the cover, shot by Steven Meisel, with the cover line "Jodie Rules." A number of other cover lines ran down the right side of the cover, stories on Yasser Arafat, Willem de Kooning, Jerry Seinfeld, New York senator Daniel Patrick Moynihan, and Helen Mirren. Those cover lines perfectly illustrate what *Vanity Fair* was: an international general-interest culture magazine—movie stars, television stars, international politics, domestic politics, midcentury art. It appeared that the magazine went both a little high and a little low, with art, theater, politics, business, celebrity, and gossip.

A few minutes later another woman approached. She had a white bouffant hairstyle and was dressed brightly but conservatively, and could have been anywhere from her fifties to her seventies—when you're in your early twenties, everyone over the age of fifty looks the same.

"Hello, Dana, I'm Pat," she said in that soft English accent that I'd gotten to know over the phone. She smiled. I stood and shook her hand. I followed Pat down the long hallway to Graydon's office. We passed a line of windowed offices on the right—editors, art directors—looking out onto Forty-fifth Street, with assistants outside in their little cubicles. They looked up, giving me a once-over as I passed, wondering who this kid going to see Graydon was. There was a big open space opposite the windowed offices, on the left, a pen filled with designers working on layouts. Phones were ringing, people were having animated conversations, young staffers were rushing around with important documents. There was a buzz in the air. The offices of *Vanity Fair,* one of the premier culture shops in the world, were alive, vibrant, and exciting. As nervous as I was, it gave me a rush, the thought of being part of this.

We reached the end of the hallway and Pat led me into Graydon's smoke-filled office. Although I'd been in his presence at the Dakota, exchanged the occasional pleasantry, in my mind he was still that towering figure sitting in that corner booth at 44, holding court. He looked up, a Camel Light in his mouth, and smiled, unfolding his long frame as he stood to greet me. He was tall, a shade over six feet, and towered over me. He was an intimidating figure. He wore a dark double-breasted suit, a white shirt with a spread collar, and a blue polka-dotted tie with a small knot cinched tightly around his neck. His hair was parted on the left, the unmoored end of the part finishing with a floppy flourish resembling Nike's swoosh logo or a ski jump, or like it was trying to run away from his head.

"Nice to see you, Dana. Thanks for coming." He shook my hand. "Jesus, you're sweaty."

I smiled, humiliated. "Nice to see you, Mr. Carter."

"Please. Call me Graydon. Have a seat. Smart suit by the way."

I misunderstood the meaning of "smart suit"—he was telling me in his Canadian-Anglophile way that it was a nice suit. I thought he was making fun of me for wearing a silk-lined wool suit on an eighty-degree day. I shrunk in my chair.

The office was covered in wood, dominated by a long desk with more than half a dozen chairs opposite his big office chair, wood paneling on the walls, wood bookshelves stuffed with books and magazines. There was a green couch against one wall and a small bathroom. Having your own bathroom, in your office, was one of those perks of being a Condé Nast editor in chief. There was a glassless window cut out behind his desk, with Pat's desk on the other side of it.

I sat at one of the chairs opposite him. He looked me over.

"How's Brian treating you?"

"Really well."

"Do you know why you're here?"

I knew why I was there, but I was unsure why *I* was there. "Brian told me you were looking for a new assistant."

"And do you know why I wanted to talk to you about it?"

"Honestly, I have no idea."

He laughed. "Have you thought much about a career?"

"Not really."

"Do you have any great ambition?"

In that moment I cursed myself for not thinking more about some of the questions he might ask me, prepared a little more. But the fact was I hadn't thought much about a career and I definitely didn't have any great ambition. I hadn't really allowed myself to envision anything in terms of my future. I had dropped out of college three years earlier, with the vague idea that I might go back at some point, but that was looking less and less likely. I answered as honestly as I could.

"This is probably not the thing to say in a job interview, but . . . no. I always hoped something would eventually reveal itself to me. If I was lucky. I guess I'm just waiting for that—for some kind of spark."

Graydon looked at me, appearing satisfied with that answer. When asking that of other young prospective employees, I'm sure he usually heard some rehearsed speech about how they first fell in love with magazines at the age of eight and decided it was what they wanted to do when they grew up, their life taking on a singular mission from that day forward. Me, not so much.

"The reason I wanted to talk to you is I noticed you at those dinners. The way you carried yourself, the way you interacted with people. You're respectful and humble. You're a hard worker. You have a good head on your shoulders. You're perceptive. You're smarter than you think you are. And you pick things up quickly."

I was taken aback. Astounded not only because he had noticed me, and paid attention, but because this was the nicest thing anyone had ever said to me. And while I did think some of those things might have been true, I'd never had anyone say them to me. It was like he saw something in me that nobody else had. I can't understate the impact of that one moment.

"Human resources keeps sending me candidates. Harvard, Princeton, Columbia, journalism degrees, Rhodes scholars—and I've hired those kids before, and sure, some were good. Some were great. But I always sensed that they thought the job was beneath them, thought they should be writing feature stories, not getting me coffee and typing up thank-you notes and filing papers. They didn't have any of those qualities that I've seen in you in the few interactions we've had."

He paused for a moment.

"Look, Dana, this is a great business. It's creative, it's fun, it's never boring, and journalism is an important service. I promise, if you work hard and pay close attention, you can learn every-thing you'll ever need to know working for me for a few years."

I nodded along. It was almost like he was selling *me* on the job. Was I witnessing that spark, in real time, that I'd been waiting for?

"So what do you think?"

What did I think? I was speechless. Here was a man I hardly knew, one of the most powerful people in New York media, who had not only noticed me but seen something in me, and was now seeming to offer me what could be a potentially life-changing job. A job that was one of the most sought-after positions for anyone trying to break into the publishing business. I was in complete shock. Eventually, "Yes" emerged from my lips. That was all I was able to get out.

"There's a few hoops to jump through still. I want you to talk to a few other editors. They like to be involved in these decisions. Then you'll have to go talk to Human Resources. Just do your best, be yourself. And listen. Sound good?"

I nodded, still in shock, and we stood, we shook hands, and he called Pat in. She collected me and took me to meet with the man-aging editor, Chris Garrett, Graydon's second-in-command. Like Pat, she had a soft English accent, though of a more posh variety. Chris had an old-world elegance and a *very* English manner, like a character from one of those *Masterpiece Theater* costume dra-mas. Her nickname among some of the staff and writers, I would later learn, was "the Velvet Hammer," as she was often the one who had to pleasantly deliver unpleasant news. After a brief and friendly conversation with Chris, I was handed off to another editor, then another, and another. I was like a product moving on an assembly line, trying to get stamps of approval from the in-spectors, as I made my way slowly down the conveyor belt of the *Vanity Fair* masthead. They asked me more probing questions than Graydon had, a cultural quiz that I didn't quite know the answers to. *What's your favorite magazine? What was the last book you read? What's your favorite play?* Graydon had told me to be myself, but that wouldn't work, so I stretched the truth as best I could, throwing out answers ripped directly from that issue of the magazine I had studied for the previous few weeks. I've still never read *The Alienist*.

Everyone was friendly, a few more encouraging than others. Some spoke to me slowly, like you would to a child, or a foreigner for whom English was their second language. But I held my own, did my best not to raise any red flags.

My last stop was the Human Resources department, and what would turn out to be the most difficult part of my day. Condé Nast was the premier upscale luxury magazine company, which meant that its Human Resources department had a standard to uphold, a reputation to protect. It was hard enough to get an *interview* without an Ivy League education or the proper lineage. And now suddenly one of their top editors, one of their stars, was sending *me* to see them, a college dropout, no social pedigree of any kind, a barback from 44 for fuck's sake!

I was met by an assistant in the reception area. She probably had blond hair and wore pearls and was somewhat uptight.* She asked me for my résumé. I told her I didn't have a résumé. This confused her. She eventually moved on and informed me that I would have to take a typing test. This terrified me. The tense standoff ended with her eventually leading me to a little room with a handful of small desks, each one holding a massive, hulking *beast* of a typewriter. She gave me a page of text to type.

Now, it's not like I hadn't typed before, or used a typewriter, or computers by then. If you grew up in the 1980s, learning to type was part of the high school curriculum. There was typing class. Which seemed like a great class to skip out on and instead go smoke pot somewhere to get ready for seventh-period chemistry because Bunsen burners are even more awesome when you're high. And why would I need to learn how to type? It's not like I was ever going to have an office job or anything. So while I had

---

* This might sound unfair, but it describes at least half of Condé Nast at that point in time, so I like my odds.

typed before, the term "hunting and pecking" would have been a generous description of my abilities. And I'd certainly never done it with someone standing over me with visible contempt and a stopwatch.

It felt like she shortchanged me by a few seconds, but I did the best I could. The assistant ripped the sheet of paper out of the typewriter and led me into the office of a woman named Sarah Slavin, one of the toughest HR gatekeepers in the company. I nervously sat down across from Sarah as the assistant handed her what I'd just typed up, then left us alone. Sarah looked at the sheet, counting words in her head. She put the paper down on her desk quickly—*Wow, she's a really fast counter,* I thought—and looked up, staring at me for a few uncomfortable moments before she spoke.

"Fourteen."

From the look on her face I assumed that wasn't great, but having no context about how typing tests were scored—maybe fourteen was good, or it was like golf, and a low score was what you wanted?—I asked her what I thought was a reasonable question: "Is that good?"

"No, it's not good. And you misspelled half the words."

So technically, I had typed seven words a minute.

Sarah glared at me.

"In all my years, I've never come across a less qualified applicant for a job than you. I don't know what Graydon sees in you. If he decides to go through with this—and I will urge him not to—you'll last a few weeks, *if that.* Thank you for coming in. I'll be in touch."

In an instant, all those nice things Graydon had said to me seemed to vanish. I was back to being that kid who couldn't do anything right, who wasn't good enough.

Chapter 6

I woke up the next day actually relieved. Getting the job would have been the easy part. Succeeding was another story. What if Sarah Slavin was right and I only lasted a few weeks? It would be far less humiliating to return to 44 after having failed to *get* the job rather than a few weeks later after having failed *at* the job.

It was at that moment that the phone rang. Sarah, with clear disdain in her voice, told me that I was officially being offered the job. I was as surprised as she was, and without giving it a second of thought, I accepted. My first day would be Monday, April 25. She told me that my starting salary would be $16,500—

Wait, *what*?! In all the excitement and anxiety and fear and self-loathing, I'd never once asked how much money the job paid. I never liked to talk about money. It makes me uncomfortable, to this day, which is idiotic when you're talking to someone about a job. Usually that's one of your first questions. Many of the young Condé Nast assistants received a supplement to their income from their families. That was not to be the case with me. But while this was a steep pay cut, I knew I couldn't back out. This was the opportunity of a lifetime. I had to look at it as a long-term investment. I'd have to accept the short-term loss and sacrifices to my lifestyle and look at the big picture. Now that I had actually been offered the job, I needed to succeed. I needed to prove Sarah wrong.

I gave my notice at 44 to Brian and Jonathan, both of whom couldn't have been happier for me. It reflected well on them, to send a kid up to the big leagues. In the week or two before I started my new job, I picked up extra shifts to buy a few suits, shirts, and ties from the discount rack at Century 21. I bid farewell to my 44 colleagues and promised to stop in for a drink now and then, as I'd be working only a few blocks away.

On April 25, I showed up at eight A.M. at 350 Madison, suited, tied, and ready to go. It was an odd transition, having to get up early, shower, get dressed, head to the subway. More often than not, I was stumbling home at that time of the morning, eyeing with disdain and pity the stone-faced office drones heading to midtown or Wall Street. Suddenly the shoe was on the other foot, and it was an uncomfortable fit. I was one of those poor bastards now.

I got off the elevator and said good morning to Bernice, who welcomed me to the *Vanity Fair* family. Pat eventually came to the reception area and greeted me with a warm smile, offering congratulations and encouragement. It was quiet, the workday not officially kicking off until closer to nine or ten, though some of the more junior staffers milled about. We did a slow lap around the office, which took up almost the whole floor. The rows of editors' offices; the art department; the planning room, where layouts of the next issue were covering the walls, awaiting Graydon's approval or changes. I caught a glimpse of the June cover, a close-up of Tom Hanks's head, the rest of him submerged in blue water up to his chin. The *Vanity Fair* logo was orange, the cover line "Tom Terrific" in white, below his floating head.

We continued on to the production department, the photo department, the research department, the copy room, the back-issues closet. She took me upstairs to the mailroom, introduced me to the guys—and they were all guys—who, in stark contrast to the rest of the lily-white Condé Nast, were mostly Hispanic and Black, the office-tower caste system similar to the restaurant world's. She took me down to the lobby, to the newsstand, to introduce me to Helmut and Margit, the German couple who ran it, then up to the small cafeteria. Pat finally took me to the Human Resources office, leaving me there for orientation along with a group of five or six recent college graduates, mostly young women, bright-eyed and bushy-tailed, primped and preened. They must have thought I was just like them, sitting there in my suit and tie, and now I guess I was, though my route in had been of a different variety. I'd snuck in through the service entrance.

I don't remember any mention of discriminatory hiring practices, diversity, sexual harassment policy—there was no sensitivity training, as I'm sure corporate orientations nowadays are legally mandated to do. There might have been a video. We were given our health insurance packets, asked to fill out some forms, and told about the company.

Condé Nast has a rich history. It was founded in 1909 by Condé Montrose Nast, a New York–based veteran of the publishing business, when he bought *Vogue* that year. Nast would add to his list of titles in the coming decades—*House & Garden, Glamour,* and *Vanity Fair,* which was originally launched as *Dress & Vanity Fair,* and would be shut down in 1936. (It was merged with *Vogue* before being brought back to life in the 1980s.) Nast assembled a stable of upscale magazines, each targeting specific readerships of the high-net-worth variety, attracting upscale advertisers—*duh*—which was where the revenue would come from. This simple business model would continue on into the next century, until it would run into a steamroller called the internet.

In 1959, Si Newhouse's father, Samuel Irving Newhouse—who passed on not just his name to his eldest son, but then Condé Nast, in 1975—bought the company as an anniversary gift for his wife, which thankfully isn't on any anniversary-gift-by-year list I've seen. (The rich *are* different from you and me.) Samuel *père,* who had been born on the Lower East Side, a child of Jewish immigrants, went into the newspaper business. Like so many immigrants of that era, he started young and worked his way up from the bottom. In 1922, Samuel cobbled together enough money to buy the *Staten Island Advance,* a newspaper you will hear very little about except in the story of the Newhouse family. Starting with that small, local paper from New York's redheaded stepchild of a borough, Samuel would build a media empire, a vast fortune, and in the process create endless wealth for many future generations of his family. A kid went from the Lower East Side with nothing to creating one of the country's premier dynastic families in one generation, the kind of American success story that has drawn so many to our fair and fertile shores over the years.

Now, in 1994, the family's core businesses were magazines and newspapers under the umbrella of Advance Communications, although early investments in the Discovery Channel and cable providers would add a few more zeroes to the family's net worth in the oncoming boom of the information age. Si ran Condé Nast, the magazines—and briefly books, owning Random House publishing from 1980 to 1998—while his younger brother, Donald, ran the newspapers, which were mostly local papers spread around the country. Advance and Condé Nast were privately held—still are—so their revenue, and the family's net worth, were closely guarded secrets, whispered about in hushed tones like that mentally unstable sibling in the institution who is never discussed openly around the dinner table. But it was well known that the newspapers made the real money, while Condé Nast was the show pony.

Once indoctrinated into the cult of Condé Nast, I returned to Pat and my new little L-shaped desk perpendicular to hers, across from the door to Graydon's office. On top of the desk sat a typewriter; a large, faded PC; and a circular Rolodex, with names and numbers written in hand on each card: the florist, the liquor store, Graydon's driver, the numbers to his home office at the Dakota and his country house in Connecticut. There was a dish full of black-and-silver binder clips, in varying sizes. Graydon hated paper clips, Pat told me sternly. They were never to be used under any circumstances.

The first day in any new job is overwhelming. Especially if you're in an office and you've never worked in one before. The simple things are confounding. For instance, not only had I never used a copy machine, I hadn't even seen one since the late seventies, in grammar school, and that one had a hand crank and made me feel light-headed. You're meeting so many new people, and being told what exactly they do, that you couldn't possible retain any of it. On my desk was a sheet of paper that Pat had typed up with the details of my responsibilities throughout the day and week. Aside from a few of the more simple ones—"Make sure there is always a fresh pack of Camel Lights in Mr. Carter's desk drawer"—I didn't know what any of them meant or where to begin.

Graydon arrived and stopped in front of my desk, a wide grin on his face. He started laughing at the sight of me sitting at that little desk. I couldn't help but laugh along. A few days earlier I had been toiling behind the bar at 44, cleaning glasses, wiping down the bar, restocking the shelves. Today I was an assistant to the editor in chief of *Vanity Fair*. I was Cinderella, and he was both the Fairy Godmother and Prince Charming. The absurdity wasn't lost on either of us. He looked at me and gave the advice he would give me hundreds of times over the coming years: "Don't fuck it up."

The hidden meaning of this simple directive was clear, and always would be. I had a lot riding on this, but so did he. Graydon had gone to the mat for me, insisted on hiring me against the wishes of the company, with nothing but instinct and a gut feeling. *Don't make me look bad. Succeed. Don't fuck it up.*

He entered his office, pulled out a stack of papers from his green Hunting World bag, placed them on the window ledge, and lit a Camel Light. This was how each day would begin.

Every morning, when Graydon would arrive in the office, he would hand a stack of papers through the little window to Pat. This might include manuscripts of articles he'd read the night before, with notes for the story's editor; galleys of magazine pages for the next issue; marked-up, ripped pages from newspapers and magazines for editors with "Let's discuss" written on them; or a potential story idea. Pat would take the pile, sort through it, and extract what was for her, and I would get handed what remained, to be distributed to the staff or filed.

It was an odd transition over those first few weeks. In many ways I was living a double life, still spending my nights in ratty T-shirts playing guitar in downtown clubs like CBGB and the Mercury Lounge or rehearsing in Williamsburg. After a few hours of sleep I'd roll out of bed at seven, put on a suit and tie, comb my hair, and make my way to 350 Madison, all the while keeping my other life a secret from my new boss and colleagues. They were two completely different worlds, and I wanted to keep them separate.

I slowly began to find my footing. I figured out how to use the copier, got to know the names of the staff in the mailroom, was on a first-name basis with the guys at Blue Meadow Flowers, in the East Village—Graydon sent flowers constantly, to every staff member and contributing editor on their birthday, to fashion designers, celebrities, authors, the subject of a story who was upset, the subject of a story who was thrilled, Donald Trump once (because of something I did; more on that later), all accompanied by a handwritten note, or one typed up by me on that old typewriter, then signed in his looping signature. His penmanship was a throwback to an earlier age, well before the industrial revolution, when people wrote with quills and wore soft velvet hats, an elegant calligraphy with some words so hard to decipher, I became a translator, servicing a queue of editors throughout the day wondering what the hell they were being tasked with.

I got to know Margit and Helmut at the newsstand downstairs, where we had an account. I tried to hand them money for a pack of cigarettes for myself one day—Winston reds, soft pack—and they refused it. They just put it on the account, told me not to worry about it. That sole pack soon became a weekly carton, then two. It was "free," so why not up my habit to two packs a day? When I told friends that a perk of my new job was free cigarettes, they couldn't believe my good fortune.

And then magazines, free magazines. I immersed myself in my new field. I got them all, *Esquire, New York, The New Yorker, Harper's, Time, Newsweek, The Atlantic, Rolling Stone, Spin,* and all the British magazines, like *The Face, NME, Mojo,* and a new one called *Loaded,* which was unlike anything I'd seen before and was the beginning of the lad mag craze, which would hit hard one day, saturate the market, influence the rest of the business to an absurd degree—*Shorter pieces! Charticles! Numerous entry points on a page!*—then virtually disappear within a decade.

There was a new magazine called *Might*, published out of San Francisco and edited by a young Dave Eggers. It was beautifully designed, well written and modern, clever and culturally edgy, like a younger, West Coast *Spy*, and way ahead of its time—which is why it only lasted for three years. *Might* and *Loaded* were clearly something new, created by my generation, for my generation, which felt revolutionary, and I was now part of that revolution. The inside jokes and references were generation specific, and they were aimed right at me. There were so many magazines in 1994, so many new magazines, and so many *great* magazines. All the young talent of the moment was eschewing other industries and flocking to the business. It was the coolest place to be. The center of the media and cultural universe. I'd accidentally and happily landed in the right industry at just the right time.

Chapter 1

O ver the years, these are some of the people I've found myself
seated next to at dinner parties: Kevin Spacey; Debra Mess-
ing; Gwen Stefani and her then soon-to-be ex-husband, Gavin
Rossdale; Tom Ford; Megan Mullally and her husband, Nick
Offerman—after Bill Hader asked to switch seats with me so he
could sit next to his wife; one of the Olsen twins (don't ask which
one; couldn't tell you); Natalie Portman, the first person I ever
interviewed, when she was on the cover of *Vanity Fair*'s 1997
Hollywood Issue—her mother picked up the phone in their Long
Island home, saying, "Let me see if she's home from school. . . .
Natalie? Natalie?"; Chevy Chase; Ian McKellen; Nick Rhodes—
Nick Rhodes again!—be still my seventh-grade heart; Conan
O'Brien; Sam and Aaron Taylor-Johnson; Snapchat founder Evan
Spiegel; Uber founder Travis Kalanick; Yelp founder Jeremy
Stoppelman—three and a half stars at *most*, and that's being gen-
erous; and the supermodel Natalia Vodianova.

Now, these are not people I would say I've had dinner with.
They're not people who left their house or hotel that evening say-
ing, "I'm so looking forward to having dinner with that Dana
Brown tonight. He's clever, delightful, and such good company."
In fact, they arrived at dinner having no idea who I was or that
they were about to be stuck next to me for a few hours. They were
attending a function thrown by *Vanity Fair*, and whether it was in
Los Angeles to celebrate the Oscars, Cannes for the film festival,
London, New York, San Francisco, or Paris, the time and place
are immaterial; what isn't is that I was not the draw.

While it sounds glamorous—and sure, it *was*, sitting there
overlooking the Mediterranean or in a roomful of Hollywood's

A-list—it was also just another part of my job, and occasionally challenging.* Where do you take the conversation after introducing yourself to Nick Offerman and, attempting show-business small talk, ask him if he has any interesting projects on the horizon and he says, "I'm thinking about making a birdhouse"? What's a natural response when a discussion of newborns with Chevy Chase becomes a story about his squirting streams of milk across the room from his wife's nipples while she was lactating? In fairness, Offerman and Megan Mullally were two of the loveliest and funniest people you could hope to spend a couple of hours with; Chase excused himself a few moments after the breast milk conversation, never returned, and checked into rehab soon after. *Was it something I said?*

For many of these dinners, especially early on in my career, I wasn't really an official guest. I was a call-up, like a minor leaguer brought up to the majors to temporarily fill in for an injured star. If someone didn't show up, I was called to action. Because: *No empty seats.* When the name on the place card is Brad Pitt, or Madonna, or Stevie Wonder, and then *I* sit down—those looks of disappointment just cut you down to the quick and are something I'll not soon forget.

So over the years, I had to up my game, try to be interesting, interested, charming, talkative and cultured, engaged and engaging—and *drink*. I became a character that I could call on at will, hiding my insecurities, fears, social anxiety, and lack of education, tapping into my id, that Freudian survival mechanism buried deep in the recesses of one's subconscious. I can give good table, make that person sitting next to me think they're as interesting, charming, cultured, engaged, and engaging as they hope

---

* Let me get this out of the way: Regarding my use of the word *challenging* here, to be clear, I have enough self-awareness to know that if someone asked me what some of my work responsibilities as an editor at *Vanity Fair* were and I replied, "I drank excessively at dinner parties so I could pretend celebrities were interesting," you'd immediately think, *Beats working in a coal mine, you insufferable privileged twat*, and want to punch me in the face. And you would not be wrong. But please, keep an open mind. And if you can't, maybe it's not too late to exchange this book for something deeper and more emotionally satisfying.

they are. Ask lots of questions, pretend the answers are interesting, reveal as little about myself as possible. It was a transaction, and one that I got good at. Looking back at my first experience in the role of a dinner-party call-up, just weeks into the job, when a mix-up on my part led to something I'm still, to this day, ashamed of, I had nowhere to go but up.

It was May 19, 1994, and I had been at my job a few months then. I was returning to a familiar scene: Graydon's Dakota apartment for one of his dinners. Only now, I was on the other side of the equation.

On this particular night, the guest of honor was Dan Rather, the *CBS Evening News* anchor. In 1994, being the anchor of one of the three evening network news broadcasts was the most visible—if not the most important—job in journalism. At that time it was Rather, Tom Brokaw at NBC, and Peter Jennings at ABC. It's not a stretch to say that before the rise of the cable news networks, the internet, and the twenty-four-hour news cycle, much of America tuned in to one of these three every night. Network news anchors were America's conscience, the trusted voice of reason, a constant cultural presence with an outsized influence on public opinion going back to Edward R. Murrow and Walter Cronkite. So, it felt like a big deal to be in the same apartment as Dan Rather.

These dinners were managed behind the scenes by Sara Marks, *VF*'s director of special projects, whose attention to detail was executed with military precision. Sara was in charge of all of *Vanity Fair*'s events and is the most organized person I've ever met, to the point where you almost worried about her and felt sorry for her exhausted label maker. Sara and Graydon would huddle before dinners like these, to figure out the seating; go over minute details; discuss which guests were feuding with each other and make sure they were at separate tables (or at the same table, if spicing things up was on the menu), and which guests were secretly sleeping together or trying to close a big business deal and so should be seated next to each other; note what kind of cigarettes each guest smoked and make sure to have backup packs at the ready, or what specific brand of liquor guests liked to drink and make sure it was stocked. For instance, there were a few bottles of Princess Margaret's preferred whiskey on hand at that dinner I had worked the year before in case the princess, a renowned imbiber, wanted a tipple or two. (The Famous Grouse. She did. And did. And did. . . .)

My job at these dinners was to help Sara behind the scenes to make sure the "trains ran on time"—tables were set up in the right places, the correct chairs and tablecloths were retrieved from storage, dietary needs were met, caterers were let in through the service entrance, all the guests showed up. Again: no empty seats.

The tables were set up; the guests were mingling over cocktails; Dan Rather and his wife, Jean, had arrived; and everything seemed to be running smoothly. I sat in the back, out of sight, at the kitchen table, overlooking the Dakota's courtyard, hanging out with Graydon's young sons, helping with homework or playing a game, catching up with my old friends from 44, who were rushing around with trays full of drinks and hors d'oeuvres. Geoffrey Zakarian and his sous chef were preparing to plate the appetizer course, awaiting word that the guests were about to sit. Brian, often a guest at these dinners, would pop his head in every so often to check on everything, punctuating the end of each sentence with a Cockney-accented question-as-statement: *knowwhatahmean.*

Once all the guests were seated, I was off the hook for the night. In stark contrast to this fancy uptown dinner in a seven-figure apartment full of important and glamorous people, it would be back to my East Village dump and my recently rescued pit bull puppy, Otto, who desperately needed a walk.

At that moment, Sara came rushing into the kitchen. *There was a problem.* Everyone was ready to sit for dinner, but someone was missing: Diane von Furstenberg. She was supposed to be seated at Graydon's table in between Graydon and Dan Rather! I needed to try to find her. In the *Vanity Fair* universe, an empty seat at a dinner, especially at the host and guest of honor's table, *in between them, no less,* was a Chernobyl-level disaster.

If I wasn't quite prepared to handle a moment of crisis at such a young age, I somehow sensed the importance of optics in these situations. Don't panic. Remain calm. Take control. Solve the problem. Or at least make it appear as if you're doing your best to.

"I'm on it." I swung into action, rushed into the Situation Room—Graydon's home office off the kitchen—riffled through his Rolodex, and called Diane's home number. After a few rings, someone picked up.

"Ellaaaaooooo." It was Diane's unmistakably upscale European drawl; imagine Dracula as a chic woman, vowels misplaced and elongated elegantly. To this day I still don't know the correct pronunciation of her name—some Americanize it and say *Dieanne,* others Euroize it and say *Dee-ahn.* She responds to both, like Dwayne Johnson/the Rock.

"Hi, Diane, it's Dana from Graydon's office. I'm at his apartment, and he's expecting you for dinner tonight, like, *right now.*"

"Oh; pleeeease send my raaaaagrets, I'm not feeeeeling well and eeeen for the night."

"You're . . . but . . . I . . ."

"Thank yooo, daaarleeeng." Click.

Fuuuuuck.

I ran and told Sara, who rushed off to talk to Graydon. I imagined they were removing a chair, reorganizing the table's seating chart. She came back a minute later.

"Graydon wants you to sit—in Diane's place. At his table. It's too late to remove a chair."

What?!

I let this sink in for a moment or two.

"I . . . *What do you mean? Are you crazy?! Is he fucking crazy?! I can't do that!*" I was in a panic. This was not something I was prepared to do.

"Sweetie, you *have* to. Graydon wants you to. And it's your *job.* And everyone's about to sit." She grabbed my arm and started pulling me. I held on to whatever I could to anchor myself, dug in my heels, hoping there was some way out of this.

"Please, Sara. He's making a huge mistake! I'm completely out of my depth, I'll embarrass him. It'll be a fucking disaster!"

My protests were getting me nowhere. Before I knew it, she had begun frog-marching me down the long hallway to the living room like I was a death row prisoner headed to the gallows, my short, inconsequential life flashing before my eyes. The tables came into view. Everyone was now sitting, looking at this one empty chair. There was no turning back.

I took a deep breath and slowly lowered myself into my seat. The configuration had been shifted, and I was between two women, Graydon smiling and winking at me from across the large round table, taking a perverse joy in throwing me to the lions, to see how I'd hold up, the beginning of a frightening pattern.

I introduced myself to the two lionesses who were about to make a meal out of me. The one to my left was Jean Rather, Dan's wife—he was seated across the table. I had no idea who the other woman was, and as she introduced herself it went in one ear and out the other. I looked for a place card, but there wasn't one. She was middle-aged, heavily made-up, with big waves of red hair and billowy bosoms. I looked around. Although in the coming years, after some cultural and social seasoning in the offices of *Vanity Fair*, I would know who everyone in this room was in order of their importance, their job titles, their net worth, and the names of their yachts and who they were sleeping with, in this moment, I had absolutely no clue who anyone was except for a few of my new colleagues and my old colleagues from just a few weeks earlier, who were now filling up my wineglass, an uncomfortable turn of events to say the least.

Jean couldn't have been nicer. She and Dan had a weekend home in upstate New York, in the western Catskills, where my father also had a house and where I had spent a lot of time during my childhood; my sister and the Rathers' daughter had even gotten married at the same place a few years earlier—great, a connection, a common thread. In sharp contrast to Jean, the billowy-bosomed woman to my right was loud and animated. Something about her look and the way she carried herself told me she must have been from a state that produced oil. She dominated the conversation. The main topic that night, the name on everybody's lips, was Jackie O—at that moment, just across Central Park from the Dakota, at 1040 Fifth Avenue, another iconic New York address, Jacqueline Bouvier Kennedy Onassis, riddled with cancer, lay on her deathbed. Then my tablemate segued to politics without taking a breath, going on a long rant about what a terrible and corrupt president Bill Clinton, who had been in office for a little over two years, was. She insisted to Jean and me that his would be a one-term presidency. She was also confident that Dan Quayle was a shoo-in to win the Republican nomination and the 1996 election. Jean and I immediately burst out laughing, bonding over the absurdity of that statement.

A spirited debate about politics and the state of the world would take us through the next hour or so, after which the woman apologized, said she had to leave early to attend to a family matter, and got up and left as the entrées were being cleared. Jean and I looked at each other, relieved.

As the meal was winding down, Graydon's phone rang—his house phone; this was of course pre–cell phone. He gave me a glance that I took to mean *Answer it.* "Excuse me," I said to Jean, shot up, and ran to the phone.

"Hello, Carter residence."

There was a serious-sounding man on the other end of the line. "We're looking for a guest of Mr. Carter's this evening. Lee Radziwill. It's an emergency." *Lee Radziwill . . . Lee Radziwill.* I had no idea who Lee Radziwill was, or even whether Lee was a he or a she.

"Okay, um, this Lee . . . is a . . . lady . . . or . . ."

"*Excuse me?* Who is this?"

"It's uhhhh . . . so I'm kind of new—"

"Obviously . . . Look, I don't have time for this. Is she there or not?"

Aha. She. I thought for a second, looked around the room.

Somehow in my confused young mind, and after more than a few glasses of wine to calm my nerves, I made an absurd logical leap and figured that the woman who had been sitting next to me, and had left early to attend to a family matter, must have been this Lee Radziwill. In the moment, it was also the easy way out, so I took it.

Without thinking too much more about it, I said, "Oh, *that* Lee Radziwill. . . . Of course. Miss Radziwill just left."

"Thank you." Click.

I was pleased with myself. I had read the sign, taken the initiative, answered the phone, solved the problem. Maybe I'd found my calling and this whole assistant thing was going to work out.

The tables were cleared away; a few of the guests left, others lingered in the living room. I stuck around, had another drink or five, made passable conversation, talked with a few of my new *VF* colleagues, eavesdropped on what I assumed were important conversations between important people. No longer feeling completely out of my depth, I suddenly felt accepted, or at least not so out of place. Could I somehow fit in here, in this world I had stumbled into, after all?

It got later and later, and the party began thinning out. I happened to be chatting with Graydon when an elegant woman, on her way out, stopped by to thank him. As I stood awkwardly next to him, Graydon turned to me. "Did you two meet?" I shook my head. I reached out my hand confidently and for the first time introduced myself as I would thousands of times in the coming years, as my name and place of employment became inseparable and intertwined parts of my identity: "Dana Brown, *Vanity Fair.* Very nice to meet you."

She took my hand, smiled. "Lee Radziwill. It's a pleasure to meet you, Dana."

"Oh, so *you're* Lee. Funny, but there was a . . ." *Wait a minute.* I stopped myself for some reason, like Elmer Fudd realizing he'd been outsmarted by that damn rabbit again, the gears in my head grinding to a halt. *Uh-oh.* "Have a good evening," I said through clenched teeth, forcing a smile. And she was off.

"Jackie O's sister," Graydon whispered sadly as Lee walked out the door.

Oh shit. The puzzle pieces quickly assembled in my brain, the picture becoming clear.

I had a sleepless night. One of those awful, tossing-and-turning, pillow-flipping, anxiety-riddled nights when you've done something wrong and it's weighing on you so heavily, your mind wandering from one imagined scenario to another, one imagined consequence to another, and you know whatever happens it's all going to reveal itself in the light of day, and it's not going to be good. A few weeks earlier I had been handed a key, and now, before I even made it to twenty-two, it was going to be taken away from me, that door slammed shut. I wasn't ready for responsibility or adulthood. It would be over before it began. It was back to 44 for me.

Jackie died that night. Her spirit left her body around ten-thirty P.M. It was announced the next morning. She was sixty-four. To this day I don't know if her sister made it across town in time to say goodbye. As I would later learn, theirs was a famously complicated relationship, as it often is with siblings, so I hope she did. I read every obituary I could get my hands on, trying to find one that placed Lee by Jackie's side at the time of her death, but none did. *The Washington Post* reported that the two had spent the day together, which gave me some comfort. I was always too ashamed to ask Lee, whom I crossed paths with occasionally over the years, or to even tell anyone that story until now, partly out of self-preservation, partly out of guilt. Lee died in February 2019, at the age of eighty-five.

Jacqueline Bouvier Kennedy Onassis would grace the next cover of *Vanity Fair* with the cover line "Forever Jackie." The issue was a big seller and the beginning of a winning formula: dead Kennedys. Inside was a lengthy piece by Dominick Dunne. That issue, July 1994's, would be the first with my name on its masthead, listed as editorial assistant.

In case you were curious, the flame-haired, billowy-bosomed

woman sitting to my right at dinner, whom in that moment I mistook for Lee Radziwill, was Georgette Mosbacher, a cosmetics executive, minor social figure, and Republican Party fundraiser and insider. She was married to Robert Mosbacher, who had run George H. W. Bush's successful 1988 presidential campaign before serving as Bush's commerce secretary. Georgette would go on to become Donald Trump's ambassador to Poland. For those without a well-developed social-world palate, mixing up Georgette Mosbacher with the elegant and pedigreed Lee Radziwill is like confusing a corn dog with caviar.

Chapter 8

During my first few months, I began to study magazines, new and old, like they were religious scrolls, trying to understand them, their key components, how they differed, who the reader was, how they did what they did, pull quotes and captions jumping off the pages. I was still going out most nights, hitting the town, staying out late, but I occasionally began to call it a night a little earlier, refusing that final drink that might push me over the edge. I was beginning to spend some nights in, too, surrounded by piles of magazines, trying to unlock their magic, hoping some would rub off on me.

Pat was a professional and lifelong executive assistant, and had been in Condé Nast's Human Resources department before being assigned to Graydon when he started. She was his first assistant, and I was his second. Her role was more passive, mine more active. I was always on the move, running errands, distributing papers. Pat spent most of the day sitting at her desk, covering the phones, making sure meetings happened on time and that Graydon got to his outside appointments and knew where he was meant to be, coordinating the day with his driver—a coveted Condé Nast perk.

I would watch Pat closely, study her like I had those patrons at 44. She was an old pro, great at her job, putting her boss's needs before her own. She made lists of what she needed to accomplish each day and would methodically go about doing so. I too began to make to-do lists. And when she asked me to do something, I would put whatever I was doing on hold and jump up and immediately get it done. I knew that keeping Pat happy, and pleased with my work and effort, was as important to my success as anything, because it would no doubt get back to Graydon. I was aware that I was under a microscope, more so than the other assistants.

But there was only so much I could learn from Pat. She was an executive assistant and had little interest in the inner workings of the editorial operation. So my morning routine of distributing manuscripts and galleys and other notes became an hour of study, as I'd go office to office, having a cigarette with those editors who smoked, which was half the staff—the other half constantly complained about it—talking about magazines, writers, politics, movies, books, and gossip. This would eventually be interrupted by Pat, who would call office to office, down the line, looking for me, needing me to run an errand or get Graydon a coffee. I'd rush back, out of breath, ready for duty.

Because I worked for the boss, I was treated differently than the other assistants. I was given access, free rein, not dismissed like other entry-level types might have been. I was a good ally to have. This was all a very strange feeling—I'd never been considered important before, or maybe "important-*adjacent*" is a better term, and it felt good. I took advantage of that, learning as much as I could, absorbing information like a sponge, those words of Graydon's a constant refrain in my head, like Obi-Wan's voice in a young Luke Skywalker's: "If you work hard and pay close attention, you can learn everything you'll ever need to know working for me for a few years." I wasn't going to let this opportunity pass me by. I was going to learn the ways of the force.

I did work hard, and it didn't go unnoticed. Graydon would pull me aside and with a nod of encouragement tell me, "Keep doing what you're doing, and don't fuck it up"—or give me a knowing smile after watching me from his desk, Camel Light hanging from his lips, as I accomplished my latest task. I was there every morning at eight A.M., sometimes not leaving until twelve or thirteen hours later. I'd be there alone, after eight P.M., typing up thank-you notes or filing correspondence. I *wasn't* going to fuck this up. What I lacked in knowledge, experience, and training I was going to make up for with blood, sweat, and tears.

About six weeks into my tenure, on June 12, there was a grue-some murder in Los Angeles that made national news. Initially, it wasn't because of its victims, a thirty-five-year-old woman named Nicole Brown Simpson and a twenty-five-year-old waiter from a nearby Brentwood restaurant, Mezzaluna, named Ron Goldman, but because the woman's ex-husband was O. J. Simpson, the Hall of Fame NFL running back, and he was a suspect.

The murders were the talk of the office. Well, they were the talk of *every* office *everywhere*. America loves murder mysteries, crime stories, and celebrities, even more so on their way down than up—this one was hard to pass up. Simpson went from being suspected of the murders to the prime suspect, and a warrant was issued for his arrest. Five days later, on June 17, as I was watching Game Five of the NBA finals, Knicks-Rockets, O.J. was scheduled to turn himself in. Suddenly, they broke into the game with the news that O.J. was on the run, in the back of his friend Al Cowl-ings's white Ford Bronco, with Cowlings at the wheel, Simpson pointing a gun at his own head. Los Angeles news helicopters had zeroed in on the white Bronco, trailed by an armada of LAPD squad cars. There were people cheering him on from highway overpasses. It was like watching the news, but it felt like some-thing different too, like watching a television show or a film, but it was also like sports, because it was happening in real time, and there were people who had seen this news coverage and left their house to go watch it unfold live, and root for O.J. from overpasses. It was a postmodern, meta, televised clusterfuck. Every major network broke away to show this slow-speed chase, NBC splitting the screen between it and the game.

Everyone was glued to the television. Almost one hundred mil-lion people tuned in to watch O. J. Simpson blow his head off. Which of course he didn't. He eventually turned himself in, later that night, setting up the Trial of the Century, which would begin in January 1995 and end with Simpson's acquittal in October. It would become the biggest story in the world, dominating the news cycle in 1995, and have lasting cultural repercussions. It wasn't the first modern trial to be nationally televised—that honor goes to serial killer Ted Bundy, in 1979—but because Simpson was already famous, and Black, it hit the trifecta of combining crime, celebrity culture, and race.* Every moment of that trial was televised, every day, on every broadcast network, and it's all anyone did during the day for those eight months. Then every night, when the courtroom went dark, that day's proceedings were dissected, picked apart, obsessed over. The media was on it like flies on shit. It was the only game in town.

Vanity Fair's Dominick Dunne would spend much of 1995 holed up in the Chateau Marmont and that L.A. courtroom, covering the trial for the magazine. He made perfect sense: The murders and subsequent trial had similarities to the case that launched his career as a writer after his daughter's murder in 1982 at the hands of an ex. It was personal. He was an avenging angel—for his daughter, Nicole Brown Simpson, and Ron Goldman.

Dominick found a way into a story that was covered in the macro and the micro in the newspapers, in weekly magazines, and on television, which he was on every day; the courtroom cameras constantly caught him scribbling in his notebook, then he'd make the rounds of the cable news circuit at night. But a monthly magazine works on a longer lead time than other print mediums (except books, of course). Text needs to be in weeks before it actually hits the newsstand as a finished product. The twenty-four-hour news cycle was on warp speed compared to us, and it was getting faster in real time thanks to the rise of cable news. Dominick had to find a way to write about the Simpson trial without simply rehashing the events from the courtroom, because that would all be yesterday's news by the time his story hit newsstands a month later. In order to make people want to run out to the newsstand, plunk down $3.99 for information that was weeks old, he needed a different take. Dominick did break news regarding the case occasionally, but he also wrote as much about what was happening outside the Los Angeles courtroom as what was happening inside,

* The acquittal of the four LAPD officers accused of beating Rodney King and the resulting L.A. riots in 1992 were still a lingering source of racial tension in the city.

the effect the trial was having on the culture of the city and its inhabitants. He wrote about the bit players, the hangers-on, what he'd overheard at a fancy restaurant or Beverly Hills dinner party—and most important, he made himself a character in the story. So there was Dominick, in the courtroom, on television; then there was Dominick, on CNN that same night, talking about what we'd all seen earlier that day; then you'd read the story a month later, in which he'd write about where he went to dinner after that appearance, whom he sat next to, what he overheard. It was behind the scenes, after the scenes, jump cuts to different scenes, flashbacks and flash-forwards to different movies altogether, noir and porn, a B movie recut as an art house murder mystery with a disjointed narrative. Dominick's stories were gossipy, name-droppy, trashy, smart, fun, kind of upscale, and kind of down-market. High and low and everything in between. It was the convergence of the perfect writer and the perfect story at the perfect moment.

And readers loved it. America loved him. He was already a well-known writer, had written bestselling books, but those stories, and the courtroom cameras, made him into a legitimate cultural superstar, one of the most famous writers in America, if not the world. He was in high demand for the nightly cable shows that rehashed that day's events. He would even get his own television show in 2002, *Dominick Dunne's Power, Privilege, and Justice,* on Court TV, which ran until his death in 2009. One of the most famous and lasting images from the Simpson trial is Dominick's face, in the gallery, his chin almost hitting the floor as that not-guilty verdict is read. In that moment, with much of America responding in a similar fashion, we were him, just as he was us. As a journalist, Dominick had managed to form an unbreakable connection with his readers and viewers that was indelible.

When it came to filing Dominick's O.J. copy, it was always down to the wire. His would be the last pages out the door, the last ones shipped off to the printer. During the end of an issue's close, when the copy editors were dotting every last *i*, crossing every last *t*, and undangling all those danglers, when the lawyers and fact-checkers were making last-minute revisions, I'd stay late into the night, get handed a final galley, and jump into a waiting Lincoln Town Car to take the pages to the Dakota, so Graydon could read them, sign off.

The O.J. trial was the biggest story in a generation, and I was thrust in the middle of it, however tangentially, and it was exciting. I felt like I was a part of something. Dominick was on television, in the courtroom; then his voice was on the speakerphone in Graydon's office, talking about the day's events and discussing the topic of his next column; then he was standing in front of me, in the office, gossiping about the trial; then I was holding the first draft of his story, devouring it, unable to put it down, hanging on every word. And then a week or two later that stack of first-bound issues would arrive in the office, with the finished product ready to go out into the world, to be eagerly consumed by millions of people. I'd watched the process from start to finish, from idea to end product. I was in the belly of the beast, behind the scenes, learning along the way, about how the media works, how stories come together, how narratives take hold, and the cultural power of celebrity. It was like a drug, and I was hooked.

Dominick may have been the first celebrity I knew personally. When his semi-fictionalized book about the trial, *Another City, Not My Own*, was released a few years later, he mentioned my name in passing: "I had Dana check with Garcetti's office, and it's going to be a three-day weekend at the trial. . . ." It was a throwaway moment in the book, but it meant everything to me.

The Simpson trial would change so many things, influence popular culture in innumerable ways. It turned regular people—lawyers, cops, a judge, limo drivers, Kato Kaelin, and even a dog, an Akita also named Kato*—into celebrities. Reality was suddenly so much more interesting than the scripted stuff. It was real life with the twists and turns of cheesy soap operas, which were bumped from their network time slots to make way for the trial, a move they would never recover from, their audience moving

* Really.

seamlessly from soap to grime. It wasn't a huge leap for some executive somewhere to say, "Hey, wait a second, look at these ratings, I think there's something here."* At that same moment there were three little girls sitting at home watching Daddy on television each day, and here of course I'm talking about Kim, Khloe, and Kourtney, and their father, Robert Kardashian, who was part of O.J.'s defense team. The O.J. trial was the urtext of reality television, the beginning of a cultural infection that would spread like cancer in the next decade. A shit show if ever there was one.

I don't want to rehash the O. J. Simpson trial here, because what else is there to say about it? But the rush and thrill of playing even a tiny part in the biggest global news story of the age was the most exciting thing to ever happen to me at that time.

But I'm getting ahead of myself. As much as Dominick's coverage of the trial would help the magazine, goose newsstand sales and subscriptions, which would increase advertising and revenue, there was something else going on in the summer of 1994 that would have an even more lasting effect. Something that none of us knew about at the time, the germ of two future ideas that would help turn *Vanity Fair* into the most influential general-interest magazine of the next two decades.

---

* In fairness, MTV's *The Real World* debuted in 1992, predating the Simpson trial by three years, and the genre's roots actually go further back, to PBS's 1973 series *An American Family*, but the modern incarnation of what would become one of America's biggest contributions to twenty-first-century culture began with the Simpson saga.

Chapter 9

I hit something hard at the end of that last chapter, dangled a cliffhanger that I'm not paying off immediately, and for that, I'm sorry. But while it sounds like I was doing great over those first few months, working hard, getting the job done, not fucking up—and I was—it was an uphill battle for me, internally.

Being surrounded by a group of really smart young co-workers, as I was at *Vanity Fair* and Condé Nast, I lived in a constant state of fear that I would be found out, exposed. I had a secret to keep. I was still embarrassed about my backstory, would change the subject if any questions about my past came up. I struggled with basic grammar. My spelling was atrocious. I didn't know the correct places to put commas in sentences and apostrophes in words when I was typing up notes and letters, and would have them returned to me from Graydon unsigned, with edit marks on them, needing to be retyped. Graydon never mentioned it, left it there on paper, but it was humiliating. Hard work alone could only take me so far.

I was constantly intimidated by my colleagues and the writers and editors I encountered each day. These were people, kids and adults alike, who had sparkling résumés and superior educations, had gone to the best high schools and universities, had graduate degrees in journalism. Literary references dropped into conversations would go right over my head—*It's just like when Jane leaves Lowood for Thornfield Hall!* I'd nod or laugh along, as if to say, *Of course, I get it.* But I didn't. They were well read and well bred. They had been the editors of their school papers, been champion debaters, written award-winning essays, and were highly trained to be writers and editors, pursuing careers in their chosen profession. They were built for this shit.

Of course there was also another group, a whole different animal, the future fashion editors and stylists, who were the daughters of either fashion icons or famous socialites, or were just simply so beautiful, with such great style, that Condé Nast couldn't *not* hire them—and here I'm being vague, but I'm mostly talking about *Vogue* and its assistant corps. I didn't fit in with them either, obviously. They were intimidating too, but on another level, totally unapproachable, like the popular clique in a 1980s teen movie, and I was no quarterback.

I refer to myself as a college dropout, which technically I am, because there's a certain romance to it, like I stormed off in frustration because I was so far ahead of all those petulant and petty undergrads, had learned all I needed to learn and was ready to tackle the real world. Both Graydon and Si Newhouse had dropped out of college (which may be why Graydon had more patience with me than most others would have), as did Steve Jobs, Bill Gates, and a long list of boldfaced names. There's a certain cachet to it nowadays that didn't exist back then.

But calling myself a college dropout is being generous and certainly doesn't tell the whole story. I wasn't simply a bad student. I was one of the worst, ever. A slow reader, bad at math and science, easily distracted. I was constantly tested for learning disabilities, but none were ever found, so it was just assumed that I simply lacked intelligence. I also avoided speaking up in class, afraid of being wrong and the humiliation that would follow. My fear of judgment and my insecurities took total control of me. I had terrible handwriting, so I hated writing. I struggled to learn in a traditional way, and a traditional education was all that was available to me and most kids of my generation.* These frustrations compounded and grew into a disdain for school and learn-

---

* As much as my generation romanticizes it now, growing up in the seventies and eighties mostly sucked.

ing. I was the youngest of four and my older siblings were all great students, excelled, never struggled in school. I was the fuckup. School just never clicked for me.

All this failure at a young age, not surprisingly, led to isolation and loneliness, which became a direct route to self-loathing and hopelessness. As a result, I began to look inward, to try to understand what was wrong with me, which of course couldn't be fully examined or understood at a young age, so I would get frustrated and uncomfortable around other people. I would eventually look outward, and into the future and the great beyond, becoming unmoored from my own life, fantasizing about what might be out there in the world, just waiting to be discovered. Believing that there was always something better on the horizon, just beyond reach. This is often the foundation of anxiety, addiction, alcoholism, depression, codependency, and maybe worst of all, creativity, and a future in some creative field, which leads right back to some combination of those others. But of course, I was stuck at home, in the suburbs, still a kid, under someone else's roof and rules, that passage into adulthood—*which was going to solve everything!**—still years away.

I needed an escape. The first thing I discovered that scratched that itch, filled that void, connected with my teenage angst, was music and books. Music was easy to experience, as I had older siblings, so three record collections to beg, borrow, and steal from. The Beatles, the Stones, Neil Young, David Bowie, Lou Reed, the Clash, Elvis Costello, Blondie, the Police, the Pretenders. Books were readily available too, and also offered other worlds that I was desperate to be part of. They offered characters I could idealize—*I want to be just like him.*

In high school, being a middle-class white kid, I became particularly attracted to twentieth-century American counterculture writers like Jack Kerouac, Kurt Vonnegut, Tom Robbins, John Irving, Hunter Thompson, and Charles Bukowski, and books like John Knowles's *A Separate Peace* and Robert Pirsig's *Zen and*

---

* It didn't.

the Art of Motorcycle Maintenance. They existed in a different world, a more vibrant version than what was available to me in my sad little bedroom. The characters were adults, but they didn't seem like any of the adults I knew. These books gave me hope that there was freedom just around the corner, and that freedom was adulthood, and it would no doubt be as great as I'd imagined it would be. A vision of adulthood that is so captivating to teenage boys (and so completely unrealistic—fiction).

And if you were a teenager mired in a constant existential crisis growing up in America in the second half of the twentieth century, there was one book and one character that spoke to you like no other: J. D. Salinger's *The Catcher in the Rye* and its protagonist, Holden Caulfield. Salinger put into words, through the voice of Holden, what we were feeling. Holden Caulfield was smart, sensitive, misunderstood, lonely, and cynical. He was able to express what we were not. He made it okay to say to yourself, *Holy shit, everything is bullshit, just like I thought*. Which is really appealing because it's comforting, it confirms your deepest suspicions, and it's kind of true (and also kind of not).

While idealizing Holden Caulfield, who attended and was expelled from the fictional Pencey Preparatory School, I began to romanticize boarding school. Boarding schools make appearances in a lot of John Irving's books too. It makes sense. It felt like an answer, an escape, a geographic cure. It seemed like attending boarding school was cheating at the game of life, getting a head start on adulthood, on being on your own. On finding yourself.

Before email and the internet and Google and algorithms, when there was just regular old mail, among the piles of letters and postcards and bills and magazines and catalogs, boarding school brochures would occasionally arrive in our mailbox. I would sit and read them from cover to cover, fantasizing about being in those small classrooms, grass and flowers and sunshine or piles of snow out the windows. They looked nothing like the classrooms or schools I had been in. The teachers and students seemed so engaged and interested in learning. There was always a picture of a really stunning WASPy-looking girl, an action shot of her playing a preppy sport like lacrosse or field hockey; we would fall in love and she would be my girlfriend and we'd summer on the Cape together. There were photos of great-looking groups of kids, stretched out on lawns, all wearing J.Crew roll-neck sweaters and L.L.Bean duck boots, books of poetry strewn around them. They all looked so happy. Those boarding school brochures were my porn.*

The second thing a sensitive, introspective, and lonely teenager discovers after books is drinking, quickly followed by drugs, which were harder to get your hands on than booze or a book— they don't sell drugs at the library, although in the 1980s, they *did* sell drugs in Bryant Park, right behind the New York Public Library—so you had to work your way up to that.

I liked how drinking made me feel immediately. It gave me the confidence I lacked, so I could socialize, loosen up and talk to people. It made me funnier and better looking.† It brought me closer to all those hard-drinking characters I loved, and drinking was what adults did. (This is also why I started smoking cigarettes at about twelve, which must have looked ridiculous.) It had the effect of taking me one step closer to the future and somewhere else. And on top of that, I was good at it, *really* good at it, and I wasn't very good at anything. If drinking were a professional sport, I would have gotten endorsement deals.

I smoked pot for the first time also when I was twelve—I stole it from my older brother like everyone else—and immediately took to that, too. It wasn't long before coke entered the picture. It turned out drinking and smoking pot were just flings on my way to falling in love, which I did the first time I snorted a line. It gave me energy, focus, and confidence, made me chatty while I remained totally in control. And cocaine was everywhere, readily available even to a fifteen-year-old, sold on the street a ten-minute car ride away in the Bronx.

A year later, my obsession with boarding school and my bur-

---

* Metaphorically speaking, of course. I didn't . . . you know.

† Still does.

geoning drug habit were about to collide into one narrative thread. Because with all that drinking and all those drugs, which were my main pursuit by then, my grades had begun to slip below passable. A D-minus would have been cause for celebration because at least it wasn't a failing grade. The decision was soon made that I should be shipped off to boarding school, before the jaws of life were needed to get me out of the car crash my life had become.

This was welcome news to me. After all, it had been my fantasy all along.

But what school would offer me a place, with my spotty grades? As it turns out, there was one, a small school called the Putney School, set on five hundred pristine wooded acres in southern Vermont. Oddly, I was accepted at the very last minute for the next fall. It was a progressive boarding school with a rich history and illustrious alumni, especially in the arts and letters: photographer Sally Mann; filmmaker Errol Morris; television writer and producer Carlton Cuse; Pulitzer Prize–winning journalist J. Anthony Lukas; actors Téa Leoni, Felicity Huffman, Ken Olin, Tim Daly, and Wallace Shawn (son of longtime *New Yorker* editor William Shawn); and LinkedIn founder Reid Hoffman.

Founded in 1935, Putney was one of the first coed boarding schools in the country. It had a functioning farm where the students did much of the grueling work that began at five A.M. and left you smelling like cow shit all day. The assumption was that I struggled within the confines of a structured, traditional public education, so why not give a progressive school and its small classes, collaborative and liberal approach to education, and emphasis on creative thinking and the arts a try? It might be just what I needed. And that's not a bad assumption—but unfortunately, it just so happens that in the eighties, the Putney School had gained the reputation as one of the most renowned fuckup schools in the country, a den of sin and transgression. And at that time, they would pretty much accept anyone. Case in point.

The Putney School's per capita drug use would have been off the charts, if such a chart existed, and my arrival only pushed those numbers up. It was *The Catcher in the Rye*'s Pencey Prep as written by Hunter Thompson. As the eighties turned into the nineties, the Putney School would begin to turn itself around—not coincidentally timed to my graduating—and is now often included on lists of the best boarding schools in America, with a price tag of more than $60,000 a year.

With a little more than a hundred students, class sizes were small, and I quickly became engaged and took an interest in learning, which was new to me. And thanks to a pass/fail grading system, I appeared to be a good student, at least to my parents.

The teachers at Putney were far different from any previous teachers I had encountered. The French teacher taught a class in French film and introduced me to Godard and Truffaut and the French New Wave. I took a sculpture class where I learned how to weld. My English teacher, Dave Calicchio, was a former boxer, a playwright, and a novelist, like a character dreamed up by Hemingway. He'd tell us stories about hanging out with Jack Kerouac and Allen Ginsberg in New York in the fifties and had us reading books by all those writers I'd grown to love. Dave was lifelong friends with John Irving, who lived nearby, and it's said that he would read all of Irving's manuscripts, before the novelist turned them in to his editor. This was heady stuff for someone who had never taken much interest in teachers or their lessons.

But while I was suddenly engaged academically and interested in learning, getting to watch *Breathless* and *The 400 Blows* and weld shit, my appetite for drinking and drugs also blossomed.

There's an art to drinking and doing drugs at boarding school, as any alum will tell you, and its guiding principle is "Don't get caught." This was not an art form I managed to master. I got caught almost immediately, within my first few weeks, smashed and stumbling through the halls of a neighboring dorm, well after curfew. Strike one of a three-strikes policy. I grew more cautious, learning the system, figuring out how to get fucked-up undetected by the authorities, although not quite cautious enough, as strike two would arrive that winter, soon after I returned from break. After strike two, the policy was to issue random urine tests for the offender. Every few weeks or so, I would get hauled out of a class to the nurse's office and have to pee in a cup. But I tempted fate; I didn't curb my illicit activities. I made a totally unscientific assumption and leap of faith that the urine testing was just a deterrent, convinced the samples weren't actually tested for traces of drugs. As far as I know, this irresponsible calculation proved to be correct, as I never heard about a positive test.

In the spring, when a bong was found in the crawl space underneath my dorm, suspicion immediately fell on me. And for good reason. When the whole dorm was called into the common area for an all-dorm meeting, with the bong sitting on the coffee table, this question was put to the group: "Whose is this?" I looked around the room nervously. A few eyes turned to me. Was someone going to give me up? To my surprise, like in that famous scene in *Spartacus,* a hand went up. "It's mine." It was the weird anarchist kid who was probably from Greenwich, Connecticut. As was his habit, no matter the context or situation, he was making a political stand. Then another hand shot up, and another, until everybody's hands were up, claiming ownership of the bong. Though it would turn out my struggle was far from over, this battle had been won cleanly. But that good feeling, and my salvation, wouldn't last long.

The next day I was called into the head of the school's office, which was never a good thing. I was told that it was assumed it was my bong; they had heard I was still doing drugs and drinking, even though I hadn't been caught and they had no evidence. I tried to protest. But it was clear to them I had a problem and I needed help. They gave me a choice: Attend drug counseling at the Brattleboro Retreat, a well-regarded rehab nearby, and finish out the year, or don't attend and get thrown out now. My thoughts turned to Holden Caulfield—getting expelled from school set the whole plot of *The Catcher in the Rye* in motion, and there was something sexy about that. But before I could answer, I was informed that my parents had been called and that they would be driving up the next day to either take me home for good or attend the counseling sessions with me. This was not going to go my way.

I should mention two things here. One, my parents had gotten divorced four years earlier, and they were not getting along. In fact, they weren't even on *non*-speaking terms at that point. The idea that they would have to see each other, sit *next to* each other, in a room, with me and a drug counselor at a rehab facility while I was being asked about my drug use—this was not exactly something I was looking forward to. Second—and this sounds random, like a non sequitur, but I promise it pays off *big*—I had been in rehearsals the previous few months for the big spring play. It was a musical, written by Kurt Weill, called *Down in the Valley*. It was about a love triangle between a lovestruck teenager, Brack Weaver; the object of his desire, Jennie; and a wicked businessman named Thomas Bouché, who also digs Jennie, whose father is in debt to him. You can guess the rest. It ends with Bouché dead and Brack Weaver sitting in a jail cell awaiting the business end of a rope. If you ever get a chance to see it, don't. It's an awful play, pure Americana kitsch. I'm surprised Weill allowed his name to be attached to it. Not only was I in it, I played Thomas Bouché, the baddie. And opening night was a few days away.

The head of the school didn't want to disrupt the play and urged me to go through with the drug counseling. It would just be a day, I would make it back in time for that evening's rehearsal, and the show could go on. I begrudgingly agreed. I was already in trouble and my parents were going to kill me; one way or another I was going to have to face the music. It was the only choice out of two really bad options.

In an adolescence full of bad decisions, what I did next stands apart. I went back to my room. I paced. I might have cried, maybe screamed into my pillow at the top of my lungs, punched a wall. (In the film this is a montage sequence.) I didn't sleep. Tomorrow would be perhaps the worst day of my life. I lay awake all night, hopeless, out of options. As the sun was coming up, my thoughts turned to Holden Caulfield. What would he do if he were in this situation? It didn't take long for me to realize that he would get the fuck out of there. After all, Holden on the run, on the move, is the motor of *The Catcher in the Rye*. There was my answer. I leapt out of bed and began packing my backpack.

It was a straight shot from the dormitory's back door into the woods. A few hundred yards down the hill from the tree line there was a path that would take me to the main road. This being Vermont, a state full of hippies and old people, hitchhiking was common and easy, so I would stick out my thumb and get a ride into town, Putney, or close to it. Once in Putney I would figure out a ride to Brattleboro, where there was a Greyhound bus station. I'd buy a ticket to Worcester, Massachusetts, and catch the next train to New York. I had just enough cash in my pocket to get me to the city. Once there, I'd figure it out. That, at least, was the plan, and the early stages of that plan went off without a hitch. I somehow made it to Brattleboro and the Greyhound station. I bought a ticket to Worcester, looking around nervously as I did, to see if I had been tailed, but I seemed to be in the clear.

I got on the bus and took a seat in the back. I knew my parents were on their way up to Vermont that very minute—separately, of course—and imagined I might pass them on the highway, the two of them going north, me heading south. I thought about the looks on everyone's faces when they realized I'd outsmarted them, like the end of a prison-break movie when the warden and the guards find nothing but pillows stuffed under the inmate's blanket—cut to me, on the bus, a broad smile on my face, squinting at the sun, tasting freedom. That's the awesome movie-ending version of this story. That didn't happen. Here's what did:

Before the bus's doors closed, a state trooper got on and started walking up the aisle slowly. He was holding a piece of paper, looking closely at every passenger, then glancing down at the paper as he walked, studying every face as he made his way to the back of the bus. I could have saved him time, stood up, said, "Hey, copper, I'm the fella you're looking for," but I was frozen, terrified, or hoping that maybe, just maybe, it was someone else they were after, a real criminal. Would they really send a state trooper after me? Weren't there real crimes and criminals they should have been attending to? Probably not; this was Vermont, with one of the lowest crime rates in America. It's possible I *was* the most wanted criminal in the state at that moment. Finally, the trooper got to me. We made eye contact. He looked down at the piece of paper, then back at me. I looked up at him, and he flipped the piece of paper around, as if to say, *Gotcha*. And he did. It was a photograph of me—in character, as Thomas Bouché, from rehearsals. I had a cowboy hat on and one of those Colonel Sanders ribbons tied around my neck and was wearing a white blazer. I *literally* looked like Colonel Sanders, and about as dangerous as an eight-piece bucket with two sides and four biscuits. This was the most humiliating arrest in the history of law enforcement.

The trooper reached for his walkie-talkie and spoke into it proudly, as if he had just grabbed Al Capone.

"Got him."

I didn't technically get arrested. They didn't put handcuffs on me. They *could* have done both. I was just "taken into custody." As I found out, because I was an enrolled student at Putney and under eighteen, the school was my legal guardian, and I was apprehended by the police as a "confirmed runaway (RAW)." I was "evading the person or proper authority having legal custody."

Putney's dean of students picked me up at the police station in Brattleboro and took me directly to rehab (*do not pass go, do not collect $200*), where my parents were waiting for me. They were about as thrilled to see me as I was to see them. I tried not to make eye contact, looking past them, out the window, at an expansive and stunning view of the Green Mountains, right where the West River and the Connecticut River meet.* I told the drug counselor what he wanted to hear, was contrite and apologetic. For a parent, there's a point where a badly behaved fuckup of a child, whom you can just simply get angry at and punish, suddenly becomes one with a serious issue and real problems who needs help. At sixteen, of course, I didn't think I needed help, but it was clear to everyone else that I did.

I was given rehab-and-school-mandated therapy for the rest of the year, which meant weekly sessions with a local Putney psychiatrist. He was a lovely old New Yorker who had moved up to

---

* It is a beautiful rehab, if you ever find yourself in need of one.

Vermont in the 1970s (which was like half of Vermont's population), and I grew to really like talking to him. I don't think I was ready to understand my own head, the root of why I did the things I did, or to have those kinds of conversations about myself that make therapy worthwhile, but it kept me from getting kicked out of school.

After the trauma of rehab, my parents decided to stay in Vermont for a few days to catch opening night of *Down in the Valley*. It was held in a tiny theater, so when I came onstage for the first time, it was hard to miss them, sitting together, about ten feet away. Apparently, I killed.

So that, in a nutshell, was high school. And when your list of extracurricular activities begins with state troopers and ends with rehab, getting into college is going to be difficult.

I wasn't that interested in continuing my education, at least at that point. I just wanted to get to New York City, where I somehow knew my future was waiting. I did take a year off, moved out west, and when my mother suggested a place called the Eugene Lang College of Liberal Arts, which I'd never heard of, I didn't think much of it. When she told me it was located in Greenwich Village, my ears perked up. I filled out the short application, by hand, and mailed it in.

Eugene Lang was a tiny college that was part of the New School, which is a progressive conglomerate of small schools that are mostly arts oriented—Parsons School of Design being the most famous—and the New School for Social Research, which offers graduate classes and continuing education for adults. The New School had a well-regarded acting program, aligned with the Actors Studio, and a few music schools, its jazz program most famously. But Eugene Lang was for kids who couldn't get into, or afford, NYU.

There was a dorm on East Twelfth Street and Third Avenue, mostly for the Parsons students, that I moved into. Briefly. Because the whole of the East Village in 1991 was essentially an outdoor drug market. You could get anything you wanted just by walking out the door. And the bars didn't check IDs in that era.

Once again, I had been enrolled at the worst place possible for me. I went to a few classes for the first week or two, then just stopped going. The night, and the streets, and the bars won out. And that was the end of my short college career, which meant I was on my own, needed a job and an apartment. That eventually led me to the kitchen at Union Square Cafe and that dump of an apartment in Little Italy.

Which is all to say, among the young staffers at *Vanity Fair* and Condé Nast, I was the definition of an outlier. On top of that, when Graydon said, "Don't fuck it up," I don't think he realized that was all I'd ever known how to do.

Chapter 10

One of my daily tasks as Graydon's assistant was to file correspondence and other papers in the giant wall of filing cabinets stationed behind my desk. Every evening, once the office emptied out, I would file the stack of papers and notes that would accumulate on my desk throughout the day. Early on, as I sat there filing, I'd read through old correspondence, congratulatory notes, and press clippings. It was like reading a biography, as I assembled a portrait of my new boss piece by piece, note by note. It was almost voyeuristic, like going through someone's medicine cabinet at a dinner party.

By the summer of 1994, Graydon had been at *Vanity Fair* for almost two years. The first issue under his editorship had been November 1992, Liz Taylor on the cover, holding a condom, with the cover line "Liz Aid" in black lettering. Many of the personal notes were dated 1992, from well-wishers congratulating him on that first issue, from celebrities, writers, fashion designers, and other media figures. Somewhere, some kid just like me had probably typed them up, had their boss sign it. There was a file labeled PRESS that contained copies of all the articles that had been written about Graydon and *Vanity Fair,* from when he first took over, including a *New York Times* story from July 1992, right around the time he was hired. It was less about Graydon than it was about *Vanity Fair* and Tina Brown and the magazine's success, although its financial picture was still hazy. Did it make money? Did it lose money? Did Si recoup the $50 million he spent relaunching it? As I mentioned earlier, when it came to Condé Nast's profit and loss, especially title by title, it was impossible to know unless you were in the innermost circle or a Newhouse.

The media was obsessed with trying to figure out Condé Nast's financials. According to the *Times, Vanity Fair* had made a profit of somewhere in the three-to-six-million-dollar range in 1991 after turning its first profit in 1988, of under a million dollars. It was charging $48,000 for a page of color advertising, $30,000 if it was black and white (color ink is more expensive), and had run 1,440 pages of advertising, which is where the bulk of *Vanity Fair's*—and most of Condé Nast's—revenue came from. The *Times* story reinforced the idea of what a star Tina was and how much she had achieved during her run. It cited figures from the second half of 1991, when circulation—a combination of subscriptions and newsstand sales—hit 991,178, a 25 percent increase from the previous year (those numbers were inflated by the sales of the Demi Moore naked-and-pregnant cover, still considered one of the most iconic magazine covers ever). Newsstand sales jumped 15 percent for all of 1991, to 313,948, and newsstand sales are the best indicator of a magazine's vitality and appeal to consumers, its heat in the marketplace and cultural reach. Both those figures showed impressive growth year over year and a magazine still on the rise, not cooling down.

Graydon was an afterthought, not mentioned until the sixth paragraph. Tina was in the lead, above the fold, mentioned in the second sentence, following this: "*Vanity Fair* might be the hottest magazine on the market, but does it make money?" Tina was given all the credit for *Vanity Fair's* success, and rightfully so; Graydon hadn't even put out an issue yet. But I mean, how do you follow *that*? Graydon was left with mop-up duty, quoted in the last paragraph of the story after this editorializing from the *Times:* "Ms. Brown clearly developed an appealing formula for *Vanity Fair.*"

"[*The New York Observer*] is a great raucous noisy dinner party," Graydon told the *Times.* "*Vanity Fair* is a more formal setting, with liveried servants standing at every elbow. It is a very smooth elegant dinner party and I hope to maintain that. The mandate is to make it my own magazine. But I like it as a reader and my changes will be gradual."

In other words, he had an immense amount of pressure on his shoulders. Sure, he had to maintain Tina's formula so as not to alienate the magazine's readership, make the changes gradually, but the key quote here is this: "The mandate is to make it my own magazine." And therein lay the problem. How the hell do you do that? It was an almost impossible task following Tina, who had not only helped *Vanity Fair* rise from the ashes in 1985 but had been its savior and had turned it into a publishing industry success story, if not *the* publishing industry success story, of the eighties. She cast a long shadow. And she walked away on top, with *Vanity Fair* on an upward trajectory—clever—a hard act to follow. Graydon had to thread the needle of keeping the status quo while making the magazine his own.

He wasn't coming from some other major national magazine, wasn't a star editor, hadn't yet succeeded on the national stage like Tina. *The New York Observer* was tiny, a local paper for knowing Manhattanites. *Spy* had been a success, but a small-*s* success. It was a cult magazine. It put Graydon on the map—and Kurt Andersen, *Spy*'s co-founder, who would go on to edit *New York* magazine—but it wasn't a major player in the magazine world outside of New York. (Graydon and Kurt sold *Spy* in 1991.) When he was handed the reins of *Vanity Fair,* it was already a well-funded, well-oiled, successful machine. He was given a championship team after succeeding in a small market. But even teams with high payrolls can stumble; the game is won on the field, and there are plenty of examples of star-laden organizations stumbling, and not just in sports. He wasn't a scrappy upstart anymore. He could have whoever he wanted, hire whatever writer, photographer—he was now at the top of the food chain. And while that sounds incredibly appealing, it's also dangerous and difficult.

On top of that, *Spy* had been ruthless to *Vanity Fair* and Condé Nast, skewering its affected culture, especially Tina Brown and *Vanity Fair*'s slavish and obsequious devotion to the rich and powerful. Graydon had stumbled behind enemy lines. In 1994, as I watched him in that corner booth from behind the bar, according to the gossip, the whispers at 44, "stumbling" is the exact word that may have been used. There were rumors. He was out of his depth, Si was getting impatient. Graydon was finished before he could achieve that mandate. The vultures were circling.

I don't know how much of this I was aware of at the time. I was so focused on my own transition and survival that it didn't even occur to me that Graydon might have been struggling. But he was, as he would tell me later.

When a new editor takes over a magazine, the first thing they need to do is clean house. While it may sound cold, ruthless even, it must be done and is de rigueur. You have to figure out who's a partisan from the previous regime and get rid of them. It's standard practice in a lot of businesses, but nowhere is it as pronounced as it is in the magazine business and at Condé Nast. While Graydon brought in a handful of new staffers from the *Observer*, some of whom had been at *Spy* with him previously, he also made some other key hires, along with inheriting a handful of Tina's staff, a few who were enemies in his midst. These bitter dead-enders decided to wage a campaign against him, of both the whisper and shouting varieties. Graydon didn't know what he was doing, he was on the verge of being fired, his covers sucked, his sales figures were low, he wasn't as good as Tina. That *Times* story had some information only someone on the inside would have known. It was less a piece celebrating the success of *Vanity Fair* than it was an attempt to take Graydon down, smother him in his infancy.

These Tina holdovers had toiled away for her during her rise but felt left behind, slighted, when Tina didn't take them to *The New Yorker*, or thought they should have gotten the top job themselves, not this Canadian yahoo from *The New York Observer* and *Spy*.

Magazines aren't democracies. Editors in chief are dictators, ruling by decree. The whole operation, from top to bottom, is their vision, and they shoulder the responsibility of every single thing in every issue, and its success or failure. The buck stops there. Graydon would approve every word and photograph that went into every issue of the magazine—every caption, every pull quote, every photograph, every headline, the running order of the stories, who was writing those stories, down to the placement of the page numbers. All those papers and galleys and manuscripts that I was delivering every morning to the staff, all those notes and directives scribbled in the margins, were the final say on the matter. There was even a "Banned List"* of words that Graydon had decided were not to appear in the magazine under any circumstances, that he would add to on a whim, because a particular word had done him wrong and needed to be punished. And that was his right. But if you're a dictator, and your troops aren't in line, if there are some saboteurs among your ranks, you need to execute them publicly before they get footing, turn everyone against you, and overthrow your rule.

Graydon had a secret weapon to root out these saboteurs: Brian McNally. Every day, Brian oversaw a dining room full of catty Condé Nast editors, bouncing from table to table, schmoozing and gossiping. Brian knew more about what was going on at Condé Nast than maybe anyone inside or outside the company. One afternoon, a *Vanity Fair* senior editor, a Tina holdover, was talking shit about Graydon to Brian. What that editor didn't know was that Graydon and Brian were very close friends. A call was placed, a decision made.

Graydon was a benevolent dictator and highly empathic; he avoided confrontation. Which might have made him a good per-

---

* The Banned List: *a.k.a.; à la; bed-sitter* (for *apartment*); *boasted* (as in "had" or "featured"); *boîte* (for *restaurant*); *bond* ("I felt a strong bond with my mother") and *bonded; brilliant; centered* and *grounded* (to refer to a film star); *chic; chortled* (for *said*); *chuckled* (for *said*); *condo* (*condominium* was permissible); *cough up* (as in "to spend"); *doff; donned* (as in "put on"); *eatery* (for *restaurant*); *executive-produced* and suchlike; *flat* (for *apartment*); *flick; freebie; freeloader; fuck* (okay as an exclamation, not for having sex); *funky; garner; genius* (adj.); *gig; glitz; golfer; graduate* (as a transitive verb without *from*); *grown-up; guy; holler* (all forms); *honcho; hooker; joked* (for *said*); *legendary; lover* (for men and women); *moniker; of course; opine* (in any form); *paucity; pen* (used as a verb); *plethora; purloined; quipped; row* (meaning "to fight"); *sci-fi; scribe; sleaze; small screen* (for *TV*); *sported* (as in "wore"); *star turn; take* (as in a "comedic take"); diminutives for titles of books, movies, plays, etc. (i.e., not *Prince* for *The Prince of Tides*); *tome* (for *book*); *trendy; wanna; wannabe; weird.*

son but made him a bad dictator. Now he was cornered, had no other way out, had to cut all the heads off the Hydra before they multiplied. I remember the week he took control and fired a few of these saboteurs, including that senior editor. They were called down to his office late in the day, one by one. They would emerge a few minutes later, pale, shell-shocked, walk back to their office with their heads down, on full public display, a walk of shame. I'd never witnessed someone get fired before, had never been fired myself, and it was jarring. I was the first person they would see when they walked out of his office, would make eye contact. Even though some of them must have expected it, they looked like they'd just experienced the horrors of war or seen a ghost. They were told to clean out their desk immediately and escorted out of the building by security, soon to be replaced with less toxic blood. This was step one in Graydon's mandate to make *Vanity Fair* his own. I didn't realize it at the time, but step two was already in motion.

Graydon had a little brown leather-bound address book, around ten inches by eight, full of pages and pages of blue three-hole-punch paper. His weekly calendar was in there, at the front, and that was Pat's responsibility. The bulk of the book was his Rolodex, thousands of phone numbers and addresses that were added to constantly. Every Friday, it was my job to print out the updated address list on the sheets of little blue paper and replace the old Rolodex, so he had the most up-to-date version. Behind the Rolodex were pages of future stories, some assigned to writers, others broad sketches, which it was also my responsibility to update. The stories were arranged by month, followed by a section behind that labeled "Future." Eventually, a wall in Graydon's office would have a giant grid painted on it, like a Luddite's Excel sheet, broken down by month, from left to right, and by topic—COVER, CRIME/SCANDAL, HOLLYWOOD, INTERNATIONAL, SOCIETY, etc.—from top to bottom, and I would type up that information in big letters, print it out, trim it to size, and pin it to the wall. This board was a visual representation of each upcoming issue.

I would get a piece of paper handed to me, sometimes ripped

from Graydon's *Vanity Fair* notepad, sometimes scrawled on a cocktail napkin, with a month or the word *future* written on it, a story title, an author's last name, an editor's initials in parentheses, all separated by slashes. Sometimes there would be a photographer's name attached to these future stories, usually "LEIBOVITZ" (Annie) or "RITTS" (Herb) or "NEWTON" (Helmut), who were the magazine's most famous photographers. I would input the data into the document on the computer, and every Friday, along with the Rolodex, would replace the previous week's version.

There were two of these notes that were handed to me early in my tenure that meant nothing to me at the time but would turn out to be key to Graydon's not only fulfilling his mandate but finding his footing and righting the ship before it hit an iceberg. I didn't think much about these two entries when they landed on my desk, just entered them into the document like all the others. One read: "OCTOBER/NEW ESTABLISHMENT/HALBERSTAM (DS)." Halberstam was David Halberstam, the Pulitzer Prize–winning journalist who had covered the civil rights movement and went on to make his name with so many other journalists of his generation during the Vietnam War. He was one of the most celebrated journalists in America, a peerless "chronicler of the postwar era." The "DS" was Doug Stumpf, Halberstam's book editor, whom Graydon had hired around the same time I had arrived.

The story had come out of a conversation Graydon and David had over lunch one day that Graydon put a name to and decided would become the anchor for a larger package—meaning a number of stories thematically linked—in that October 1994 issue, which would arrive on newsstands that coming September, with an Annie Leibovitz photograph of Tom Cruise on its cover. Halberstam's story was about a shift in American power as the industrial age waned and the information age began to take hold.

"In this issue, *Vanity Fair* has taken on the challenge of redefining the power center of America as it enters the Information Age," Graydon began his Editor's Letter. Some of the members of this new establishment who were highlighted in the issue, also photographed by Annie, were Bill Gates, David Geffen, Rupert Murdoch, Oprah Winfrey, Barry Diller, Ted Turner, Michael Ovitz, and, weirdly, Barbra Streisand. They were in technology and media, the rising moguls of the information age, replacing the Rockefellers and Mellons and Carnegies, the titans of the industrial age. I had seen this issue taking shape but didn't quite understand it or its relevance. I'd even typed up letters to each of the names I just mentioned, pitching them the idea for the feature and asking if they would pose for a photograph.

Over the coming years, a list would be added to this yearly feature, a ranking system, that would create a frenzy among the members of this new establishment. (If there's one thing the rich and powerful need, it's public affirmation of their power and wealth, and they want nothing more than to be on top of a list, *any* list.) This New Establishment package would become a defining yearly feature of the magazine and, as Graydon told me years later, would save his job. It would make him not just a kingmaker in the halls of Condé Nast and at the tables of 44, but also a member of this new establishment that would only grow in influence and power over the coming years and decades and include names like Jobs, Bezos, Zuckerberg, Musk, Page, Brin, and more.

The typical reader of *Vanity Fair* that Graydon inherited was an urban, professional woman, or at least that's what *VF* was selling to advertisers, and what advertisers wanted (sure, there were male readers, but it's safe to say at least 75 percent of *VF*'s readership was women, if not more). Fashion and beauty and luxury advertising were Condé Nast's stock-in-trade. This was key to Tina and *Vanity Fair*'s success. She tweaked the formula and found an audience for a magazine that was struggling to find its position in the marketplace, and that was with celebrity, upscale gossip, crime, and aspiration. It was a formula that was tailor-made for the eighties, and its striving yuppies.

Graydon had never edited a magazine with an overwhelmingly female readership, nor should he have. This goes back to his stumbling—of course he was stumbling. If you're a man, and not only a man but a straight man, and not only a straight man but one of the straightest you'll ever meet, editing a magazine for an audience of women you have no idea how to talk to, you're in trouble. So why not try to attract male readers and some of the advertising categories that go along with them: cars, (brown) liquor, (big) watches. Men traditionally didn't buy magazines with celebrities on the cover; they stuck to the newsweeklies and business magazines. So, attracting male readers meant covering news and business. Among other things, that was exactly what the New Establishment began to accomplish.

At their best, magazines define cultural shifts. This New Establishment was a major cultural shift. *Vanity Fair* not only identified and defined this shift but gave it a catchy name. The New Establishment had arrived, and so had the beginning of a new era for *Vanity Fair,* leading to the marketing tagline a few years later "The Biography of Our Age." Little did we know at the time that we were also beginning to write our own obituary.

And that second little scrap of paper that was handed to me around the same time? It read: "APRIL/HOLLYWOOD ISSUE/ LEIBOVITZ/VARIOUS (JS)."

Hollywood Issue.

Those two words, initially scrawled on a cocktail napkin, would become more important and influential than any of us could have ever imagined.

Chapter 11

By the end of 1994, I had the basics of the job down and had established myself as one of the hardest-working members of the young staff. I was a quick learner, didn't have to be told twice to do something, and was still humble and thankful that I had been given this opportunity. I wasn't going to lose sight of how lucky I was that I had gotten this break, forget where I came from. And maybe most important, I felt like I belonged, had been accepted by this world and culture that had been so foreign to me just eight months earlier. I was still playing in a band, was still juggling these two identities, had a foot in two worlds, but I was beginning to change. While retaining some of that downtown edge, I started to feel as comfortable in a suit and tie as I did in jeans and a T-shirt playing guitar in a dingy basement rehearsal space. I wasn't as intimidated walking into the office every morning. I was coming into my own and felt at home. For the first time in my life, my confidence was on an upward trajectory. And it showed. Even the way I moved around the office was pointed to as the appropriate hustle expected of assistants—I walked "quickly and efficiently, with a sense of purpose." I was held up as an example to the other assistants. That was such a big deal to me that I remember it so vividly all these years later.

Because my desk was outside the office where everything happened, where decisions both big and small were made, I knew everything that was going on and was occasionally consulted on what the "kids" thought about something, questions being yelled to me out of editorial meetings—*What do you think of a Courtney Love cover?* (Sure.) When Courtney Love appeared on the cover a few months later, in June 1995, in angel wings, bathed in baroque lighting, I felt a sense of pride knowing that my one little nod of approval had played a minor part in setting the wheels in motion on what turned out to be a major media event.*

I would listen closely to those meetings, and others with editors and writers, gleaning what I could. These were mostly high-minded discussions about stories and pitch meetings. I made mental notes about what made a *Vanity Fair* story based on what made it through and what didn't, paying close attention to Graydon's responses to pitches. Knowledge by osmosis. I was adjacent to the center of it all, and in a short time, my institutional and operational knowledge was unparalleled.

My relationship with Graydon deepened. He liked having me around and would summon me into his office to smoke cigarettes, talk about what makes a great magazine piece (characters, conflict, conclusion), give me life advice. He'd tell me about the arc of his career, starting his first magazine in Canada (*The Canadian Review*) while still in college, moving to New York and writing for *Life* and *Time* magazines, then founding *Spy*. He'd suggest authors to explore and books to read. He gave me a first edition of the playwright and screenwriter Moss Hart's autobiography, *Act One*, about Hart's rise from an impoverished childhood in the Bronx and Brooklyn to becoming one of the most successful playwrights of the twentieth century and a towering New York social figure, assuring me I would learn everything I needed to know about life from that one book.

The message was clear and gave me some insight into why he had given me this chance. Graydon and I may have been at different points in our careers and stages of reinvention, but we were similar. Like Moss Hart before us, we were both outsiders. And that meant something at the beginning of the journey, but it could also hold you back. As Hart put it: "The only credential the

---

* There was some history here: In a 1992 profile of Love in the magazine, when she and Kurt Cobain were the reigning queen and king of American pop culture, the author of the story, Lynn Hirschberg, reported that Love had used heroin in the early days of her pregnancy. Love would later publicly blame Hirschberg for Cobain's 1994 suicide.

city asked was the boldness to dream. For those who did, it un-locked its gates and its treasures, not caring who they were or where they came from." I wondered if Graydon had come across someone when he first arrived in New York, a mentor who took a chance on him, offered him opportunity and advice, gave him that same book, that same speech, and this was his way of paying it forward.

This moment triggered me in some way, awakened something. I spent much of that first year keeping my head down, working hard, focused simply on making it through the day. As 1994 was coming to a close, that spark that I had been waiting for before the job began to ignite something bigger inside me. I started to believe that I could make this work, that a career in the magazine business wasn't so far-fetched. Where I came from and my lack of a résumé and a formal education didn't matter; it was now more about where I was going. Why *not* me?

In addition to working hard, I was also having fun. I think Graydon was too, having me around. We had a similar sense of humor where nothing was off-limits. He could be playful and mis-chievous. One day he called me into his office with a directive. There was an unauthorized biography of Si Newhouse being pub-lished that was embargoed by the publisher—they were keeping a tight lid on the book, desperately trying to keep it out of the hands of Si and anyone from Condé Nast before it hit bookstores. A call was made, a ruse created so we could get our hands on a galley. I dressed up as a messenger and went to pick up a copy from a book editor in the Flatiron Building, with the backstory that I was from Hearst, a rival publishing company, picking up a copy of the book for one of their magazines. It worked, and Gray-don triumphantly delivered a prepublication galley to Si.

Another day he called me into his office with a wide grin on his face.

"Check this out."

He held up what looked like a pen.

"A pen?"

"Nope!"

He clicked a button on the "pen" and pointed it at the ceiling, and a red dot appeared.

"It's a laser pointer."

"That's cool." I'd never seen a laser pointer before.*

"Let's mess with some people!"

He went to his window and beamed the little red dot out onto an employee of a bank on the corner of Forty-fifth and Madison. When the man looked up from his desk, we ducked, giggling like schoolboys.†

We took turns, getting more bank employees and people on the street, hiding and laughing when one would freak out and look up our way. A few days later we were visited by police detectives investigating a laser beam that was coming from one of Condé Nast's windows, and we were prime suspects. We played dumb to the cops—*What's a laser pointer?*—collapsing in hysterics after they'd gone, like true idiots.

When Christmas rolled around, Graydon turned into a real-life Santa Claus, and the *Vanity Fair* assistants his elves. We had to spend a weekend or two in early December wrapping his Christmas gifts for staff, contributors, advertisers, family, and friends. It was an endless pile, hundreds and hundreds of boxes and books and bottles of champagne and clothing. I even had to wrap my own gift, which that first year was a case of—*really expensive*—wine, and a cashmere sweater and a pair of shoes from Prada, gifts that cost more than my monthly salary.

It was around this time that I landed a girlfriend. Well, not quite, but I was working on it. I first saw her in the office, on one of those late nights when I usually had the place to myself as I filed that day's correspondence or typed up thank-you notes. Her name was Aimee, and she was roommates with a colleague, a fellow assistant named Riza Cruz. They had gone to Northwestern

---

* At that time, a laser pointer was cutting-edge technology. And we were easily amused.

† Again, easily amused.

together and moved to the city after they graduated, a year apart, and were now sharing a little two-bedroom apartment on East Twenty-fourth Street.

Born in Taipei, Aimee had moved to Ottumwa, Iowa, a small town in the southeastern part of the state, which is literally in the middle of fucking nowhere, a grain silo probably its tallest structure, when she was eleven. To emigrate from a major metropolis in Asia to a tiny rural town in America's heartland, not speaking a word of English, must have been jarring, dreamlike almost, and hardened her in some ways. But she was a city creature, the desire to get out of small-town America and back to a big city taking hold at some point, first leading her to Chicago—well, adjacent—for college, then New York.

Aimee worked at Miramax Films, in the publicity department, as that company and independent film were in the midst of their meteoric nineties rise. She had a side gig at *Vanity Fair* a few evenings a week, putting together for the staff the Culture List, a constantly updated list of every cultural event going on around the world in the coming year or two, broken down by category (gallery and museum openings, theater, dance, literary festivals), month, and location. It was Aimee's job to collect the endless piles of culture-related press releases that arrived by mail every day by the truckload, sort through them, and input the information into a document that was then distributed to the editors. Once a month, the senior staff would hold a meeting and go through the list page by page, deciding which upcoming cultural events were worth covering in the magazine.

But secretly, Aimee was there for a more covert reason. She and Riza had come up with the idea of starting a magazine, a proto-hipster, female-centric downtown culture magazine called *Tart*, which they were in the process of launching, and the empty *Vanity Fair* office after dark offered them access to the supplies and technology—copy and fax machines, computers—needed for assembling a magazine that weren't available to twentysomethings outside of an office, especially for free.

I was instantly intrigued by her, with her short hair, androgynous style, and complete lack of interest in me. There was something almost European about her, an indifference and unstudied cool that was neither here (America) nor there (Asia). I found her mysterious, like a quiet character in a foreign film.

I didn't officially meet Aimee until Riza dragged her to my twenty-second birthday party dinner at the Odeon, thrown by a few of my co-workers, by which point she had abandoned her moonlighting gig at *Vanity Fair*. I liked the way she smoked her cigarette, sitting there that night, bathed in the perfect golden light of the restaurant. It took some convincing before she believed I was more like her than what I appeared to be in the office, that I wasn't really of that world, that the suit and tie, my office uniform, were just a costume, a pose, my daily game of dress-up, and in reality, like her, I was an outsider, in on the joke and there purely by accident. After a few nights out in the safety of a group, she finally agreed to go out with me.

Overall, things were going pretty well in my new life. I felt a sense of ownership over myself for the first time, pride even, and was able to shut off the constant loop of that voice in my head that had always told me I wasn't good enough.

You never knew what awaited you from day to day at *Vanity Fair*. One afternoon, word traveled around the office that any smokers who wanted to quit should assemble in the conference room. Of course, every smoker wants to quit, always, or at least claims they do, including Graydon, so twenty or thirty of us gathered in the conference room. A famous Boston-based Russian hypnotist who specialized in helping smokers quit had been flown in. He was a *thing* at the time, well known for his hypnotic powers, and spoke to us as a group before meeting with us one-on-one for a minute or two, during which he mumbled some Russian mumbo-jumbo and then smacked you in the forehead with the palm of his hand—"No more you smoke." As I was standing there, listening to this crazy Russian talk about the inner workings of the brain, addiction, and the power of the mind, the door behind me opened and in walked Lou Reed. I don't know how he got there, but I was starstruck, standing next to one of my heroes,

New York's unofficial poet laureate, while the Russian went on and on.

I couldn't resist. I turned to Lou and whispered, "Do you think this is going to work?"

He looked at me and, in his gruff New York accent, replied simply, "No."*

My concerns about money and the dramatic decrease my income had taken the moment I accepted the job proved to be unfounded. That was partly due to overtime, which we all inflated to absurd degrees. Plus, I had discovered the petty cash economy, which operated like a black market in the assistant underworld of Condé Nast. Its currency took the form of petty cash, receipts, and car service vouchers, which made it possible to live on such meager salaries. Of course, so many of the kids at Condé Nast weren't concerned about money, living off trust funds or parental allowances. For the rest of us, we had to find opportunistic ways to game the system. This included selling books and CDs that were submitted to the magazine for review—and these were lying everywhere around the office, piles and piles of them discarded like trash—to stores like the Strand and downtown record shops. But the key to supplementing your income, and survival, was the petty cash economy, which was like the dark web of its time.

Condé Nast's expense accounts were mythologized, tales of excess and consumption passed down from generation to generation as if they were verses from the Bible. And not just in the magazine business, but outside too. It was one of the draws of working there. If you were an editor in chief, especially for the higher-profile titles, it seemed like there was no limit to your spending. Senior editors and other corporate executives had an expense account for meals, travel, and anything else they could justify. And I use the word *justify* gently—it was never clear if

---

* None of us quit smoking that day. A decade later, in an interview with *Esquire*, Reed said, "What I really want more than anything else is to quit smoking. That's what I want. I've quit a lot of things in my life, and this one's the worst. Maybe 'cause it's the last."

there was actually a review process. Expense forms would be submitted, with receipts attached, and a week or so later, a check for
the full amount would be received. It was like the greatest magic
trick you'd ever seen. You'd hear tales of editors paying their
rent, kids' school fees, nannies, even prostitutes and drug dealers,
somehow figuring out a way to get those charges reimbursed. But
for the assistant class, it was more clandestine.

Everything throughout the typical workday and week was paid
for. Coffee, lunch, newspapers, magazines, taxis. But no one
wanted to use their own cash, submit an expense report, and wait
a week to get reimbursed. Especially us assistants, who were operating on tiny salaries and minuscule personal monthly budgets,
with no disposable income, just scraping by. We needed every last
bit of our own cash, couldn't spare a penny of it to run out and
get our bosses coffee, or lunch, or a pile of magazines. So at the
beginning of the week, you would submit a petty cash form to the
business manager, requesting $250, or maybe as much as $500.
They'd usually sign off, no questions asked. This was just the cost
of doing business. You would then take it upstairs to a little window, like Condé Nast's in-house bank teller, and exchange it for
the amount requested. This was the cash used not only for your
boss's needs but for your lunch and coffee, too. And maybe more.
And that's where the problem would come in. Because when
you're in your early twenties and have an envelope full of cash in
your desk drawer, it's awfully tempting to dip into it for, say, a
nice dinner, getting drunk, cigarettes, a pair of shoes, rent, or
God forbid some dirtbag bought drugs with it! You see where
I'm going with this.

So let's say you ended the week short $100, meaning you had
receipts for coffee, sandwiches, and magazines for you and your
boss that added up to $400, but the advance was $500, and you're
$100 in receipts short. And you couldn't take out more petty cash
if you hadn't cleared the previous advance. Stray receipts became
currency. If you were in a cab and noticed a roll of receipts from
previous customers, you'd kindly ask the cabdriver for all of
them. But you couldn't submit receipts that were time-stamped

consecutively and so close together like that. No one's going to buy that. (Although to be honest, they would, as I would find out over years of risky scientific expense account experiments—no one was checking into that kind of detail.) So, every week assistants would walk around the office, bartering receipts for receipts, trying to make up the difference. Some receipts were more convincing than others, and so more valuable. This was before credit cards were widely accepted for small purchases (not that I had a credit card), so many receipts were old-school, of the handwritten-on-an-old-receipt-pad variety. And who's to say those were always legit?

Then there were the car vouchers. Condé Nast used a Brooklyn-based car service company called Big Apple—editors in chief and other executives used a more upscale company called Manhattan Limousine; cars were lined up in front of 350 Madison at all times. Condé Nast was such an important client for Big Apple that they had an on-site car dispatcher whose sole job was to locate cars for Condé Nast employees. There were so many Lincoln Town Cars double-parked and triple-parked, clogging traffic on Madison Avenue, that they needed a full-time employee to find which car was yours. The Big Apple cars only accepted the vouchers, which had spaces to write pickup and destination addresses. Or you could write "as directed" or "time job" instead of putting in addresses, which was helpful when the pickup or destination wasn't the office and you were, say, keeping a car all night to go from restaurant to club to club on a Saturday night, or you had a Big Apple car take you to the Hamptons. There was a tacit agreement between the drivers and Condé Nast's employees—a win-win for all involved. (Well, except Condé Nast, which ultimately footed the bill.) There were sheets and sheets of these vouchers around the office. We might not have had enough money to take cabs everywhere, but who needed taxis when you had vouchers and Big Apple cars on standby? They were essentially free rides anywhere, anytime. I mean, why use that last ten-dollar bill in your pocket for a taxi when you could pay $50 on the company, ride in luxury, and keep that tenner?

It was also around this time that email appeared on our ancient PCs. Or maybe it had been there for some time, and we just discovered it, stumbled on it one day. *What's this?* It wasn't yet a useful tool for business—it would have been had anyone known how it worked. But no one important was using it; there weren't emails about scheduling meetings or other announcements, and it was used mainly by the younger staff who were in the process of discovering the internet, although our office computers weren't hooked up to the internet yet, the email just an internal system. The internet was seen as some newfangled trend—like email, not considered useful—and mainly accessed from home, on an old dial-up modem hooked up through a phone line and used for fun on your old Mac from college.* There wasn't much on the internet; websites were in their infancy. It was mostly crudely animated bananas singing about "peanut butter jelly time" and creepy chat rooms full of early-adopting techie pedophiles and other perverts and conspiracy theorists. And while *they're* still there, I guess it has gotten more useful.

The younger staffers, the assistant corps, took to email. It was a way to communicate secretly under the noses of our oppressors, emailing one another office gossip, flirting, making drink and dinner plans for after work. But the email system wasn't password protected. There was a centralized system in order to get into your incoming message inbox, meaning anyone could log in to anybody else's email account. This led to practical jokes that might now be considered a felony, where you would send an email from one unwitting staffer to another, saying, "Hey, can you stop by my desk? I have something to run by you," or "Can you do me a favor and grab me a Snickers bar? I'm starving and slammed." We'd then watch what unfolded, as a confused photo assistant would approach a junior designer, Snickers in hand. Two married fact-checkers were carrying on what appeared to be an affair, their clandestine arrangements being made over email. We would log

* I mean, not that I had an old Mac from college. I just had a shitty tribal tattoo on my right shoulder.

in every day and read their latest missives, a novel whose narrative was developing in real time.

On a particularly busy day, I was emailing with another assistant, complaining about how busy I was. I ended with this: "I'm going to kill myself." The next day, I was called into the office of Chris Garrett, the managing editor. Pat had gone into my inbox and printed out the email thread that ended with me threatening suicide. Chris told me that if I needed help, the company could arrange for me to talk to somebody, and if I was being overworked, she could look into lessening the load. I had to explain that it was a figure of speech, I wasn't a danger to myself, wasn't being overworked, I was fine, really, and she didn't need to worry. It was a valuable lesson about email and electronic communication, and context, that I would never forget.

Soon after my attempted suicide and intervention, Pat was in Graydon's office, going over his weekly calendar, planning upcoming travel arrangements, having him sign papers that needed signing, when I was called in and told to sit down. They both had serious looks on their faces, and my first instinct was that this was about my suicide note, or that I'd done something else wrong. (I'm very fragile.) Before I had time to panic, Pat began to speak. In hushed tones she told me that her mother had taken ill back in England, and that she needed to take a leave of absence to take care of her through the end of the year. I was relieved that I wasn't in trouble, then felt immensely selfish and guilty that that was my first thought. I told her how sorry I was and that whatever she needed, I was there for her.

Graydon looked at me.

"Do you think you can handle this alone for a few months?"

He gestured around the office.

Honestly, I didn't think I could—it was a two-person operation, handling his personal and business needs, his calendar, the phone sheets, all those urgent galleys and papers going in and out, scheduling meetings, the thank-you notes and flowers and lunch reservations and RSVPs. It would mean working fourteen-hour days, probably some weekends. Not to mention someone always had to be at one of those desks, answering the phones, which rang nonstop. I'd be tethered to that desk. But then "Of course I can" came out of my mouth almost immediately, the confidence surprising even me. I had proven myself capable in my role up until then, mostly figuring things out on my own. Maybe this wouldn't be any different. And it seemed like an opportunity to really prove myself.

Graydon looked at Pat, then back at me, and took a long drag from his Camel Light. By now he trusted me. He had no reason not to. So far, I'd made him look good. He nodded, assuring himself that I was up to it, and smiled.

"Don't fuck it up."

At the same moment I was preparing for my solo flight, Annie Leibovitz was in Los Angeles for a photo shoot related to that slip of paper I'd received the previous summer and have taken forever to get to in this story. Annie was shooting ten actresses for the cover of the April issue. It was part of an idea Graydon had come up with around the time of the first Oscar party the previous March, which was this: What if *Vanity Fair* produced a single yearly issue devoted to Hollywood? A special issue, then the party, all timed to the Oscars. We could own Los Angeles for the month of March every year, during Oscar season, potentially valuable real estate. An issue that was cover-to-cover nothing but Hollywood. Stories from the golden age of the old studio system to the cutthroat business it had become, a photo portfolio of its stars, fronted by a parade of them, maybe as many as ten!

But how the hell do you squeeze ten people onto one cover? They'd be so small they'd look like ants. You could do a gatefold cover—a cover that folds out, so you have essentially two covers, with the benefit of an extra page of advertising to sell hidden behind the foldout. But ten—it's still tight. What about a *three-page gatefold*? It sounded audacious. It was. And then *there it was*. On that first panel of that inaugural Hollywood Issue, on a crisp white background, from left to right, Jennifer Jason Leigh, Uma Thurman, and Nicole Kidman, then Patricia Arquette, Linda Fiorentino, and Gwyneth Paltrow on the second, and finally, on the third, Sarah Jessica Parker, Julianne Moore, Angela Bassett, and Sandra Bullock. A mix of established stars and up-and-comers, familiar faces and new ones, and more than a few who would achieve a level of fame that would last until today. Okay, sure, in retrospect we dressed them up like tarts, and it looked like a police lineup of prostitutes more than a magazine cover, and we would rightfully catch some grief for that, and let's not even talk about the lack of diversity. But it was a hit.

And inside: a portfolio shot by Annie Liebovitz and Herb Ritts, a who's who of Hollywood talent, a casting director's dream. Schwarzenegger, Cruise, Hanks, Julia Roberts, Robin Williams, Brad Pitt, Michael and Kirk Douglas, Harrison Ford, Denzel Washington, Whoopi Goldberg, Liza Minnelli, Ellen Burstyn, Dennis Hopper, Christopher Walken, Clint Eastwood, Michelle Pfeiffer, Jack Nicholson, Warren Beatty, Sophia Loren, Robert Mitchum, Johnny Depp, Daniel Day-Lewis, John Travolta, Quincy Jones, Jack Lemmon, Tony Curtis, George Burns—*even God was in there!* Movie stars, screenwriters, directors, agents, Oscar winners, Oscar losers, old Hollywood, young Hollywood, over-the-hill, climbing up the hill. Then the stories: behind the scenes of upcoming movies; William Randolph Hearst; Larry Gagosian and L.A.'s art-collector wars; Dominick Dunne on O.J., of course, still the talk of Los Angeles. An issue thick with drama, and, just as important, ads, page after page of ads. This issue would expand with ads in the coming years like an accordion, becoming *Vanity Fair*'s answer to *Vogue*'s phone-book-sized September issue, bringing in substantial revenue. An anchor issue.

The initials *JS* on that scribbled note that had been handed to me the previous summer belonged to Jane Sarkin, *Vanity Fair*'s longtime features editor, whom Tina had hired in 1985 to wrangle celebrities for the magazine. Jane, along with our West Coast editor, Krista Smith, would spend the next two decades assembling this puzzle every year, tweaking the formula, fielding calls from Hollywood publicists pitching their clients or complaining about the placement of their clients, fighting for that first panel, or maybe the second. Some years the cover would be all men, sometimes all women, sometimes a crop of unknowns, or statement covers with nothing but mega movie stars. It was a yearly event when we released the issue—an unveiling that would see that cover picked up by press around the world like a natural disaster or a coup. It could make or break careers.

The timing of that first Hollywood Issue, in 1995, couldn't have been better. The film business was going through a cultural revolution in the 1990s the likes of which had not been seen since the late 1960s. The 1980s was a decade known for Hollywood blockbusters and action stars, obsessive market testing and studios chasing the four-quadrant film (male, female, under twenty-five, over twenty-five). But as the eighties became the nineties, suddenly quirky and interesting films started getting made. This was in part due to the success a fledgling Miramax had with Steven Soderbergh's *Sex, Lies, and Videotape* in 1989. It was the first independent blockbuster, made for $1 million and grossing almost $40 million. It would pave the way for a new generation of auteurs who grew up on the films of Hollywood's post–Hays Code golden age in the sixties and seventies, the French New Wave, and seventies and eighties horror and comedy, thanks in part to the arrival of VCRs and the availability of VHS rentals in the eighties. Quentin Tarantino (who worked in a video store), Richard Linklater, David O. Russell, Todd Haynes, Allison Anders, Todd Solondz, Paul Thomas Anderson, Christopher Nolan, Darren Aronofsky, Robert Rodriguez, Lisa Cholodenko, Abel Ferrara, Wes Anderson, Kevin Smith, David Fincher, Nicole Holofcener, Gus Van Sant: Throughout the nineties these directors would write the films and roles that would create a new crop of young movie stars who would become household names.

Vanity Fair and the Hollywood Issue would become an important part of this new ecosystem, recognizing and pushing this up-and-coming generation of movie stars on our covers and in the magazine. They began replacing models in the luxury advertising in our pages, signing lucrative contracts with the fashion houses, pushing those brands on the red carpets of premieres and awards shows. It was around this time that the question "Who are you wearing?" was first uttered. When it came to the intersection of celebrity culture and fashion, *Vanity Fair* was the traffic light. Even *Vogue* began abandoning cover models for celebrities in the nineties.

Demi Moore, Sylvester Stallone, Michelle Pfeiffer, Bruce Willis, Kim Basinger, Kevin Costner—*VF*'s cover mainstays in the eighties began being pushed aside by Gen X flag bearers: Brad Pitt, Kate Winslet, Keanu Reeves, Sandra Bullock, Leonardo DiCaprio, Gwyneth Paltrow, Ben Affleck, Uma Thurman, Matt Damon, Natalie Portman, Heath Ledger, Cate Blanchett. There were so many newly minted stars and Hollywood was hot, full of rich stories and personalities. This new generation of stars would anchor *Vanity Fair*'s covers for the next two decades. They would open up to our writers, pose for our photographers, socialize with our editors, wear our advertisers' clothes, hire our stylists, announce weddings and divorces in our pages and show off newborns on our covers, show up at our parties. They trusted us with their narratives, and we played our part. It was a perfectly symbiotic relationship.

"This is the magazine's first-ever special issue," Graydon wrote in his April 1995 Editor's Letter, "and it is a natural extension of last October's report on the New Establishment. Hollywood, and all that it produces, is a cornerstone of the Information Age." The information age. There it is again. A term the magazine would take and twist, remake until it became our own. Recognize the cultural shifts, create a narrative, package it, and sell it at a premium. That's what successful editors do. Give the people what they didn't know they wanted. The Hollywood Issue was the magazine equivalent of a blockbuster film that would spawn yearly sequels, a valuable franchise both culturally and financially. Its three-panel gatefold cover would become a *Vanity Fair* signature, iconic and often copied, surviving well into the next millennium.

Chapter 12

While I'd toned down my antics somewhat, settled down a
bit, and was taking my responsibility to my job more seriously and staying in occasionally, I still couldn't have a normal
night out, couldn't just meet up for a drink or two. Instead, it
would usually end with my stumbling home, falling into bed—
fully or semi-dressed—miraculously remembering to set my
alarm to wake up a few hours later, making it into the office on
time, stinking like booze, tie askew, shirt misbuttoned, socks mis-
matched, shoes untied. *You look like you had an interesting
night.*

That kind of behavior might get you called into Human Resources for a stern talking-to these days, but it was pretty standard operating procedure back then, considered normal if not
expected behavior in the publishing business in the nineties. I
might have taken it a little further than most, went a little harder,
always stayed a little later, but a culture of drinking and excess
wasn't just prevalent but celebrated. I remember staff Christmas
parties where people had to literally be carried out of restaurants
at the end of the night. When I had interviewed with Graydon,
he'd told me how much fun working at a magazine was, and he
was right. This might be another reason why I fit in so well and
was flourishing. It turns out the only skill I had, one I had spent
years developing during a misspent youth, was transferable to the
magazine world.

A typical night out for me, in the midnineties, would go something like this: I had been invited by one of our fashion editors,
Kate Harrington, to join her and a few colleagues for dinner.

She'd booked a table at the Bowery Bar, on East Fourth Street and the Bowery, an old gas station repurposed as a multi-hyphenate, hybrid restaurant-lounge-club like so many others that began popping up in the nineties.

I had stopped by a friend's house earlier in the evening for a drink or two and noticed a recent book on his coffee table that I'd been meaning to read, or at least pretend to read. It was a biography of Richard Nixon, big in both literal size and literary stature, a *Times* bestseller that *Vanity Fair* had excerpted. I asked if I could borrow it, he said of course, and off I went to the Bowery Bar, with my five-pound Nixon book in tow.

There's something magical about being young and out in a vibrant cultural capital like New York.* You just never know what's going to happen; however the evening begins, something totally unexpected lies around every corner.

The Bowery Bar was packed that night, as it was every night in those years. The crowd in the bar area bled into the restaurant, which bled into its back-room bar. It was full of celebrities and artists and writers hopping from table to table. I checked in and was led to a banquette along the windows on the north side of the restaurant, one of the prime tables. But instead of being met by Kate and a group of *Vanity Fair* colleagues, I found her sitting with the hip-hop mogul Russell Simmons and a slight-framed, androgynous-looking man whom I didn't recognize, and a few other hangers-on, one of whom might have been future producer and director Brett Ratner, who was Simmons's assistant around that time. Simmons was one of the most famous music moguls in the world, the man who helped define and popularize hip-hop with Run-DMC and the Beastie Boys on his Def Jam label in the eighties. He was in the process of conquering the fashion world with his clothing company, Phat Farm, which ushered in a new kind of street style that still thrives today. Simmons sold Phat Farm in 2004 for $140 million.

* Or maybe it's just wonderful being young *anywhere;* I forget.

Kate greeted me, kissed my cheeks, told me how excited she was that I had come.

I sat down, uncomfortable and intimidated. I was expecting dinner with a group of co-workers, mostly kids, who I knew.

I introduced myself to Russell, who was friendly and animated, and then introduced myself to the others, including the androgynous-looking man, who was beautiful, with delicate features, and sat quietly across the table from me. He shook my hand gently, and as quietly as possible in a soft English accent introduced himself as "Jaye." I quickly put together that he was Jaye Davidson, the breakout star from the film *The Crying Game*, the Irish thriller directed by Neil Jordan that had been a massive hit a few years earlier.

For some reason Russell took an instant liking to me. I still looked about twelve, I could drink like a seasoned veteran—and I *had* to that night, otherwise I might not have said a word and might have just sunk into the banquette—plus I was carrying a giant book about Nixon that perhaps made me seem intelligent, or at the very least odd. And *Vanity Fair*—those two words, and the simple fact that I worked there, were a signal to Russell; they gave me some gravitas even though I was just a lowly assistant. Naturally, he decided to call me "Nixon."

Jaye didn't say one word throughout the rest of dinner, though in fairness none of us did, as Russell didn't seem to pause for breath, jumping from one topic to the next with abandon and non sequiturs. Eventually he decided it was time to move to the next happening location and leaned over and said to me, "Come on, Nixon, let's go to the Tunnel!"

As dinner was coming to a close, and having had quite a few drinks, I wasn't in a clear state of mind to say no, on top of which his chauffeured Rolls-Royce—maybe it was a Bentley?—was parked outside, and I'd never been in one before. So I grabbed my weighty Nixon book and we headed off into the night for the next adventure.

While "peak nightclub" in New York has always been more

closely identified with the late seventies and eighties, nightclubs still thrived and were a big part of the social scene in the nineties, the last gasp of New York's true clubs, mostly because of the popularity of ecstasy, which had taken over from cocaine and disco at some point in the mid to late eighties, house music being the bridge. The drugs and the music had changed, as had the crowd (club kids) and culture (rave) surrounding the clubs, but they had adapted.

The Tunnel opened in 1986 in the desolate West Twenties, which was full of warehouses and not much else. Its entrance was on the corner of the West Side Highway and Twenty-seventh Street, across from the massive Starrett-Lehigh Building. I wasn't much of a club guy, though I'd spent too many nights to count at the Tunnel and other clubs (Limelight, Palladium, Club USA) because that's what you do when you're young and in New York City. But my previous trip there, with some fellow *VF* assistants and Aimee—who by then was officially my girlfriend—a few weeks earlier, had led to a tale about me that had circulated around the office and cemented my reputation as being somewhat *excessive*.

It began with a Saturday night plan among four or five of us to meet up, have dinner, go to the Tunnel, do ecstasy all night, then sleep it off on Sunday before the workweek began. This was pretty standard fare for a group of people in their early to mid-twenties on a Saturday night in midnineties New York. I was the one with the ecstasy connection, so I went to see my drug dealer in the East Village early that evening and got the supplies. But as I was headed out the door, he stopped me.

"Hey, I forgot. . . . I have some quaaludes. Do you want some? They're really rare, I probably won't get them again."

I'd never taken quaaludes, the "disco drug" synonymous with the seventies and Studio 54; I'd only heard and read about them. Their manufacture had been discontinued in 1985, and they'd just disappeared. It sounded glamorous in a retro kind of way, so, my curiosity piqued, I bought two of the big white pills. When I got home, before heading out to dinner, I took one, washed it down with a glassful of vodka, then thought better of it and took the second one, washing it down with another tumbler of vodka. What could go wrong?

About halfway through dinner, after a few more cocktails and bottles of wine, things started to get a little hazy. Then my memory of the night just stops cold. There is a roughly eight-hour gap from that moment until I was standing at the front of the long Tunnel coat check line at around six the next morning, with the coat check woman giving me a confused look.

"*What!?*"

"Can I have a small root beer, please?"

She looked at me with concern. "Are you okay?"

I was asking for a small root beer at a nightclub coat check at six in the morning, so no, I probably wasn't okay.

Aimee, who was standing next to me, fished through my pockets as I stood there wobbling, found my ticket, and helped me with my coat, and we walked out into the blinding sunlight. From what I heard later, I was not only semi-functional but really fun that night, even danced, something I'm not known for, though "small root beer" became the defining narrative of the night.

Now, a couple of weeks later, I was headed back to the scene of that embarrassing crime. I got into the front seat of Russell Simmons's Rolls (or Bentley), and we headed to the Tunnel. It wasn't late, maybe eleven or so, and there was a big crowd of clubgoers trying to get in. We pulled up, got out of the car, and the crowd parted like the Red Sea—a fancy car at a nightclub will do that, like a shark swimming into a school of fish. As I stepped away from the car with Kate, Russell Simmons, and Jaye, I held the biggest book you've ever seen with a photo of Richard Nixon on it. The bouncers unclipped the velvet rope from its stanchion and led us in.

The thing about being somewhere, especially a nightclub, with someone famous—and here I'm talking less about Jaye and more about Russell, who was at the peak of his fame—is you not only get everything for free, but you're suddenly *interesting*, surrounded by people who want the contact high from that celebrity.

The power of celebrity is something to behold in real time. And even though I had only met Russell a few hours earlier and would never speak to the man again, on this night, sitting with him, being introduced to random people, being slipped cassette tape demos to pass on to him, I was part of Russell Simmons's entourage. ("Yo, meet my man Nixon.") Which is absurd, as is the remainder of the story: At some point I realized I had lost the book. I turned to Russell.

"Russell, Russell, I lost my book!"

"What book?"

"My book. My Nixon book!"

He seemed concerned. "Oh shit. Well, you better go find it, Nixon."

He's right.

In an inebriated panic, I began my quest to recover my quarry. I retraced my steps through the club to find it. Looking back, I really don't know why—I could have just bought another copy pretty easily—but in the moment it felt important; my new identity was wrapped up in that book. How could I be "Nixon," the newest member of Russell Simmons's entourage, without my namesake book? I made it my mission to find it. I spent the better part of an hour stumbling around, looking in bathroom stalls, in every corner and crevice of the place, between separated drywall, behind the DJ booth, at one point even crawling around on the floor. I went from bartender to bartender, asking if anyone had found a big biography of Richard Nixon, but no one had, or seemed to care. One of the bartenders told me there was a lost and found at the coat check, so I quickly headed there.

I approached the woman manning the check window.

"Excuse me, excuse me, I'm looking for a book, it's very important, it's a big book, a biography of Richard Nixon."

The woman looked at me, utterly dumbfounded. "You were here a few weeks ago."

"Yeah . . . probably . . . I think."

She turned to the other coat check women. "He was standing

right here a few weeks ago and asked me for a small root beer, now he's asking for a book about Richard Nixon!"

They all started laughing.

I was humiliated.

She turned back to me.

"You need to get your shit together."

Chapter 13

Pat never returned. Or, well, she did briefly, in late January, only to announce her retirement. She would stay on for a month or two, then ride off into the sunset. Meanwhile, still one of the youngest members of the staff, I had gained a reputation not only for my late-night antics, but for somehow balancing that with my responsibilities running Graydon's office, which I had done single-handedly for a few months without issue or drama. I was managing twelve-hour days and double the workload on a few hours of sleep most nights, working so hard during the day, giving so much to my job, desperate for approval, while also attempting to hold on to that other part of me, which I knew was slowly getting pushed out. I wasn't quite ready to be an adult, but that's exactly what was happening. Which is ironic because I had hated being a kid and always dreamed of being an adult and the freedom that came with it. But sitting at a desk in a suit and tie wasn't part of that vision of the future. And that scared me. It's why I couldn't bring myself to quit playing music, even though there was really no chance of success and my heart wasn't in it like it once had been. It's why I stayed out late. I needed something to connect me to who I thought I was going to be. I was barely twenty-two. I wasn't going to go down without a fight.

Pat's leaving meant that for the time being, until Graydon could find a suitable replacement, I was his lead—and only— assistant. Which meant doing everything, including traveling with him. Which meant Los Angeles in March. Which meant the Oscar party.

I had only been to Los Angeles once before, in 1983, when I was eleven, for a family vacation—my father had a great-aunt,

Aunt Ella, who lived there. Her former husband, a man named Billy Blask, who was by then deceased, had been in vaudeville in the 1920s. Which sounded glamorous, going to visit a distant relative in Los Angeles with a connection to show business, however tenuous it may have been. The fantasy of California and Los Angeles was deeply embedded in the subconscious of kids who grew up in the late seventies and early eighties. It was the realization of the American Dream. Desert became oasis, which begat strip malls and swimming pools, fast food and drive-thrus, movies and music.

So much film and television was shot and set in L.A. that it felt like the center of the universe. All the cool popular culture that was on kids' radar seemed to be blossoming there, Los Angeles a visible part of its DNA. Skateboarding and surfing. Shopping malls. Guess jeans. Van Halen. *Repo Man* and L.A. punk. Frank Zappa's song "Valley Girl" had been a hit the summer before, as had *Fast Times at Ridgemont High* and *E.T.,* both set and shot in Los Angeles and the San Fernando Valley. Those two films right there are the arc of mid–Gen X boys' adolescence and coming-of-age, maybe the two most important films for my generation, released two months apart in the summer of 1982. You're just a prepubescent kid, rooting for this other kid your age, who looks just like you (and in my case, he really did), to save his sweet alien friend, a metaphor for the innocence of youth, having to battle against adults and adulthood, the system, and societal pressure to grow up. It was a film about trying to hold on to childhood. Then all of a sudden, two months later—*Oh my God, what are those?*—you see Phoebe Cates's breasts in *Fast Times*, it makes you feel funny, and before you know it you've forgotten what E.T. even stood for. The leap from childhood to adolescence in the darkness of a movie theater over the course of one summer.

I remember the city's lights stretching as far as the eye could see as the flight made its descent into LAX, the entry point to the dream factory. I remember going to a place called Chuck E. Cheese, created by one of the co-founders of Atari, where you could eat pizza and play video games at the same time—*This is the greatest place on earth!* They didn't have this in New York. I remember the rows and rows of billboards on Sunset Boulevard. I remember seeing one for *Synchronicity*, the new album by the Police, my favorite band at the time. There was probably one of these in New York, but it didn't matter. This was Los Angeles, this was California, and this was the Sunset Strip.

The reality was that Aunt Ella lived in a cinder-block ranch house near the airport. We spent a few nights in a hotel in Hollywood, one of those two-story motor lodges with the rooms arcing around a pool in a U. The pool was filled with syringes and used condoms. Los Angeles is all about stagecraft and optics, a façade. What you see in the frame and not much else. The emptiness of the American Dream.

But there was another side of L.A., and this trip with the magazine was going to introduce me to it, and be a completely different experience than that one more than a decade earlier. We were staying at the Hotel Bel-Air. I'd never stayed in a nice hotel, let alone one as fancy as the Bel-Air. I rented a car for the very first time. It was a convertible—a BMW. I'd never driven a car that nice. I had thousands of dollars in cash for myself and maybe ten thousand dollars' worth of traveler's checks in case Graydon needed cash. Yes, this was going to be a different version of Los Angeles.

The Bel-Air is tucked away in the foothills of the Santa Monica Mountains, in the neighborhood it takes its name from, north of Sunset Boulevard, east of the 405. Along with Beverly Hills and Holmby Hills, it makes up Los Angeles's Platinum Triangle. Prime real estate in a town full of it. Driving my BMW with the top down, a giant map unfolded in my lap, exiting the 405 on Sunset, then turning left into one of the most beautiful neighborhoods I had ever seen, a sanctuary with winding roads and ancient tree cover, felt like a fantasy, like stepping into a movie.

The hotel was spread over twelve acres, a little more than one hundred rooms in small buildings connected by paths winding through beautiful gardens, the trickling sound of fountains following you wherever you went. It was like Versailles, or the Hellbrunn Palace in Salzburg, or stepping back in time to 1946, when it opened, a feverish dream of old Hollywood.

I was met at check-in by the hotel's manager, assistant manager, and concierge. They all called me Mr. Brown. I was handed business cards and told that if there was anything, *anything*, Mr. Carter or I needed during our stay, I should not hesitate to ask. I was led to my room, the most beautiful hotel room I had ever seen, an impressive suite overlooking a courtyard surrounded by other rooms, each with a little patio. I tipped the bellman generously as he put my bags down.* He thanked me—*Mr. Brown, again!*—he left, and I dove onto the king-size bed, the most comfortable mattress I'd ever lain on. I opened the curtains and the double doors and stepped out onto the patio, met by the sounds of a trickling fountain, the smell of flowers, and, to my right, Sean Penn and Woody Harrelson deep in conversation on the patio next door, Penn with a cigarette hanging from his mouth. I smiled, nodded, as did they, and, not wanting to disturb their conversation, quickly retreated back into my room, which would be my home for the following two weeks.

Graydon, who would be arriving a few hours later, had a giant suite right off the patio of the restaurant. It made my room look like peasant quarters and was at least three times the size of my New York City apartment, with endless bouquets of fresh flowers filling its many rooms. His wife, Cynthia, and their four kids would be arriving for the second week of the stay, timed to their school holiday. I set up his desk for him, a mobile office—pens, pencils, notepads, stationery. Everything was personalized and highly curated, down to the hardbound folders with their contents embossed on the front in a sans serif font—MANUSCRIPTS, GALLEYS, DISPLAY TYPE, CORRESPONDENCE—and the *Vanity Fair* logo. I'd spend the next two weeks running back and forth

---

* Having come from the service industry, living off of tips, I became a profligate over-tipper during my years at Condé Nast. It's not like it was my money anyway. I was like Robin Hood.

between his room and mine, weighed down with papers and manuscripts, faxing noted-up manuscripts back to New York and re-
laying directives on layouts and galleys.

I doubled as a babysitter, too, watching the kids if Graydon and
Cynthia were headed off to dinner or a party. I adored his kids
and didn't mind having an excuse to stay in, order room service, and watch movies with them. Early one afternoon, as Graydon and Cynthia were headed off to a lunch, he asked me if I
minded hanging out with the kids by the pool for a few hours. Of
course I didn't.

"Great. Thanks so much."

He then handed me a giant syringe.

"Spike"—his youngest son—"is really allergic to bees. If he
gets stung, just jab him in the chest with this and depress it, and
his heart will start again. It's not a big deal. Thanks again and
have fun!"

Not a big deal?! I spent the next two hours gripping the
EpiPen, keeping a close watch on all the bees in the vicinity—*and
there were fucking millions of them!*—wondering what would
happen if his son was killed by a bee on my watch. Is *that* a fire-
able offense?

A team of staffers had flown out to handle the Oscar party, and
they'd make the trek up to the Bel-Air for daily meetings, go
through RSVPs, add to the list of invitees, gossip about the B-list
stars who were begging for an invite. I'd sit in and listen. The
other big Oscar party was Elton John's, which he had begun hosting a year before *Vanity Fair*'s started, in 1993. The competition
was fierce to land the better crowd, the bigger stars (never mind
that John's party doubled as a fundraiser for the Elton John AIDS
Foundation).

The Oscar party was in its infancy, headed into its second year,
and hadn't become the big-ticket Oscar-night destination yet. It
was held at Mortons restaurant, in West Hollywood, on the corner
of Robertson and Melrose. Mortons was one of the hottest restaurants in L.A. at the time. We eventually outgrew the restaurant, a
few years later blasting a hole in its back wall and erecting a giant

tent behind it, then rebuilding the wall the next day as if it never happened, like a yearly Brigadoon.

But our Brigadoon was two weeks away. And while my days were busy with my job, my nights were free. I was twenty-two and had a stunning hotel room, a nice car, and thousands of dollars in cash. This was going to be fun—and trouble.

I had a few friends in L.A., many of whom I hadn't seen in a couple of years, so I made some calls, arranged some get-togethers. I'll admit now that I was less interested in actually catching up with any of them than I was in showing off my newfound wealth and success. This wasn't supposed to have happened to me, of all people. I'd invite them up to the bar at the Bel-Air, where we'd get the best table, and the waiters would call me Mr. Brown. I'd flaunt my newfound "wealth," order the most expensive whiskeys and cognacs and bottles of wine to audible gasps. We'd shut the place down. I'd sign the check to my room with a flourish. Maybe I'd head down to West Hollywood or Silver Lake, to a party at a friend of a friend's, or get together at the Chateau Marmont with the young *VF* staffers who had made the trip west. On more than a few occasions, I'd be off in the wilds of L.A., no idea where I was, miles away from the Bel-Air; notice that the sun was coming up; and suddenly panic like a coked-up Cinderella as midnight approached.* I needed to be back at the hotel to start dealing with the East Coast any minute, or Graydon would be calling me at seven A.M. to come to his room with that day's marching orders. In no shape to drive, I'd leave my BMW, take a taxi back to the Bel-Air, having to retrace my steps the next evening to find the car.

One night I went with a friend to the Viper Room, Johnny Depp's bar on Sunset Boulevard, which had become infamous a year and a half earlier when River Phoenix overdosed and died there. Phoenix's death had apparently made the Viper Room a little more sensitive and cautious about potentially illicit behav-

* Just a reminder: It's 1995, so no cell phones, no iPhones, no Uber; life back then was like being a homesteader on the frontier.

ior. When I emerged from the bathroom with my friend—let's just say we weren't *literally* going to the bathroom together— a bouncer was waiting for us and physically collared us and dragged us out of the place. I was always back at the Bel-Air in time to gather the galleys and manuscripts and correspondence from the constantly screeching fax machine in my room, delivering them to Graydon first thing in the morning, looking no worse for wear.

While a handful of the magazine's staff—including the boss, who needed to sign off on everything—was out in L.A., there was still a magazine to put out, an issue to close, and it was my job to make sure that happened. I'd stand over Graydon as he made notes with his pencil, eventually handing me back a stack of marked-up papers that I would take to my room, sort through, and fax to New York, or I'd call editors with yeses and nos, word changes and headline choices. Watching him make all these seemingly minor decisions, I was always struck by the ease with which he made them and how a simple word change could so dramatically alter the meaning of something. Even the display type, captions, pull quotes, headlines, and decks—the text that runs under headlines describing what the piece is about—all told a little story, or were critical parts of telling a larger story, whether with two words, ten, or twenty. There's a story in everything. That's all writing and editing is: finding, or recognizing, the story, figuring out the best way to tell it, then assembling the words in the correct order. That may be oversimplifying it, and it's harder than it looks to do well, but once you have that ability, develop that muscle, you can't help but find the story in everything. I wanted to have that ability.

That said, I don't think Graydon knew I was out all night every night, or how wild I was, although as long as I got the job done, I don't think he would have cared, and he might have even gotten a kick out of my sordid tales. After two weeks of stumbling around L.A., it was time for the main event. Our Brigadoon was about to make its annual appearance.

Chapter **14**

S o I'm smoking a joint with Seth Rogen and Danny McBride.
        This might sound like the setup to a joke, and it would
probably be a good one, but this is what the Oscar party was like.
At least for me. Over the years, whenever I told anyone I worked
at *Vanity Fair*, nine times out of ten, their first question was
"Have you ever been to the Oscar party?" The Oscar party grew to
be so successful, so monolithic, its own brand, that it became as
big as the magazine itself. I only missed one between 1995 and
2017, in 2005. (In 2008, it was canceled due to the writers' strike.)
At a few of those early Oscar parties, clipboard in hand, I worked
the door, a miserable rite of passage for *Vanity Fair* assistants.
Once you'd served your time as a grunt on the front lines, you
graduated to fill-in—*no empty seats*—although sometimes you
weren't called on, eating dinner while leaning against the bar with
fellow fill-in rejects and other staff members. After a few years of
that, if you were still around, you became an invited guest, sitting
in front of a place card with your name on it. But before I get to
the Oscar party, I forgot to mention something about that first
trip to L.A. in March of 1995, a moment that, to me, was more
important than anything else over the course of those two weeks.
It was a tale Graydon told me, the origin story of his taking over
Vanity Fair.

    That first day we arrived, as I was sitting with him in his room,
running down the schedule for the coming week, the phone rang.
He picked it up. It was Hamilton South, *Vanity Fair*'s editor at
large, whose role was more like Graydon's chief of staff than an
actual editor. He had his hand in almost everything. Hamilton

was young, smart, funny, and connected. He was one of Graydon's closest advisers, and Graydon trusted and adored him. I did too—his office was one of my favorite places to hide out during the day, to smoke cigarettes and gossip. Hamilton knew how the world worked, and I soaked it up like a sponge.*

They caught up for a few minutes as I sat there, Graydon howling with laughter at whatever gossip Hamilton was passing on. Then Graydon went silent for a few moments.

"Maybe. Hold on, let me ask Dana."

Graydon put the phone down.

"Do you want to go to Vegas?"

"Yes."

What else are you going to say when your boss asks if you want to go to Vegas? It's not like I was going to say no.

"I mean, like right *now*. Hamilton has a plane. It's leaving in an hour. We'll come back later tonight."

Again: "*Yes.*"

I'd never been to Vegas. I'd never been on a private plane either.

He got back on the phone, told Hamilton we'd see him at the Van Nuys Airport in an hour, and hung up.

"You've got five minutes. Go put a suit on and meet me out front."

I ran back to my room and put on a suit and tie, trying to channel the Rat Pack as best I could. I opened the safe where I'd stashed all the cash I'd brought and grabbed $1,000, instantly thought better of it, and grabbed another $1,000. It was Vegas after all. And I was going to come back a winner.

When I got to the front of the Bel-Air, Graydon was already there, in a white linen suit. He looked like something out of a Tennessee Williams play. A car was waiting for us. We got in and were driven over the hill and into the Valley, right onto the tarmac of the Van Nuys Airport and up to the plane. Hamilton was waiting for us, along with Sara Marks and Krista Smith and her boy-

---

* That's Hamilton sitting next to me on the cover of this book, from this era.

friend. We squeezed into the jet, which was tiny.* There was no door to the cockpit, so as we took off, you could see everything through the windshield. It was like being in a flying minivan.

It was a forty-five-minute flight to Vegas. We were met by a small armada of Lincoln Town Cars and driven to the Mirage. Steve Wynn, the billionaire casino magnate who owned the Mirage, had given us a suite on the top floor, just about the size of a football field, even though we weren't even going to be spending the night. In the 1970s, in his early thirties, Wynn had become the youngest casino owner in Las Vegas when he bought the Golden Nugget. The Mirage, which Wynn opened in 1989, was the first mega hotel-resort-casino to open on the Vegas Strip, the beginning of modern Las Vegas. I remember Wynn from the Golden Nugget TV commercials with Frank Sinatra when I was a kid. Wynn was legally blind. He'd had a meeting with Graydon at 350 Madison Avenue a few months earlier, and I had been dispatched to the lobby to bring him up; although Wynn could barely see, I was instructed not to help him in any way, so as not to call attention to his sight issues, which he was apparently sensitive about. I did as I was told, watching helplessly as he bounced off walls and people and elevator doors like a pinball.

Wynn was also an avid art collector, which is either hilarious, tragic, or just ironic. In 2006, he made headlines when he accidentally bumped into one of his Picassos, 1932's *Le Rêve*, worth $140 million, elbowing a hole in the canvas, which is hilarious, tragic, *and* ironic. Although he went on to sell *Le Rêve* seven years later for $155 million after it was restored. The casino mogul's empire would come crashing down in February of 2019, when he was #MeToo-ed, accused of sexual misconduct, and had to step down as CEO of Wynn Resorts.

The slogan "What happens in Vegas stays in Vegas" wouldn't debut until 2003. You know what else stays in Vegas? Your money. That's all that city's about. The family-friendly version of Vegas

* I'm not *complaining*, I'm just saying it was small.

would appear around that time too. That they convinced tens of millions of dopes a year to holiday in Vegas with their families, so they could spend even more money by bringing their kids, is such an insidious and brilliant piece of marketing that I almost have to respect the scumbags who pulled it off.*

Not only had I never been to Vegas, I'd never gambled before. I knew how to play cards, knew the rules to blackjack and poker, but it turns out I didn't really know how to play blackjack and poker. Life's full of all sorts of little lessons. They lurk around every corner. And that night, I quickly learned a new one: I shouldn't be a gambler. I blew through two grand in less than an hour. I should have quit while I was behind, but I began borrowing cash from Graydon, which led me to a second lesson that night: I'm quite possibly a gambling addict.

At some point in the night Graydon and I peeled off on our own. We were going to check out the old Strip, the playground of the Rat Pack that was beginning to fade as the new Vegas took over. We went to the Golden Nugget. After I'd borrowed a few hundred dollars more from him, which I quickly lost, Graydon, recognizing a burgeoning problem with his young charge, cut me off. It must have been around two in the morning, and we were exhausted anyway, still on East Coast time after arriving in L.A. that afternoon. We sat at a table in the Golden Nugget for one final drink before catching the plane back.

I don't know what the lead-in was or how we got on the subject, but as we settled into our drinks, Graydon told me the story of his getting the *Vanity Fair* job. I was expecting a tale of triumphing over adversity, of the underdog, the outsider, outworking and outthinking his rivals and coming out on top, grabbing the brass ring. I was assuming there was something in it for me, a life lesson, a mentor passing down some knowledge to the next generation, but I was wrong. Well, there was a life lesson, but not the one I had expected.

Graydon had gone to meet with Si Newhouse sometime around

---

* I'm not a Vegas guy and have never returned.

the time he left *Spy*, as the eighties were turning into the nineties, looking for his next act. He'd decided to start a newspaper and was looking for an investor. Si demurred, but there was obviously something about Graydon that he sparked to. Graydon wasn't able to raise the money to start his own newspaper, so agreed to edit the newspaper *The New York Observer*, which had launched in 1987—though no one was paying much attention to it—and turned it into a must-read. Everyone was talking about the *Observer*. Si must have taken notice of this.

Around that time, Si was growing impatient with one of his recent hires. In 1987, he had hired Robert Gottlieb, a well-known book editor with a string of major hits on his résumé—most famously, Joseph Heller's *Catch-22*—to replace longtime *New Yorker* editor William Shawn. Shawn was legendary, a towering figure in the magazine world, and had been the editor since 1952. He was a tough act to follow. To make things worse for Gottlieb, 150 *New Yorker* staffers had signed a letter to Gottlieb asking him not to accept the job. Tough crowd.

In 1992, after five years on the job, Gottlieb was floundering, so Si began looking for a replacement. He called Graydon. I don't know if he called others too, but somewhere during that conversation, or conversations, Si decided Graydon was the guy to replace Gottlieb. He asked him if he would be interested in taking over *The New Yorker*. Would he be interested in taking over *The New Yorker*!? It was one of the most respected and storied magazines *ever*. Editor of *The New Yorker* is one of the biggest jobs in the magazine world. Of course he was interested. The leap from the *Observer* to *The New Yorker* was like going from town council to president of the United States. It was a major move into the big time.

Si told Graydon to keep the news to himself. Don't tell a soul. Gottlieb wasn't aware that there was a plot under way to overthrow him. Graydon did as he was told. This was some Mafia-like omertà shit, Condé Nast style. If Gottlieb saw the hit coming, it could jeopardize the whole operation.

Graydon must have been excited, like a kid in a toy shop. He got to work, toiling away until all hours of the night, excitedly scribbling notes and writing plans for his vision of *The New Yorker*. With a healthy budget and a brand name behind him for the first time, he would be able to attract whatever writers he wanted, a dream come true for a magazine editor. Story ideas must have been feverishly appearing in his head. He was about to make a high-profile, life-altering leap.

Somehow, this news made it to Tina Brown. Nothing ever stays a secret for long at Condé Nast. It must have gotten her thinking. She'd turned *Vanity Fair* around, maybe was getting a little bored with it. Could she turn around another flagging title? Do it again for the moribund *New Yorker*, really solidify her legacy? However she came to her decision, she decided she wanted *The New Yorker*. According to Graydon, Tina went to Si, made a stink, and threatened to walk unless she got it. Whether it was an empty threat or not, Si didn't want to lose Tina; she was his star, his golden child. He had a tough decision to make, but really only one possible way out. So he made the call and told Graydon there had been a change of plans. Tina was getting *The New Yorker*. Graydon would get Tina's sloppy seconds—*Vanity Fair*.

From a certain vantage point, this doesn't sound like such a terrible thing. After all, he was going to get a high-profile job, move up many rungs on the corporate ladder, become a Condé Nast editor in chief, get a massive raise, a bottomless expense account, a car and driver, a clothing allowance, an interest-free mortgage. But *Vanity Fair* and *The New Yorker* were two very different beasts back then. *The New Yorker* was black and white, faded old WASPy money. *Vanity Fair* was saturated color, sparkling new money. *Vanity Fair* had a predominantly female readership, not an audience Graydon understood or knew how to talk to. Not only that, but he told me he didn't even like the magazine, which is why *Spy* was so merciless in its skewering of it. Graydon made no sense for *Vanity Fair*, which is why the industry heaved a collective confused groan when his hiring was announced, and the reason he struggled early on. It's a cruel trick the mind can play on you, that "What if . . ." question that's so hard to push out. He was depressed, disappointed, and didn't want to be there, having had the rug pulled out from under him.

Now, I don't blame Tina. I get it. Had I been her, I might have done the same thing. Leave *Vanity Fair* on top, try to scale a different peak. It was nothing personal. At the same time, I saw another side of Graydon that night as he told me the story. The realization that no matter what he did, he was always going to have to fight for it and prove himself. I imagine getting that call from Si changed him, and I have to believe that the chip that landed squarely on his shoulder in that moment surely remained there for the rest of his career, kept pushing him like an athlete uses that loss in the championship game.

For a moment he wasn't my boss, the powerful magazine editor, the guy in the corner office calling the shots. There was a sadness and a real vulnerability about him that I hadn't seen before. Like when Toto pulls the curtain back to reveal that there isn't a wizard, just a lost human being like the rest of us.

And maybe there was something more in that story for me, a clue as to why I was there with him. He'd taken a chance on me the way Si had taken a chance on him, and I wanted nothing more than to succeed and prove to him that I was good enough, that the faith he had placed in me was justified. His approval was my motivation. I think there was a similar dynamic between him and Si. It's a story as old as man.

Chapter 15

So I'm smoking a joint with Seth Rogen and Danny McBride. Which sounds like fun, and it was, but it was a really bad decision. Because I was on duty that night. Not only was I on duty, but I was doing something I had never done before, something that I had never wanted to do before, and something that I refused to ever do again after that night. I was working the red carpet, interviewing celebrities.

It was Oscar night 2009, our first year at our new location, the Sunset Tower in West Hollywood, after fourteen years at Mortons, which had closed the year before. A few weeks earlier, as we were trying to find new ways to cover the party for *Vanity Fair*'s website, the idea of having our own red-carpet reporter asking celebrities questions, and livestreaming it to the site, seemed like a good one. We were getting with the times. Somehow, Graydon thought it was a good idea for me to be on the red carpet. I thought it was a terrible idea, and I made it known.

Truth be told, the idea of being a red-carpet reporter was a little humiliating and felt beneath me. I have never had the desire to be on camera, to ask vapid questions of movie stars. It was my least favorite part of celebrity culture. I disliked everything about red-carpet interviews, thought they were dumb and silly ("Who are you wearing?"). I found it all so embarrassing and tacky. Plus, I'm naturally shy, at least without massive quantities of booze in me, and to be a successful red-carpet interviewer you needed to be an extrovert and outgoing. I pleaded with Graydon to find somebody else.

"I really, *really* don't want to do this."

"I think you'll be great."

"I promise you, I won't. And I'll only be able to do it if I get properly loaded, and I might do something stupid."

"As long as we get it on camera, that's fine with me."

Nothing was working to help me get out of it. Graydon was taking joy in watching me squirm, and I could tell he wasn't going to let me off the hook. It was also his way of telling me that while I might have thought I was some big shot now, by then a long-serving veteran at the magazine, he still pulled the strings. *Don't forget where you came from, kid.*

The Oscar party happens in waves. The first to arrive are the dinner guests, maybe 150 of them or so, at around five-thirty. These are usually not the biggest celebrities of the night—most of them are at the Oscar ceremony—although there might be one or two. It's more a mix of L.A. social figures, producers, studio and agency heads, faded stars who are still locally viable socially, and some old-Hollywood stars or starlets dragged out of the old-age home for the night. Dinner guests sit at tables of ten or twelve and spend the next three or four hours watching the Oscar telecast on televisions and screens set up around the room. As the Oscar ceremony got longer and longer over the years, so did the dinner. It was a *really* long dinner. When the Oscars are over, the tables are cleared away, and the party opens up to the next wave of guests, which are staggered by the hour, the time on your invite depending on your status. If you were a major movie or television star, or you were nominated, your invitation would be for nine P.M. This is when the real celebrities begin to arrive. Some are coming straight from the ceremony, others from home, or wherever they happened to watch it. As the night goes on, the caliber of stars arriving lessens by the hour, until the Oscar winners start getting there, closer to midnight. That's because if you're in possession of a gold statue, there are post-ceremony responsibilities: press conferences, photo shoots, the Governors Ball. And traffic is so bad on Oscar night in Los Angeles, it takes forever to get anywhere.

We always had two press pens set up outside the party. One was for still photographers from all of the major photo agencies, the second was the long line of news and entertainment show red-carpet reporters, who would broadcast live throughout the night. ("Let's go to Janice at the *Vanity Fair* Oscar party.") The interviews and photographs would travel around the world over the following days—it was a global event. It was right in the middle of that second pen, among all the news and entertainment show reporters, that I would spend what was going to be a miserably long night.

I put on my tux. Aimee tied my tie.* I took a Xanax. I chased it down with some vodka. Then some more. We were staying at the Sunset Tower, so I didn't have to go far, just a quick elevator ride. I took my place behind the velvet rope, right in the middle of the red carpet.

I couldn't help but think back to my first Oscar party, in 1995. I had no formal role. I just kind of hung around, watching all the action. It was the year of *Forrest Gump* and *The Lion King.* Tom Hanks won his second consecutive Best Actor Oscar, while the film took home the Oscar in the other major categories: Best Picture, Best Director, and a handful of other categories, including Best Adapted Screenplay. Quentin Tarantino won the Best Original Screenplay Oscar for *Pulp Fiction.*

Graydon would stand out front as the dinner guests arrived, in his bespoke Anderson & Sheppard tuxedo and dark sunglasses, hugging, shaking hands, being introduced to people. He was still relatively new on the Hollywood scene in 1995, but that first Hollywood Issue, which was still on newsstands, displayed prominently around L.A., had shaken Hollywood like an earthquake. The issue was like a yearbook or a house organ for the industry. It was the beginning of a long relationship between *Vanity Fair* and Hollywood that would only grow in the coming decade. We even put the cover on a giant billboard on Sunset Boulevard. You

---

* Spoiler alert: I've jumped ahead in time here, but yes, we were still together. I'll fill you in later.

couldn't miss us—we were everywhere you looked. While we didn't own the town just yet, we'd made a sizable down payment.

As I was watching Graydon doing his hosting duties, I found myself standing in front of Mortons, next to Si Newhouse. I had never really met Si. I'd obviously seen him around the building, in the elevator, coming down to Graydon's office or to look at layouts on the planning room walls. He was small and unassuming. He'd smile at me, although he seemed to smile at everyone. He had the reputation of being a cruel mogul, talked about as that monster in the closet, firing editors or shutting down magazines on a whim, but he actually seemed friendly. Si was always wearing a beat-up pair of khakis and a sweatshirt around the office. I once asked Graydon why Si dressed so poorly. He was a billionaire; surely he could afford better clothes.

"When you own the company, you can wear whatever the fuck you want."

Graydon was protective of Si, revered him. He'd taken a chance on Graydon, much as Graydon had on me. I understood the dynamic of that kind of relationship well.

Si was quiet and soft-spoken, shy. He and I just stood there, marveling at all the photographers and camera crews crowded in front of Mortons, staff running around making sure everything was perfect, Graydon, Si's newest star, the conductor of this orchestra, beaming in the L.A. sun. It was an impressive display. After Graydon had finished greeting the latest arrival, who was escorted into the restaurant, he came over to check on Si, who asked him who the man he had just greeted was. It was probably a producer or a powerful agent—someone important, but not a recognizable face to anyone outside the industry. Graydon told him. Then he had an idea. He turned to me.

"Dana, why don't you tell Si who everyone is as they come in."

What? I literally had no idea who any of these people were. *"But . . ."*

Si turned to me and smiled as Graydon rushed off, back to his greeting duties.

In a lifetime of humiliating and uncomfortable experiences,

the next half hour was certainly a contender for the top spot, as I stood next to not just the most powerful man at Condé Nast, but one of the most powerful moguls in the media world, without a clue who anybody was.

Si would lean over and quietly whisper, "*Who's that?*"

I would shake my head slowly; "*I don't know, Mr. Newhouse.*"

"Who's that?"

"No clue, Mr. Newhouse."

"Who's she?"

"Jeez, your guess is as good as mine, Mr. Newhouse."

I was hoping that at some point he would figure out that I wasn't up to this task, but he kept on asking.

"Who are they?"

"Don't know."

"Them?"

"Nope."

I must have gone 0 for 50 and was sure that Graydon would get a call the next day: *Get rid of that kid, he's a complete moron.* Someone this out of touch shouldn't have been working at one of the premier cultural magazines in the world. But I don't think Si really cared, or at least he didn't mention it to Graydon, and I lived to see another day. Now, almost fifteen years later, in 2009, at least I knew who everybody was.

As the dinner guests arrived, some of them would do the press line, others would just smile and walk on by. I managed to interview a handful of celebrities, a few of the wax-museum variety, like Joan and Jackie Collins, Robert Evans, and others like Sidney Poitier, Jay Leno, and Martin Short. I made a few decent jokes and asked mostly stupid questions, like, "What are you most looking forward to tonight?" "Who are you rooting for?" "Is Meryl going to win again?" (Meryl Streep was nominated for Best Actress in *Doubt*, although she would lose out to Kate Winslet, who was nominated for *The Reader*.)

After all the dinner guests were inside and seated, and the awards had begun, I was off the hook until after the ceremony. I hopped over the velvet rope, earning envious stares from the other interviewers and crews, and walked into the party. I sat at the bar with other staff and would-be fill-ins, had dinner, and watched the awards.

By the time I returned to the red carpet, a few hours later, when the awards were over, I'd gotten a little sloppy. I had a drink in my hand and a cigarette in my mouth. I was like the Dean Martin of the red carpet as I interviewed Jonah Hill, Jason Segel, Jon Voight, Harvey Weinstein, David Frost, and a handful of others.

My best moment, however, might have been with Leslie Mann and Judd Apatow.

Judd took one look at me, a drink in my hand.

"Drinking on the line!"

"Yes. Because this is the most horrible experience of my life."

They immediately recognized that I wasn't a professional.

Leslie asked me what I was drinking.

"Vodka tonic."

"There is no *Vanity Fair* website, is there?" Judd asked me.

"No, we just have a microphone and a fake camera."

It went on like this for a few minutes.

After the red-carpet interview with Judd, I needed a break before the final wave—the Oscar winners—so I hopped over the velvet rope and went into the party for a while. I was outside, on the terrace in the back, when I ran into my friend Matt Labov, a publicist who worked with Judd and a lot of the generation of young comedians who appeared in many of his films. Matt was standing with Seth Rogen and Danny McBride, who are as funny in real life as they are on-screen. Matt introduced us, and we chatted for a few minutes. At some point, a joint appeared. It would have been rude to say no.

I spent another half hour on the red carpet. I could barely speak. Seth Rogen smokes really strong weed. I was getting distracted by all the bright lights, like a kitten or a baby. I somehow managed to interview Kate Winslet and Dustin Lance Black, who had won an Oscar for his *Milk* script. Then I just gave up.

The next day I got a few calls and emails from friends in London. To my left on the red carpet that night was a BBC crew and reporter. Because of the time difference, they were live on one of the morning shows in the UK, and because of where I was standing, I was in their shot, drink in hand, cigarette in my mouth, often staring off into space as the night went on. Apparently I stole the show.

Chapter 16

In 1996, during Fashion Week, in early September, the Italian fashion designer Valentino Garavani was opening a new Valentino flagship store on Madison Avenue and Sixty-fifth Street. *Vanity Fair* was throwing a dinner and party in his honor after the christening of the store. We often did these dinners and events for big advertisers. This one for Valentino would be held at Le Colonial, a recently opened, high-end French-Vietnamese restaurant on Fifty-seventh Street, just east of Park Avenue. It was a midtown rip-off of Brian McNally's Indochine, though it became sort of a hotspot, at least as hot as anything can be on East Fifty-seventh Street. It was a big place, two stories, a grand dining room with high ceilings on its ground floor and a more intimate, lounge-y space upstairs. It was a good venue for a large dinner and, after clearing out the dining tables and opening the upstairs, an even larger after-party. There were a handful of movie stars and others from the literary, social, fashion, and media worlds coming. It was an *event*, something *Vanity Fair* was becoming known for.

I had been Graydon's assistant for more than two years at that point, and I was charged with working the door. It would mean hours on my feet, clipboard in hand, trying to manage the chaos, while knowing that behind me, there was a really fun party going on that I wasn't part of. Working the door was my least favorite part of my job. That night, for Valentino, the dinner was to be followed by a bigger after-party. The door during the dinner portion of the night was easy—a civilized, mostly recognizable, small, manageable crowd.

It was the after-party where things would take a turn, where the guest list went from a manageable size to hundreds. I'd have to deal with a horde of uninvited party crashers, B-list socialites, low-rent celebrities, and coked-up fashionistas pissed off that they weren't deemed important enough to have been invited to the dinner. At that Valentino party, I would have a memorable run-in with an infamous enfant terrible fashion designer whose identity I'll protect since he's been in and out of recovery for years and was clearly having a rough go of it that night. He would go on to become one of the world's most famous and successful designers, build a massive brand and fashion empire, but was more interested that night in berating me for not letting a friend of his, a veteran *Vogue* fashion editor named Candy Pratts Price, in as his plus-one, rocks of cocaine *flying* out of his nostrils as he screamed at me. "*Do you know who I am?! Do you know who she is?! Who's in charge I want to talk to who's in charge?! Fuck you, you little shit! Who do you think you are?!*" The designer's struggles with substance abuse would dog him at times during his career, although he eventually got sober.*

The day of the Valentino party, I got a call from a young publicist named Jason Weinberg. I'd known Jason for a few years—my brother worked for his eponymous PR company, which represented young actors and musicians, New York socialites, and a faded star or two. One of those faded stars at the time was Jerry Lewis, and my brother had been tasked with the thankless job of dealing with Lewis, who was in New York performing on Broadway in *Damn Yankees*. The phone system in the Weinberg office was antiquated, and Jerry would get frustrated trying to get my brother on the phone, hang up, and proceed to leave angry messages on the answering machine at our apartment. "*Where the fuck are you your fucking phones fucking suck fucking call me now! Fuck!*" (*Slam!*) I'd come home from work to numerous of these messages each day, to my endless delight, and looking back I wish I'd had the foresight to keep them. It would have been internet gold.

---

* What the hell, it was Marc Jacobs.

Another one of Jason's clients was Marla Maples, then trying to make her way as an actress. Success was thus far eluding her in that field, as she was known only for her real-life role as Donald Trump's second wife. Marla really wanted to come to the dinner that night—after all, it was a hot party during the height of Fashion Week—and Jason asked if we could squeeze her and the Donald in. It didn't seem like an outlandish request. The Donald was famous, and he and his wife had even been on the cover of *Vanity Fair* a few years earlier, just a few months before I began. I told Jason I'd ask and get back to him.

What I didn't know at the time was that Graydon had had his battles with the Donald in the eighties, personally coining the nickname "the Short-Fingered Vulgarian" for the Queens-born real estate developer in the pages of *Spy*, which drove Trump absolutely nuts and still does to this day. The small hands/short fingers meme began in 1984 when Graydon, then a freelance writer, wrote a profile of Trump for *GQ* in which the throwaway line "The hands are small and neatly groomed" sent the thirty-eight-year-old real estate developer into a rage. Over the years the Donald would occasionally mail Graydon a ripped-out page from a magazine or newspaper with a photo of himself, his hands circled in Sharpie and something along the lines of "See, not so small!" scrawled on it. This was clearly a man for whom no perceived slight went unaddressed. Their one-sided feud would go nuclear when Twitter arrived, with Trump hurling insults at Graydon constantly. Graydon delighted in the abuse. Years later, after Trump had been elected president, he had all of Trump's nasty tweets from over the years framed and put on the wall outside his office. But in 1996, Graydon's relationship with the Donald was a little more cordial.

I asked Graydon about the Donald and Marla's coming to dinner. "It's completely full, or maybe even overbooked at this point," he said, adding that we could extend an invitation to them for the post-dinner after-party, when the guest list would expand. This sounded reasonable, so I called Jason back and explained that the dinner was completely full, but we'd be happy to have them after dinner. He thanked me and hung up, and I had Marla and the Donald added to the list for the after-party.

About an hour later, Jason called me back.

"Look, they really want to come to dinner."

"I'm sorry, Jason, but they can't. It's a seated dinner and it's totally full, and it's in, like, a few hours."

"Is there *anything* you can do? As a favor to me?"

I sighed. "Okay, I'll ask Graydon again, but I can't guarantee anything."

"Thank you. I owe you one."

I went into Graydon's office and apologized for bringing it up, but Marla and the Donald *really* wanted to come to dinner. Again, no luck.

I called Jason back, said I was sorry, I'd taken it as far as I could, and there wasn't anything else I could do. He understood, thanked me for trying, and hung up.

A few minutes later my phone rang.

"He's not taking no for an answer. They're coming to the dinner."

"They can't!"

"I tried to sell them on the idea of going after dinner, but Donald's refusing. He feels slighted. They're going to show up—and you can't *not* let Donald Trump in!"

"I'm going to be at the door! And I'm telling you, *I am not going to let Donald Trump in*!"

"Look, they're coming!"

"Jason, you have to stop them!"

"I'll try. But you don't know Trump!"

We both hung up.

I didn't want to think about it anymore and hoped Jason would come up with some sort of diversion. I mean, what kind of person would just show up to a party after being told they wouldn't be let in?

Dinner was in full swing. The night was humming along. Things were going smoothly as far as I could tell. The guests had been seated and seemed to be having a good time as I stood outside with my clipboard, flanked by a few security guards. At the door, this was the lull between the dinner and the after-party, which would begin the moment dinner ended, the tables being cleared for the arrival of a much larger crowd. In a few hours, an angry mob would be in front of me, with uninvited guests trying to force their way past the velvet rope. *I know so-and-so and they told me to come!* I thought about the Donald and Marla, and assumed Jason had managed to stop them from showing up. I was relieved.

Graydon wanted a drummer—one of those kids who play the drums on white plastic buckets on street corners and in the subways that you always see in the opening shots of New York–set films—to play near the restaurant's entrance, as if it were coincidental. Sara Marks found one and hired him for the night, the constant *RAT-A-TAT-TAT-TA-TAT-TA-TAT-TAT* of the drums filling the night sky, echoing through the canyons of midtown. It was a beautiful evening, a perfect New York night, one of those nights when you're grateful the city took you in and even more grateful it let you stay. But that was all about to change.

Out of the corner of my eye I saw a stretch limo barreling across Fifty-seventh Street, headed right for us. Somehow, I knew right away. I just knew. Like when animals sense earthquakes or tsunamis and head for higher ground. My adrenaline started pumping. A confrontation was unavoidable. There was no higher ground for me to run to.

The limo pulled up to the curb, then to a stop. A driver scrambled out and opened the rear door. In my memory he was wearing one of those ridiculous double-breasted chauffeur jackets and one of those little hats with the tiny patent leather brim, though maybe he wasn't—it just seems like the sort of thing the Donald would force his driver to wear because he thought it was "classy." Slowly, the Donald, Marla, and Jason emerged. Marla was blond and perky, southern and pretty, and moved like she had spent time on a stage. In fact, she had: She'd been runner-up for Miss Georgia in 1984 before going on to win Miss Hawaiian Tropic in 1985. The Donald, who would have been around fifty and was in the early stages of his hue metamorphosis—he was closer to marigold than carrot at this point—oozed confidence, power, masculinity, and really poor tailoring decisions. Though we were firmly in the middle of the 1990s, they both appeared unable to wipe off the stain of the previous decade, and they wore it with defiance and élan. They were perfect for each other. They'd also be separated in a matter of months, divorced before the decade was over. In fact, within a year, the Donald would meet a young Slovenian model named Melanija Knavs. She would Anglicize her name, and in time, they would wed.

The Donald and Marla approached. Jason trailed behind them, nervously looking on. My back stiffened. I gripped the clipboard, my knuckles whitening. Moments later, there he was, standing in front of me. We locked eyes warily, like gunslingers in the old West. I drew first: "I'm very sorry, Mr. Trump, but this is a seated dinner, and I'm afraid you were not invited. You're welcome to come back later, at ten, for the after-party."

Gasps. From the security guards. From the other lingering flacks and hacks hanging around the door. From Marla. The Donald went quiet. His eyes tightened, his lips puckered. Silence, except for the sound of the drums: *RAT-A-TAT-TAT-TA-TAT-TA-TAT-TAT. RAT-A-TAT-TAT-TA-TAT-TA-TAT-TAT.*

The Donald stared at me. "Do you know who I am?"

That was an odd response. I had addressed him by his name just seconds earlier, so I clearly knew who he was. It must have been some Pavlovian response to being turned away from parties. I stared back at the Donald. "I am well aware of who you are, Mr. Trump, and as I explained, this is a seated dinner, and you were not invited. Even if I let you in, there would be nowhere for you and your wife to sit. You're more than welcome to come back later."

The details and specific expletives are hazy, and honestly, unimportant—but the Donald went fucking *off* on me. Throughout his tirade, I had an out-of-body experience, floating above, watching from overhead, floating up, and up, and up, the world getting smaller, and smaller, and smaller. This is apparently a common psychological defense mechanism, a way to detach one-self from being present during a traumatic experience. From above, I could see the Donald's little mouth spitting invective, his hands spinning around like tiny little propellers. And just like that, it was over as quickly as it had begun, and I fell back to earth. The Donald, Marla, and Jason walked off, Marla perhaps a little embarrassed by the Donald's public upbraiding of an underling, something she had clearly witnessed before. They got back in the limo and sped off into the night.

"I've never seen someone say no to Mr. Trump," one of the beefy security guys said to me.

The rest of the night went off without a hitch—well, except for Marc Jacobs's coke-fueled freak-out—and the party was deemed a success. Marla and the Donald never returned.

I felt sorry for Jason that night, having to deal with such a difficult client—not even a client, but a client's husband. A similar situation unfolded a few years later when Jason accompanied another one of his high-profile clients to *Vanity Fair*'s Oscar party—that client was Courtney Love, who was then trying to make the transition from musician to actress. Courtney showed up with Jason, who wasn't on the guest list, and she insisted he be let in. When she didn't get the answer she wanted, she told Jason to wait, entered the party, and proceeded to make a scene. She eventually found and corralled Sara Marks, making the case for Jason to be let in, but Sara wouldn't budge—and she was right; if she let Jason in, it would have set a dangerous precedent. *But you let Jason Weinberg in,* all the other publicists (and managers; Jason was a manager by then) would say, then suddenly it's no longer an exclusive event full of movie stars but an industry junket. Sara was just doing her part to protect a fragile and delicate ecosystem. In a tale that became Oscar party lore, Courtney was apparently livid and marched over to the line of television press covering the event, many of them beaming live at that moment, barking at them to point their cameras and microphones at her, after which she proceeded to yell at the top of her lungs, *"Sara Marks is a cunt!"*

Jason had left the PR business by then, sometime around the turn of the century, and had started a talent management company, and would go on to become a hugely successful Hollywood manager and producer (and invited guest to the Oscar party). Which is not surprising. He was immensely driven, likable, well respected, and smart, and was clearly dedicated to his clients. Whether he knows it or not, Jason also had a hidden hand in redefining fame and celebrity.

In the early nineties he had been hired by a woman named Ann Dexter-Jones. She was a British-born, New York–based, small-*s* socialite and jewelry designer, whose claim to fame was that she was married to the musician Mick Jones—not Mick Jones from the Clash, the *other* Mick Jones, guitarist for seventies and eighties lite-rock band Foreigner. According to legend, he wrote "I Want to Know What Love Is," their biggest hit, for her.* Dexter-Jones had social ambitions, wanted to turn that small *s* into a capital *S*, and somehow came to hire Jason to make that happen, to get her some press and notice in New York's social milieu. Her teenage children, Mark, Charlotte, and Samantha Ronson, from a previous marriage, seemed to be part of the package. I don't know the details of the arrangement, if they were actual "paying" clients of Jason's or not—it was unclear from the outside—but they were all of a sudden very present in downtown Manhattan and the press.

Mark, Charlotte, and Samantha were just kids at the time; they didn't really *do* anything—and I don't mean that disparagingly. They were teenagers, in high school, so I assume they did normal teenager-y things. They just happened to be the children of "Ann Dexter-Jones, wife of Foreigner guitarist Mick Jones"—which is literally how her name always appeared in Page Six, as if it were a contractual obligation—so they would tag along to parties and club and restaurant openings, then they started appearing in photo spreads in magazines, their exploits documented in Page

---

* In 2007, after knowing what love was with Ann for twenty-two years of marriage, he wanted to know what love was with someone else, and they divorced, before reuniting and remarrying ten years later.

Six with alarming regularity. They were suddenly downtown New York's "It" kids. Mark had a rock band called the Whole Earth Mamas with a group of his teenage friends—which included a young Sean Lennon on guitar at one point—that would play at Nell's and other clubs, and was sort of a novelty act. Then he started DJ-ing parties and events. He became a *thing*.

In late 1993, before I started at *Vanity Fair,* in what would turn out to be a very brief modeling career,* I took part in a fashion shoot orchestrated by Jason Weinberg for *Esquire* with Mark and three other guys. It was shot by the Danish fashion photographer Marc Hom and was during the height of "heroin chic," in the midst of the early-nineties grunge moment, when real models were out of fashion and "real people," mostly *super* skinny and *really* young looking, made up to look like drug addicts, were used in campaigns and editorials.† This shoot found the five of us splayed on, under, and around one another and a pile of dirty old mattresses, heavy dark makeup under our eyes, looking like fashionable strung-out junkies in some chic shooting gallery. The caption referred to us as "the free spirits," going on to say, "This nocturnal clique may herald an unlikely avant-garde. Ripped jeans, cut T-shirts, and shapeless oversized sweaters give them a lost-boy look."

For much of the nineties, you couldn't walk a block in New York City without stumbling over a Ronson or two. I remember watching all of this unfold, fascinated—whether it was intentional or not, Jason helped create a new kind of celebrity, taking a lump of clay and forming it into something *resembling* fame, but a kind of postmodern, post-Warholian fame where someone was famous for . . . well, nothing much, really. They were just suddenly *famous*. It was like the celebrity narrative given a page 1 rewrite with no beginning, middle, or end, fifteen minutes of fame playing on a loop.

---

* It was a onetime thing. I was young, I needed the money.

† Calvin Klein's CK One ads would become the most famous representation of this aesthetic, Kate Moss its most lasting figure.

Fame had usually been the end result of doing or creating something successful or great, or so unsuccessful you got unwanted attention and fame—infamy—for that failure (or you murdered someone or had your penis sliced off by your angry wife). Now the concepts of fame and celebrity were being reengineered, reversed, manipulated—*We're going to create the appearance of fame, you're going to get famous, then you'll figure out what to do with it and leverage that fame.* A *Field of Dreams* approach to stardom: *If you build it, they will come.* And it worked. The Ronsons, all three, got kind of famous. Mark would go on to a successful music career, Charlotte a design career, Samantha a DJ-ing career. Samantha's fame would inch toward infamy for a moment in the mid-2000s thanks to her tumultuous and very public relationship with Lindsay Lohan—but by then fame and infamy had become fully integrated, a leaked sex tape or drug arrest no longer a career ender but a career starter.

Eventually, this shift in fame and celebrity would be institutionalized with reality television in the following decade, and social media after that, like a clothing factory in China stealing designer blueprints and making cheap knockoffs of the real thing. Once you start connecting the dots, the Ronsons' running around New York City in the nineties is one of the foundations that modern celebrity culture was built upon, its Adam, Eve, apple, and snake. Without them, you don't get Hiltons, Kardashians, and Jenners, various Housewives, Bachelors and Bachelorettes, Survivors and Apprentices, Honey Boo Boo, those bearded yokels from *Duck Dynasty*, YouTube stars, social media influencers. And you sure as fuck don't get President Donald Trump.

Of course, culture doesn't really work like that; it only does when you count backward, know the end of the story first. It's never that simple, because there are too many variables to make a scientific argument. And let me be clear: I'm not likening Mark Ronson or his sisters to Donald Trump, nor am I laying "President Donald Trump" at Ronson's or Jason Weinberg's doorstep. That's not just unfair to them, it's absurd. Writing subjectively about history and culture, which it turns out any idiot can do, is like playing fantasy sports, which any idiot can do. It's kind of based in the real world, using real numbers and statistics, real players, and it takes real thought and effort; it's also kind of bullshit.

But Mark Ronson and Donald Trump do have something in common. They both came from wealthy, successful, and connected families, which gave them a little extra wind in their sails from launch. In the old days, we used to call this nepotism. Now it's been moved into a different column, the catchall *white privilege* (from which I clearly benefited, as well). Donald Trump got his start with a loan from his slumlord father, Fred—a loan Trump claimed was $1 million but has been reported as being closer to $14 million, while Mark Ronson started his career in music already a "celebrity," with the accrued cultural capital and access that being the son of "Ann Dexter-Jones, wife of Foreigner guitarist Mick Jones," comes with. They also both came with a handy "self-made" origin story. "The working man likes me because he knows I worked hard and didn't inherit what I've built. Hey, I made it myself," Trump told *Playboy* in 1990. Ronson's tale of early struggles, which he's talked about in interviews over the years, involves his lugging his own DJ equipment through a snowstorm for his first paying gig—in which he made only $50—and losing money on the night. *What horror!* No mention of having a publicist on the family payroll at sixteen.

The magazine business was full of these kinds of socially connected and wealthy kids; *Vanity Fair* and Condé Nast were swarming nests of nepotism and white privilege, evident in not only hiring practices but editorial choices. The mastheads of the company's titles read like the *Social Register*, a Dow Jones stock ticker (DuPont, Johnson), or the list of debutantes at some European ball—excuse me, *bal*. When summer rolled around, and the interns would show up, Hollywood, fashion, and society were equally well represented. *Daughter of studio chief?* Check. *Fashion designer's niece?* Of course. *Son of faded but viable star?* Yep. In print we would slobber over the children of the rich, famous, and powerful for simply being the children of the rich, famous, and powerful. Because they had great style, or so-and-so was starting a jewelry or handbag line or making traditional Austrian felt hiking hats, or opening a vegan bakery in Santa Monica, and someone got a call, and it worked its way up or down the chain. We would send a photographer and a writer, who would write 150 words that were pretty much the same 150 words as the last version, like a Mad Lib. _____ *is the* _____ *of prolific* _____ _____. *However, lest you think proximity to* _____ *is an advantage to a fledgling career in* _____ . . .

And *real* royalty? (And what *is* royalty but the foundation and institutionalization of nepotism?) Our fawning and obsessiveness knew no bounds. I lost count of how many Princess Diana covers we did. We assembled a whole issue dedicated to young European royalty in 2003, the cover line YOUNG AND ROYAL over a twenty-one-year-old Prince William, in white tie, shot by Mario Testino, in the last known photograph of William's hair. That issue was like a public service announcement for the dangers of inbreeding and European dentistry. But you know what? That cover sold; so did all the Princess Diana covers, and later those with her sons and their spouses and offspring. And once the computer algorithm machine-o-matic device told us that our readers couldn't get enough of it, and royalty equaled clicks, or likes, or whatever metric for measuring success we were adhering to at that moment, we were hell-bent for tiaras. White, middle-class aspiration is an unpredictable and powerful drug, and I learned to yield to its power. It put food on my table, after all.

I had no social pedigree or connections. The closest I came was when I was seven and a kid I went to elementary school with named Sean (his surname was something equally Irish) claimed he was related to the magician Doug Henning, and that Henning was going to perform at his eighth-birthday party. He wasn't; he didn't—an early lesson in disappointment and low expectations that would follow me through life. So, there was no Doug Henning for me then, and no jewelry line or vegan bakery for me now.

I'd always resented blatant nepotism, hated it in fact, which I think is common when something is out of reach or you're ex-

cluded from *anything*. It's plain old chip-on-your-shoulder envy.
(There's a reason it's one of the seven deadly sins; human beings
are so predictable.) *Why couldn't that have been me!* But it just
wasn't. And worse, my own family's origin story was uneventful,
a New York–centric tale that is not atypical of its middle-to-
occasionally-upper-middle-class station: My ancestors came over
sometime around the turn of the previous century, as so many did
in giant human waves. German, Irish, Russian, and Eastern European, mostly penniless and running from something—pogroms,
famine, assholes—but running *to* something, too. They landed in
New York—separately, of course—looked up a relative, a few fleeing the city for points north or west almost immediately, the others
heading off to some cramped tenement in their assigned ethnic
neighborhood in one of the city's five boroughs, where they found
a low-paying job involving pickles or eyeglasses, which might have
led to their opening a little store or starting a small business, saving up just enough money to send their kids—well, the boys—to
one of the local community or city colleges, which would get
them out of the old neighborhood, where they'd shake off the
remaining dust and lichen of the Old World, mingling with other
ethnicities, intermarrying and reproducing, muddying the ethnic
waters—from Rizzo to Richter or Ryan in one generation. At some
point, my family's Russian surname was changed from something
long and Jewish to the Anglo-sounding Brown.*

   That City College degree would allow them—well, the men—to
get an entry-level job in the mailroom at some corporation, where
they would work hard and catch the eye of some vice president
("What about that kid . . ."), which would eventually lead to a
middle-management job and see them move, maybe with the help
of a VA loan, from that tenement or row house in Queens or
Brooklyn or the Bronx to a middle-class suburb in New Jersey,
Westchester, Connecticut, or Long Island, and usually end with

---

* Meaning: Us Browns could always pass for whatever was needed in the moment, a
handy trick. Early on I think most of my colleagues just assumed I was some well-off,
educated, connected WASP, and I never bothered to dispel that notion.

their drinking themselves to death during pension-funded retirements in some exurb in Central Florida, wondering what it all meant and thinking, *Is that really it?* Except, of course, the Jews—at least the ones who didn't go west half a century earlier to build Los Angeles and Hollywood—they retired to Miami or Arizona, never really drank, and lived till 102.

Meanwhile, *that* generation's kids, the baby boomers, went to slightly better schools, maybe even an Ivy—and this is the generation where the Jews finally got in the mix, when Aaron Finkelstein from Riverdale met Ridgewood, New Jersey's Maria O'Sullivan at Cornell's freshman orientation—before going on to law or medical school, moving to a slightly fancier suburb than their parents, celebrating Hanukah *and* Christmas, joining the country club, sending the kids to private school, buying a Mercedes and a saltbox in East Hampton—Northwest Woods; nice, but nothing crazy—getting their eldest into Cornell as a legacy and a summer internship at Dad's sophomore roommate's white-shoe D.C. law firm, then divorcing, remarrying, and doing it all over again. This is not just the story of my family, and the story of the creation of much of America's white middle to upper-middle class, it's the promise of America, a country built on striving, and one generation's hard work and sacrifice paying off immediately in the next. And it's what makes this country great, even if my own family ran out of steam just before the country club–and–Mercedes bit of it.

The story of the rich and powerful isn't all that different from the story of you and me. (F. Scott Fitzgerald's theory was of another time.) Their ancestors just got here a generation or two earlier, or Great-Grandpa Joe opened that store on *just* the right block, selling *just* the right thing, at *just* the right moment, purchased the building during a downturn, or bought 150 acres of scrub outside of town that happened to be sitting on a sea of crude and decided to take the stock instead of the cash. It's the luck of the draw. No one gets to choose their parents or their family, their lot in life, and no one should be judged on that alone. This works both ways. I was lucky too, batted my eyelashes, got a break, happened to be in the right place at the right time, found a crack in the door marked WHITE PRIVILEGE—a side door, but a door nonetheless. From there it's how you carry yourself, how you treat others, how hard you work. And ultimately, that matters more than how you got there, and it's a great equalizer.

Some of those interns and assistants with recognizable and fancy last names were really smart, funny, wonderful people, raised well, who went on to do interesting things, a few becoming beloved and important members of the magazine's staff. (Of course, others were walking advertisements for the pitfalls of the aristocratic gene pool.) Some of those kids we covered in our pages created really significant things. This is something you come to terms with over the years—while it might not seem like it from the outside, most industries, and the world, have a version of meritocracy to filter out the grounds. Sure, some people have extra help at the beginning. That's just how it works. This is the standard social contract among the "elite," a word I hate to use because there's really no such thing and it's abstract and meaningless, used as a cheap weapon nowadays. We're all just a lucky break or chance encounter away from being part of this "elite," which is nothing more than the carrot dangling from the end of the stick that is the American Dream. Most people love their children and will do anything and everything to help them get started in life in any way they can, so if you can make that call, write that letter, send that email, call in a favor, work that angle, you do it. One generation's hard work and sacrifice paying off immediately in the next. The story of America.

Mark Ronson took the leg up, put his head down, worked hard, and went on to make significant music—he produced by far one of the best and most iconic albums of the 2000s, Amy Winehouse's *Back to Black*. Making music, art, and lasting culture is as important as anything as far as I'm concerned. I don't begrudge him any of his success. He is obviously talented and wouldn't have gotten as far as he did if he weren't. On top of that he was a really nice, humble kid way back when.

Donald Trump was a failed businessman, went bankrupt twice, *played* a successful businessman on a reality television show, somehow became president, has done everything in his power to upend liberal democracy, and generally behaves like a petulant and petty prick determined to tear up everything the founding fathers held so dear. As much as I can go on and on about my belief that ultimately we do live in a meritocracy, don't get me wrong: When faced with such overwhelming evidence, I admit that some grounds slip through that filter; there are abso*lutely* people who fail up and don't deserve their success, but they come in every shape and size, from every background.

Which is all to say, Donald Trump and Mark Ronson may have both been well-connected kids from wealthy families who had doors opened for them, but one of them turned out to be a loathsome narcissist intent on destroying the traditions and institutions of this country, and the other one helped Lady Gaga get an Oscar. And that too is the story of America.

The morning after the Valentino party, Graydon got a call from Steve Florio, the hard-charging, cigar-chomping, mustachioed, alpha male president of Condé Nast. It was a brief conversation, and after hanging up, Graydon called me into his office. He had a mischievous grin on his face, which turned into full-throated laughter.

"Did you refuse to let Donald Trump and Marla into the party last night?" he asked.

"Well . . . yeah. Remember, we told him he could come later, and then he just showed up for the dinner."

"Apparently he's friends with Steve Florio. They're working on some sort of business deal. He called Steve this morning and demanded you be fired."

"Ummm . . . shit, okay—so, does this mean you're firing me?!"

He smiled. "No, you moron. I'm proud of you. You were just doing your job.

"Send him some flowers. He'll get over it."

But he didn't get over it. The Donald assumed the directive to deny him entry came from on high, and the cease-fire, the fragile peace between him and Graydon that had developed over the previous few years, would come to an end, igniting a war that would escalate with the advent of Twitter a decade later.

Chapter 17

Nineteen ninety-seven was a significant year in my life. The first big change was that I quit playing music, broke up the band. My dreams of rock and roll stardom were dead. Word had spread around the office that I played in downtown clubs, and once my secret was out, it was only a matter of time before some of the other assistants started showing up at gigs. As I played one night, self-consciously, on a tiny Lower East Side stage at a small club that's now long gone, looking out at that table of my *Vanity Fair* friends, it became clear to me. It was time to move on. I couldn't deny it anymore. Those were my people and that was my world now. And while they were all polite, I could tell they thought we were terrible. And we were. It was all becoming too much—having a demanding job during the day that often stretched into the evenings, then trying to fit in rehearsals and gigs at night. I was exhausted. And after three years at *Vanity Fair*, it was really beginning to feel like home, and family, unlike the downtown rehearsal spaces, clubs, and bars of just a few years earlier. That fear that I was turning my back on my generation, and myself, that I'd felt when I first put on that suit and began working in an office had disappeared. This was who I was now, maybe who I was meant to be all along. I'd found my place.

And I was no longer living with my brother, both of us having moved on from that East Third Street apartment, taking a stab at domestication. Nathaniel had bought an apartment in Gramercy Park, and Aimee and I had moved into a loft on the corner of Avenue B and Second Street, Alphabet City, deep in the East Village. The neighborhood still had some edginess left over from the eighties and early nineties—there was the occasional stabbing on our block, junkies nodded out on our doorstep, and once in a while you were offered heroin or "sealed works" (hypodermic needles in a sealed package) on the street—but the sidewalks weren't littered with needles as they had been earlier in the decade. Things were beginning to change. It was now Rudy Giuliani's New York, safer and cleaner, the beginning of the homogenization of the city that would accelerate in the next decade. But Avenue B was still just grimy enough for us to be able to afford what was the most space either of us had ever had in New York, sixteen hundred square feet, with a wall of windows facing north, and as anyone will tell you, finding a great apartment—with great light—in New York is transformative.

It felt like a big step, Aimee and I moving in together. It would be the first time for both of us. We had been dating for two and a half years at that point, really liked being with each other, and had fun together. There was none of that manufactured drama or petty jealousy that dooms so many young relationships. A Buddhist upbringing had ingrained a groundedness and calm in her that people like me spend years trying to find. I felt more comfortable around her than anyone else I had ever met. She was exactly what I needed. I was still a little wild, and I think she liked that about me, and gave me a lot of space. She bought me a motorcycle for my twenty-fifth birthday, an old Kawasaki from my birth year (1972), and we would ride around the city, she clutching on to me, which is as romantic as it sounds.

Aimee and I were in related industries, with her deep in the independent film world after abandoning her magazine, climbing our way up the ranks, so there was overlap in our professional and social lives, although neither of us had any real social aspirations. We earned about the same amount of money—which was not much—so there were no weird power dynamics between us. She didn't drink, which helped keep my drinking in check a little bit. It was a balanced relationship all around, and it worked. We had taken a trip together the year before, our first, a week in the Caribbean, and we worked on the road too, the first true test of a new relationship. We made sense together.

That same year, *Vanity Fair* won a National Magazine Award, or ASME—an acronym for the American Society of Magazine Editors—for General Excellence, for magazines with a circulation over one million. It's the highest honor a magazine can receive, like winning the Best Picture Oscar, although no one outside the magazine world has ever heard of the ASMEs or cares. But it was a big deal in the industry. Tina Brown had won it in 1995 for *The New Yorker,* a few years into her revamping it, so the recognition from Graydon's peers was proof that in five short years, he had fulfilled the mandate and remade *Vanity Fair* into *his* magazine. It was an exciting moment for all of us, especially for me, as I'd had a ringside seat to all the action and the transformation.

The win was a surprise. Not because we didn't think we deserved it, but because of an incident that had happened the year before at the awards luncheon, which was held in a grand ballroom of one of New York's big hotels, often the Waldorf Astoria back then.

In 1996, *Vanity Fair* had been nominated for a few ASME awards—which were handed out for writing, design, photography, and other similar categories—as it was in most years, so we took up a couple of tables for the ceremony. Now, the food at those big catered affairs, fundraisers and awards ceremonies, is never good, whether it's a lunch or a dinner, a wilted salad followed by a sad piece of rubbery beef or chicken, or whatever is being passed off as the vegetarian option. It's just too many people to feed, all at once, to serve good food. But it's not about the food. At the 1996 ASMEs, Graydon decided it was. He was mad as hell, and he wasn't going to take it anymore.

The senior staff was off at the ASME luncheon; it was quiet in the office, *for once;* and I was covering the phones when the phone rang.

"Graydon Carter's office."

It was an editor, I forget which one—although it was probably Aimée Bell, who usually got stuck with these sorts of tasks—calling from a pay phone in the Waldorf's lobby.

"The food here is terrible. Do you mind getting sandwiches for everyone, from Dishes?"

Dishes was the new upscale salad and sandwich place on Forty-fourth Street we'd been getting lunch from every day since it opened. It was the kind of thing that would pop up on every city block in the coming decades with cute names like Crave, Carve, Così, Mangia, Bite, Sweetgreen, Chop'd, and 'Wichcraft, and, along with Duane Reade, Starbucks, and banks, would take over the damn city.

My response was probably something like "*What?!*"

"Just get a whole bunch of sandwiches. Then bring them up here."

"*To the awards luncheon?* Is that such a good idea?"

"I don't know. I guess we'll find out. Thanks so much."

I hung up the phone, thinking that in fact, it was a terrible idea. We were already hated in the industry, able to outspend everybody, steal whatever writer or photographer we wanted from our competitors—we were the New York Yankees of the magazine business. And worse, we were considered the ultimate snobs. And this would be an act of high snobbery, played out in front of the whole industry.

But I did as I was told. I enlisted another assistant, some poor soul, and we went to Dishes, bought bagfuls of sandwiches, and headed up to the awards luncheon.

Now, let me set the scene. Because this wasn't like walking into a buzzing room. It was pin-drop quiet. Maybe five hundred people or even a thousand. There was nowhere to hide. It was hard to be subtle, the two of us walking into that room weighed down by plastic takeout bags. Everyone was focused on whoever was on-stage speaking, presenting an award or accepting one. Tables and chairs are squeezed tightly together in those big halls. The *Vanity Fair* tables were prime tables, right in the middle of the room, in front of the stage. *Excuse me, sorry, excuse me, excuse me, sorry, can I get by? Thanks, excuse me, can I squeeze by? Sorry. Thanks. Sorry. Can I squeeze by?* This went on for what seemed like hours as we made our way to the *Vanity Fair* tables. Everyone was staring at us, not quite sure who these kids were or what the hell was going on. *Did someone order delivery to the ASME awards?* (Why yes, they did.) When we finally arrived at the table, it was clear to everyone in the audience, at least in the immediate vicinity, what was going on, as we called out orders like we were craft services on a film set. *I got tuna, tuna, tuna, who wants tuna? Roast beef, turkey with cheese—you want tuna? Okay.* And I'd hurl a tuna fish sandwich through the air.

It was not only humiliating for me, but it was really bad form for *Vanity Fair*. We were pretty sure that ASME hated us. So, it came as a bit of a surprise that we won the major award the next year. Although our success was hard to deny. By the late nineties, the magazine was doing better than ever. Our numbers were up across the board. The Hollywood Issue had become a keystone for the magazine, so full of advertising that it began to resemble a phone book, its yearly release a major media event. We were landing scoop after scoop and coup after coup. Our July 1997 issue had Princess Diana on the cover, an iconic photograph from a shoot she had done with Mario Testino. Diana would be dead within a few months, and we would return to pictures from this photo shoot numerous times over the years for covers that always sold well, adding "Dead Di" to the "Dead Kennedys" formula. The next year, Monica Lewinsky posed for Herb Ritts in another watershed cultural moment. We were going from strength to strength. Had all the heat. There was a boom in luxury and fashion advertising, and we benefited from it. I had spent more than three years sitting outside Graydon's office during the rise of the magazine's fortunes in the midnineties. And while we'd often talked about what was next for me, neither of us knew exactly what that would be. I had made myself so valuable as his assistant, the thought of losing me and training someone new must have been daunting, and inconvenient. There had been a few replacements for Pat over the years, but they kept leaving after brief stints, leaving me in the nest, alone. I was conflicted over my responsibility and devotion to Graydon, while feeling trapped and anxious to move on to the next step in what was actually looking like a possible career.

There wasn't a lot of upward mobility at *Vanity Fair*. You were either an assistant or an editor of some sort. And there wasn't much daylight in between. It was hard to make that leap to the next level, easy to get caught in the middle, and I hadn't had the experience of working directly with a text editor like the other assistants, or the foundation of an education and a degree in history or literature. That institutional knowledge I'd accrued was useful, and I was overflowing with it, but that wasn't enough to carry me to the next level.

One morning, Graydon called me into his office.

"I have an idea."

"Oh yeah?"

"What if we turn you into a photographer?"

"*Me?*"

"Yeah, you moron."

It wasn't that far-fetched an idea. I'd always had an interest in photography, liked taking pictures, as did Graydon. We would sit and talk about our newest cameras and different kinds of film, compare notes, look at contact sheets of each other's latest pictures, his mostly of his family, mine mostly of my dog and Aimee. I thought for a minute. I'd started working for him not knowing how to do anything, had never worked in an office before. I was still young, had my whole career in front of me. I didn't hate the idea of getting out in the world, not being chained to a desk. And if he was suggesting it, it might be my way up and out.

"What did you have in mind?"

"Well, you could start by going out at night, shooting parties. I think you'd be good at that. And you could be in charge of the party pages in the magazine."

We often ran a few of these pages a month, filled with socialites and celebrities and other notables at exclusive events, cocktails and cigarettes in their hands. A peek behind the curtain of a fabulous world that you could step into for a moment. From the second you opened an issue, you were transported into a fantasy of wealth and luxury and exclusivity inaccessible to most. At $3.99, or whatever the current newsstand price, it was the cheapest luxury item you could buy.

The idea of actually going out and shooting these parties immediately gave me anxiety. The taking of the pictures would probably be fine—not to diminish it; there's an art and a science to party photography, and some photographers, like Larry Fink, Jonathan Becker, or Dafydd Jones, real photographers who all shot our parties over the years, elevated it to fine art—but I was shy, and I didn't think asking strangers if I could take their photo would be my strong suit. And while my social antennae now were more developed than when I began, the party circuit the magazine covered in its pages wasn't filled with recognizable celebrities; they were socialites and figures from the art and literary worlds, but not exactly famous faces. I wouldn't have been able to identify a Brice Marden or a Ross Bleckner just yet, or tell the difference between Anne Bass and Anne Slater, and those were the types of people whose faces would land on those pages. But Graydon had a solution. A few years earlier he had hired Heather Watts as a contributing editor. Heather had been a principal ballerina with the New York City Ballet from 1979 until her retirement in 1995 and was one of the most famous ballet dancers in the world. A prima ballerina. She had often been paired onstage with Mikhail Baryshnikov. After a dazzling career, Heather was still a heavyweight in the cultural and social worlds, especially in New York.

I should briefly explain *Vanity Fair*'s contributing editors— it's a question I got often over the years as the contributing editor section of the magazine's masthead would swell to more than seventy-five names at its peak, the largest piece of real estate on the page. Many of the names were our writers', those who wrote for the magazine on a steady basis and usually had a contract. Being a contributing editor helped writers get access to stories, got phone calls returned quicker. It also meant you had achieved a certain level. It was like membership to an exclusive club, the pinnacle of the magazine world. The title alone was valuable. Of course, some of these writers were dormant, hadn't written in years, their names lingering there like the tattoo of an old lover. Then there were contributing editors from the social world, connectors, people who could make a call, help with access, get someone to show up to a party, or solve a problem. Reinaldo Herrera, the elegant Venezuelan aristocrat and socialite, whose wife is the fashion designer Carolina Herrera, was the perfect example of this type of contributor. (You don't understand the word *presence* until you've met Reinaldo, or Reggie, as he was known around the office, maybe the most charismatic and charming man to ever exist.)

We covered a lot of upscale cultural events and high-society black-tie affairs, and Heather was perfectly positioned in that sweet spot where the social and cultural worlds collide. Heather was also, like me, wild. Suddenly, we were *Vanity Fair*'s nightlife wrecking crew. Heather knew everyone, everyone knew her; I was her young sidekick, camera in hand. She would make the introductions, ask if I could take a picture with my new thousand-dollar Contax (charged to Condé Nast, of course), decided I would only shoot black and white—chic, midcentury, and arty—and we hit the town.

What looks good on paper doesn't always translate to success. Like New Coke or Quibi. Because the first thing Heather and I would do when we got to an event was find the bar. I mean, you need to gas up, oil the machine. The second thing we would do was sit at that bar for the rest of the night, smoking and drinking and laughing our heads off. People would come over, say hello to Heather, catch up; I'd spin around, grab a shot or two, photos that would get increasingly out of focus as the night went on. Sometimes I would give my camera to some random partygoer I'd just met, tell them to go take some pictures, or to take pictures of Heather and me. I may have accidentally invented the selfie, at some point. We covered a black-tie New York City Ballet gala at Lincoln Center one night, and because of Heather, we were seated at a prime table for dinner. A young Natalie Portman was sitting across from us with the fashion designer Isaac Mizrahi. I took a few pictures of them, then passed the camera around the table. I had rolls and rolls of pictures of the same ten people at that one table, and half of them I was in, smoking a cigarette, wineglass in my hand.

While Heather and I had a great time for a few months, we were producing very few pages, although a lot of great pictures of the two of us. We did get a few in the magazine, and some of my photographs weren't bad. It was a thrill seeing PHOTOGRAPHS BY DANA BROWN at the bottom of the page, in the same location, font, and point size as Annie Leibovitz, Herb Ritts, or Helmut Newton's name would appear with their features. But one night after covering an event at the New York Public Library, I left my camera in a cab, and figured that was a sign. Soon after, the magazine hired Patrick McMullan, New York's most prolific party photographer, to provide our party pictures. We needed a professional.

Graydon wasn't upset. In fact, I think the whole thing was a ruse, a plot to keep me as his assistant—give me something meaningful to do for the magazine after hours, while still remaining at his side during the day. The optics of advancement. There was also a culture of waste at Condé Nast that was accepted. Sometimes photo shoots or stories, like any creative endeavor, didn't work out. We killed stories after they were written all the time, or reshot photos. Although he did like hearing the stories of our nights on the town, howling in laughter as I recounted them, and he adored Heather, Graydon had to admit this might not be the right opportunity for me.

He suggested I try some portrait photography, a more controlled environment. I could start by photographing some contributing editors on the weekends, for the Contributors page, to get my feet wet, see how I did. I knew most of the writers by then, so I figured I'd at least be comfortable around them. And the pictures ran so small, for the most part, that it wasn't a huge amount of pressure. I could learn on the job, and that was my *thing*. He called the photo editor, Susan White, and asked if any of our writers' photographs needed updating. A big grin appeared on his face.

"Perfect."

Graydon put down the phone.

"Hitch."

"Really?"

"Yep."

"Okay. That's great."

"Don't fuck it up."

Hitch was, of course, Christopher Hitchens. I'm amazed, almost ashamed, that I've gotten this far into the book with Christopher's name appearing only once, and in passing. He was one of the most famous of *Vanity Fair*'s writers, one of its best and most versatile, and also one of Graydon's first hires when he took over in 1992. He wrote in his first Editor's Letter, in November 1992, announcing a new column: "Its author is Christopher Hitchens, a writer both cultured and ever so slightly elitist (in only the best way) and therefore one infinitely qualified to write a column on high and low culture called 'Cultural Elite.'" Christopher was an iconoclast, a contrarian, an old-school Trotskyist who hated political correctness and was a staunch defender of free speech. His outspoken defense of his friend Salman Rushdie during the ayatollah's fatwa calling for Rushdie's death was an act of absolute bravery—Christopher was a loyal friend. He was an incredible speaker and debater, and of course wrote like a dream, which seemed effortless for him. And he could write about anything. In conversation, he had the ability to reach into his brain and produce the perfect line from a classic piece of literature or poetry, or from political speeches going back to Cicero. It always amazed me—he was one of the few people who made me regret not getting a proper education and pushed me to really *read,* and as much as I could. But Christopher had no sense of entitlement or grandiosity, didn't flaunt his intelligence or make you feel stupid.* He was one of the loveliest people I'd ever met, and he was adored around the office when he'd pop up from Washington to pay a visit. On top of all that, he was fun to go out on the town

* Unless you were debating him.

with, maybe one of the most fun people ever. In that regard, Christopher and I were cut from the same cloth.

A few weeks later, on a Saturday, I jumped on a plane to spend the day in Washington, D.C., photographing Christopher. I was allowed an assistant, so I brought Aimee along for the ride, since I thought it would be a fun adventure. Plus, assistants on shoots were paid $150 for the day. Why not keep it in the family?

Christopher lived in a sprawling pre-war apartment in the Wyoming building, in D.C.'s upscale Kalorama neighborhood, with his wife, Carol Blue, and their young daughter, Antonia.* *Vanity Fair* had thrown our White House Correspondents' Dinner after-party in Christopher's apartment for a few years but had recently outgrown it.

Christopher opened the door, and I was met with his sly smile and standard greeting: "Comrade." He led us in. Christopher and Carol's apartment was underfurnished. In fact, it was almost bare, with an odd chair here or there, a couch or two in random places, and books scattered about in stacks, like an old library. I said hello to Carol. Antonia was sitting on the floor, drawing, the walls of the apartment her canvas. These were people who cared more about books and creativity and ideas than aesthetics.

Christopher and Carol invited Aimee and me to sit down with them, and we caught up. They were both warm, friendly, and funny. I shared the office gossip, they told me what was going on in Washington. We talked very briefly about the photographs I needed to get. I told Christopher that I'd like to shoot him in his office in the apartment, then go outside, use natural light.

"I am humbly at your service, comrade."

Just then, their buzzer rang. Carol leapt up to answer it. Christopher smiled.

"Our guests have arrived."

Guests?

Christopher and Carol had decided that before we got to the

---

* That Antonia grew up to be a writer is no surprise.

photographs, we should have a proper lunch. Never one to pass up a free meal, I shrugged—the pictures could wait, I guessed.

We were soon joined by four or five others, friends of Christopher and Carol. I didn't know who any of them were, but they were interesting, intelligent, and witty, and probably important thinkers or connected to the D.C. establishment in some way. Wine and Bloody Marys made an unannounced visit. Food was ordered in. Did I mention wine and Bloody Marys made an unannounced visit? We sat around, eating, drinking, and talking, with topics ranging from the Clintons to the Spanish Civil War to the oncoming age of technology. I got lost in the conversation, thrilled to be included in such a heady salon. I also lost track of time. Lunch went on for hours, then we moved into the living room, where the drinking and conversation continued. At some point, Aimee turned to me.

"Our flight is in two hours."

Shit. I hadn't taken any pictures, which was the whole reason for the trip in the first place.

I turned to Christopher.

"I need to take pictures of you! Quick!"

Christopher and I ran crookedly to his office. I didn't have any time to set up lights. He sat at his desk and smiled.

"Just sit still for a minute."

"Whatever you say, comrade."

He did the best he could, and I was able to shoot a couple rolls of film.

Soon after, Aimee and I bid Christopher and Carol, and our new friends, farewell, gathered up the equipment, and ran out the door to catch the quick flight back to New York.

When I got the contact sheets back a few days later, my face dropped. Most of the photos were overexposed or underexposed, some were out of focus, and others didn't even have Christopher in frame. One of the contact sheets was just photographs of a plant. There were a few that might have been usable, if a little arty for *Vanity Fair*'s Contributors page, with half of Christopher's face in shadow. But it wasn't the usual glamour shot.

I walked into Graydon's office, holding the contact sheets, ready to fall on my sword.

He looked up.

I dropped the contact sheets on his desk, a dejected look on my face, and he started to go through them.

"Is that a plant?" He laughed, then studied the contact sheets for a few moments, grabbing a loupe for a closer look. "This one could work. It's not bad."

He pointed to a simple headshot of Christopher, sitting at his desk, half his face bathed in natural light from the window. It was underexposed, dark, and had a vintage look, but not in a good way, more like an author's photograph on a ratty old paperback from the seventies than a contemporary image up to the standards of *Vanity Fair*. I knew it wasn't very good, and that a bad photograph was going to end up in the magazine because of where I sat and because Graydon said so. That portrait appeared in the July 1997 issue.

I was given another assignment to photograph a writer, but decided I needed professional help. I gave a friend of mine from 44, a struggling young photographer, the $150 assistant fee to lend a hand. He did everything on that shoot except press the button. I felt so guilty afterward that I was getting this chance, which felt so undeserved, and he wasn't. Having something handed to me without having to work for it made me uncomfortable and ashamed. In a quiet moment a few days later, I walked into Graydon's office.

"Look, I don't think this is going to work. I hate the idea that I'm getting preferential treatment, which I am. I also feel like I'm taking this away from someone who would kill for the opportunity. And honestly, the writers deserve a real photographer, not your assistant pretending to be one."

He seemed to understand. "Are you sure?"

"Yeah."

He nodded. "Okay. Well, we tried. We'll figure something out."

Graydon wanted to help me unlock whatever hidden talent there might have been lurking inside, wanted to reward me for putting in three years. Sweat equity. But being a photographer wasn't going to be it. And it was probably for the best. But if all I had gotten out of my brief photography career was that afternoon in D.C. with Christopher and Carol, it was worth it. It was one of the most memorable days of my young life, and I was a convert to the cult of Hitch.

I loved hanging out with Christopher over the years and learned a lot from him. One of the smartest things I might have witnessed had nothing to do with Hitch's intellect, writing, or debating, and had everything to do with his drinking. He was a seasoned pro, and I was his willing pupil, studying at the feet of the master. Almost a decade after my failed photo session with him, in 2005, he was going to be debating at Cooper Union, in Manhattan's East Village. It was the height of the Iraq War. Christopher, famous for his devout left-wing politics, had been a surprising proponent of the war and was seen as a turncoat by liberals. He had no issue with America's using its military might to overthrow despotic regimes in the name of human rights, no matter the pretenses for war, and had to defend his position constantly. This debate would be another opportunity.

Christopher's debating skills were unparalleled, and it had grown into a cottage industry for him. Michael Wolff, the savvy media reporter, who had become a *Vanity Fair* columnist that year, would be moderating.

We had considered creating a debate series for the magazine, so a group of us, Graydon included, decided to check this one out. I went to meet Christopher for a drink beforehand at St. Mark's Ale House, a shitty little dive just across Third Avenue from Cooper Union. I walked into the empty bar and saw Christopher sitting at a corner table, a white and green Starbucks cup sitting in front of him. I grew concerned. After all, this was Christopher Hitchens, sitting in a bar, drinking coffee. I ordered a pint from the bartender and headed over to see what in the world was going on.

"Comrade, you all right?" I gestured to the Starbucks cup.

That knowing smile appeared on Christopher's face.

"Let's go smoke." This was a few years into the smoking ban in New York's restaurants and bars, so we had to go outside. He stood, grabbed his Starbucks cup. I took a big gulp of my beer and left it on the table, and we walked outside.

He lit a cigarette, as did I.

"I bet right now you'd love to be having a drink with your cigarette. But because of this draconian law, you can't."

Taking a drink outside a bar to smoke was frowned upon; the bar could get fined, and so one of its employees would often stop you.

"Well, sure."

He tilted his Starbucks cup so I could see that it was almost full—of whiskey.

Christopher had gamed the system, outsmarted it.

The debate was a testy affair. Christopher was in enemy territory, a packed crowd of outspoken New York liberals, who punctuated Christopher's defense of the war with hisses and hollers. But Hitch had his defenders in the crowd too. It was mayhem, but that was par for the course whenever Christopher was talking about Iraq. Michael Wolff did his best to keep things under control.

After the debate, Graydon took a few of us, Michael and Christopher included, out for dinner, to Elaine's, on the Upper East Side. Elaine's was a mythical place among New York's older literary establishment. Open since the early sixties, it had hosted a star-studded cast each night for almost fifty years—Woody Allen, Tom Wolfe, Norman Mailer, Joseph Heller, George Plimpton, Gay Talese. By the mid-2000s, it looked like heaven's waiting room, full of so many ancient writers and other assorted fading New York characters. Elaine Kaufman, its owner and namesake, died a few years later, in 2010. The restaurant closed down the next year. But it was a favorite spot of Graydon's; he was able to express his reverence for the writers and literary figures of the generation before his in this fabled place. I'd been there a number of times with him over the years and it was always a treat. He would get excited after some old guy would stop by to say hello, then turn to me after he'd walked off.

"Do you know who that was?!"

"No."

"It was Frederic Morton!"

"Who's Frederic Morton?"

He would shake his head in disgust at the fact that I didn't know, usually delivering a book to me the next day.*

After a long, boozy meal with Christopher and the gang, Graydon decided it was time for him to take off, get home before it got too late.

"I left the tab open. Get whatever you want."

The rest of the table decided it was time to head off too, leaving me, Christopher, and Michael to continue the conversation.

After we bid Graydon and everyone else farewell, Christopher and I locked eyes, clearly thinking the same thing—*He did say,* *"Get whatever you want."* This was going to be another long night with Hitch.

He immediately called a waiter over.

"Can you bring us a bottle of green Chartreuse, please."†

The waiter looked at him, dumbfounded. Ordering a whole bottle of liquor in a restaurant is out of the ordinary, might be seen as uncouth, even a little tacky. The waiter wanted to make sure he'd heard right.

"The whole *bottle*?"

Christopher was ready with an answer. "Well, just think about how much time it will save us both."

The waiter shrugged—I mean, Christopher had a valid point— and walked off to fetch the bottle.

Michael Wolff sat across from us, staring dumbfounded, like the waiter before him. I don't think Michael was a drinker, at least not on an Olympian level like us, so it must have been jarring

---

* Frederic Morton's most famous book was a sprawling history of the Rothschild family, which was published in 1962. Graydon added him to the masthead as a contributing editor soon after this encounter at Elaine's, and he would write a few short pieces over the coming years.

† Chartreuse, for the uninitiated, is a very strong—110 proof—French liqueur that tastes like Robitussin.

watching us attack that bottle like vultures with a carcass. After some more friendly conversation about Iraq, the state of the world, and the debate, Michael called it a night and left. Christopher and I made it through that bottle of Chartreuse in what I imagine was record-setting time. We kept going for a few more hours, until most of Elaine's chairs were upside down on the tables and the floor was being mopped. They threw us out soon after, and we stumbled down Second Avenue, trying to find somewhere that was still serving.

I have mixed feelings celebrating Christopher's drinking now, because five years later, in the summer of 2010, Christopher was diagnosed with esophageal cancer, likely caused by a lifetime spent smoking and drinking. After a difficult battle with the disease, he died eighteen months later, at sixty-two, way too young. Dominick Dunne had died in 2009. *Vanity Fair*'s two star writers, who had been such a big part of the magazine for the previous decade, helped turn it into a cultural behemoth, and whom I admired so, were gone. These were holes the magazine could never fill. The age of the star magazine writer was on its way out.

Christopher's memorial service was held in April 2012 at Cooper Union, in the same room where that debate had taken place in 2005. Graydon gave the introductory remarks, followed by the poet James Fenton; Aimée Bell, Christopher's longtime *Vanity Fair* editor; Christopher's wife, Carol; Tom Stoppard; Sean Penn; Salman Rushdie; Olivia Wilde; Stephen Fry; Ian McEwan; and others. Beautiful words were put together in honor of a man who had done just that for a living. It was an emotional tribute. Afterward, I walked to the Starbucks on Astor Place and asked for an empty cup, then crossed Third Avenue and headed toward St. Mark's Ale House. I ordered a triple Johnnie Walker Black, poured it into the cup, and stood outside and had a cigarette. A fitting tribute to a fallen comrade. I decided then and there to quit smoking.*

---

* I've been addicted to nicotine gum ever since.

Chapter 18

After my burgeoning photo career ended before it really began, I hoped that when one door shut, another would open. But I was running out of doors. I was still in charge of the party pages, had an assistant editor title, which was one up from editorial associate, which was one up from editorial assistant, where I began, so I was edging my way up north on the masthead. But I was still stuck outside Graydon's office, answering phones and making dinner reservations. But I did pick up an unexpected skill during this time that made me somewhat useful.

Graydon had the most beautiful handwriting, a bold and looping cursive, and the most distinct signature. He sent personal notes out with each issue to every writer, photographer, and subject, and to every advertiser, thanking them for their support. Every staff member and contributor got flowers or champagne on their birthday with a note. This amounted to hundreds of notes each month. I would type them up on his beautiful stationery—Smythson at first, then a French company called Benneton—and he would sign them. It was a mindless but time-consuming task for him, and he asked me if I could try to learn his signature so he didn't have to do it as much.

I have maybe the worst handwriting in the history of handwriting. It's so bad that throughout my childhood, teachers were convinced I was meant to be left-handed. I gave up on script at an early age and began writing in block letters, like a kindergartner with really bad handwriting. It has never progressed beyond that level. I assumed that while this was a fairly easy task, it was one that I was not up to, re-creating Graydon's elegant cursive. Without any alternative, I studied the signature like you would a painting. The *G* was almost Picasso-like, connected to the *r-a-y* by a horizontal line shooting out from an indent in the middle of the *G*, the *r* and the *a* an afterthought before the all-important *y*, whose tail dropped well below the other letters by almost an inch. Then there was a small space before the *d-o-n*, a loop on top of the *d* that fell down, dismounting, sticking the landing right onto the *o-n*. The *C* in *Carter* was similar to the *G* in *Graydon*, the bottom becoming the *a-r*, followed by a small space before the *t* appeared, then a quick *e-r*, like an afterthought. It was topped off with a line almost touching the bottom of the *y*'s tail and running at a thirty-degree angle, trying to reach the last *r* in *Carter*, but losing steam and ending somewhere under the *t*.

I practiced and practiced, going through pages and pages of notepads, my hands stained with ink. After a week or so of this, I was ready to show my work. I marched into Graydon's office with a pad and a fountain pen.

"I'm ready."

Graydon was excited. "Let me see."

I effortlessly did his signature.

He looked at it. His eyes lit up.

"Holy shit! Do it again!"

I did it again, flawlessly.

I did it a few more times. He was in awe. I was now Graydon's official signatory. While he would still handwrite many of his notes, for the next decade and a half, unbeknownst to the recipients of notes and letters from him, I signed much of his correspondence.

But "official signatory" isn't an actual job, not on the masthead. I still needed a bigger portfolio to justify my existence at *Vanity Fair*, to free myself from the yoke of assistanthood. This appeared one day soon after, when a woman left her job as UK editor. It's an impressive-sounding title but a really awful job that nobody wanted, so it was offered to me. And so without pomp or circumstance, I was no longer Graydon Carter's assistant and had relocated into a small office about fifty feet away from my old desk to try to figure out something new.

Vanity Fair, like most American magazines, was solely distributed in North America. This is for language and cultural reasons. And financial. The cost to translate an English-language magazine into numerous foreign languages, print them, and distribute them makes no sense. Popular culture and zeitgeists vary from country to country. But *Vanity Fair*'s editorial product was appealing to British tastes—in fact, to us, London was just an extension of New York—so every month we shipped the editorial pages of the magazine to a UK printer, different ads were inserted, and what looked like the same product you'd find on an American newsstand would appear.

The job of the UK editor was to make sure this transition didn't get fucked-up, that words flowed from page to page without any dropping off, that redesigned pages looked good. It was essentially proofreading, and a monotonous and lonely back-office job, but one I picked up quickly and that taught me a lot about the process of how a magazine is made, which was something I had never really been deeply involved with. I also had to read the magazine cover to cover in close detail every month, which helped sharpen my understanding of writing. It was invaluable experience. It was also jarring. While it was technically a promotion, I'd no longer be in the middle of the action, would no longer have the power that came with having that kind of access to and relationship with Graydon. I'd be just another working stiff somewhere in the middle of the masthead. That was hard to take at first, but was soon alleviated by the fact that I would get to travel to London a few times a year on the company's dime. Aside from that, the job is pretty boring to write about, so let's move on to the more interesting things that were happening in the late nineties. Because there were two major shake-ups at 350 Madison Avenue.

First was the big Tina Brown news. In the summer of 1998, after six years at the helm of *The New Yorker,* she abruptly announced she was leaving. With the backing of Harvey Weinstein and his Miramax Films, and Condé Nast's competitor, Hearst, she was starting a "new media venture" that would include a magazine and a book publishing company, while feeding projects to

Miramax. "The first project out of the box will be a monthly national magazine, upscale, provocative, contemporary . . . from which a lot of other things can be grown," she told *The Washington Post*. An upscale, provocative, contemporary magazine. That sounded familiar. The internecine war between Graydon and Tina was about to conflagrate.

Then there was this, from the same *Post* story: "Brown also viewed the magazine as a base for other projects, including movies, television and books—a view that was not greeted with enthusiasm by some at Condé Nast." At Condé Nast, as at most publishing companies, the writers owned their stories (although this would begin to change by the mid-2010s). Meaning if there was a book or film made using a magazine story as its source material, Condé Nast wouldn't see any of the financial benefit. Magazine articles are a huge source of intellectual property for films and television series, and obviously books; unless you're a writer, this is the dumbest business model *ever*. A number of films based on *Vanity Fair* articles were produced over the years, like 1999's *The Insider*, 2000's *Proof of Life*, and Sofia Coppola's 2013 film, *The Bling Ring*, which was based on Nancy Jo Sales's 2010 Hollywood Issue story, "The Suspects Wore Louboutins." *Vanity Fair* and Condé Nast didn't see a dime from any of those projects. Tina saw a solution to this, saw a world where a magazine, a book publisher, and a film company were all under the same roof, reaping the benefits of the source material.* She had mastered buzz, was moving on to synergy. She and Harvey were going to revolutionize the article-to-film business.

Tina was ahead of her time; it would take the magazine business almost two decades to catch up. But she was a year too late to jump on a story that gripped the nation for a few months and would have paid dividends for years: the murderous cross-country killing spree of Andrew Cunanan. *The Assassination of Gianni Versace: American Crime Story*, the FX series from 2018, was based on Washington, D.C.–based journalist and longtime *Vanity*

---

* Of course, writers get the short end of the stick in this scenario.

Fair writer Maureen Orth's 1999 book, *Vulgar Favors: Andrew Cunanan, Gianni Versace, and the Largest Failed Manhunt in U.S. History,* which began as her 1998 *Vanity Fair* story about Cunanan, "The Killer's Trail," which ended with his suicide after his murder of Versace in Miami.

In the spring of 1997, Andrew Cunanan wasn't yet a household name, but he was quickly becoming one. The "Gay Serial Killer" had killed four men on his way across the country from California, first in Minneapolis, then Chicago, and most recently, New Jersey. After the New Jersey killing, Wanted posters began appearing in New York City, mostly in gay neighborhoods and in gay bars downtown, warning that a suspected serial killer was on the loose, that he was armed and considered dangerous, and—this is key—that he had friends and acquaintances in New York's gay community and might be headed to the city.

It was during all this that my brother Nathaniel called me. He sounded panicked.

"Can I come stay with you for a little while?"

Aimee and I had a spare bedroom in our loft, so space wouldn't be an issue.

"Yeah, sure. Why?"

He took a deep breath. "Remember when I lived in San Francisco for a year?"

"Of course."

"There was this guy I knew—we were friends and hung out a lot. It was Andrew Cunanan."

"*WHAT?!*"

"Yeah. And I'm afraid he's coming here to kill me."

"Did you have a thing with him?"

"No. I always thought we might, but he wasn't into me."

"So . . . he rejected you."

"He was into older guys."

"But he still rejected you."

"I wouldn't exactly put it like that."

"I would. And I am. You were rejected by Andrew Cunanan."

"So, can I come stay with you?"

I did what anyone would do when a sibling is in trouble, their life potentially in danger. He was family after all.

"*Fuck* no. I don't want to get dragged into this and get murdered. And I don't want to put Aimee in danger, either. Find somewhere else to stay, or go to a hotel. You have terrible taste in men, by the way."

I knew that Graydon had assigned a story on Cunanan to Maureen Orth, so the next day I went to see Wayne Lawson, the magazine's long-serving executive editor, who was Maureen's editor. I told him about Nathaniel and his connection to Cunanan. A source like Nathaniel who knew the subject personally is invaluable to a writer as they begin to connect the dots of a story and build a portrait of its main character. They can help with some of that backstory and might know some other sources to call. Wayne and I got Maureen and Nathaniel together, and he became a major source for her.

Cunanan didn't come to New York. He went to Miami instead, killing Gianni Versace, and then, eight days later, himself. Nathaniel breathed a sigh of relief. And Andrew Cunanan had become international news. Maureen's piece, one of those classic true-crime *Vanity Fair* stories, received a lot of attention, and she went on to write her book about Cunanan's killing spree and the murder of Versace. A few years later Nathaniel and I went together to Maureen's book party at NBC CEO Bob Wright's apartment on Columbus Circle, overlooking Central Park, in the old Gulf & Western Building, which had recently become the Trump International Hotel and Tower. As Nathaniel and I walked in, Tim Russert, NBC News's Washington bureau chief and *Meet the Press* host—and Maureen's husband—jokingly made the sign of the cross at Nathaniel to ward off any lingering evil. He did, after all, associate with known serial killers.

Nathaniel was the center of attention that night. Everyone wanted to talk to him about Cunanan. *What was he like? When was the last time you saw him?* It was like being with a movie star. Watching all this, I had to laugh. I'd finally had the chance to be one of those connectors that Condé Nast's mastheads were full of. Not because of any social connections, but because my brother knew a serial killer.

Years later, Nathaniel happened to be working at Fox when Ryan Murphy was making FX's *The Assassination of Gianni Versace*, which Nathaniel may have unofficially consulted on. In late 2017, we went to the premiere together, at the Metrograph, the groovy little art house theater on the Lower East Side, then the after-party at the Bowery Hotel. I loved embellishing the story of Nathaniel's rejection by Cunanan and did so as often as I could that night.

"See that guy over there? That's my brother. Get this. . . ."

Chapter 19

Tina threw a star-studded launch for *Talk* magazine on August 2, 1999, on Liberty Island, in the shadow of the Statue of Liberty. Guests included Madonna, Paul Newman, Demi Moore, Kate Moss, Jerry Seinfeld, Henry Kissinger, Salman Rushdie, and Joan Didion. *The New York Times* reported the next day, "The party on Liberty Island last night was as eclectic as the magazine it introduced: Models rubbed elbows with politicians, movie moguls chatted with authors, and all of them gathered at the behest of a celebrity editor. Tina Brown, the former editor of *The New Yorker* and *Vanity Fair* magazines, was the host of a party for more than 800 guests at the Statue of Liberty to introduce *Talk* magazine, a title that arrives on newsstands today."

It was treated as an era- and decade-defining event, talked about like Woodstock, referred to as "the party to end the 20th Century." It was celebrating an industry and its golden age, and Tina as much as the magazine. *Talk* was the Second Coming, Tina the Messiah. We observed from afar, like royal guards watching from the castle as an invading army assembled on a distant ridge. *Vanity Fair* didn't have that much competition at that point—very few magazines attempted to do what we did. It was hard to make a global monthly culture magazine work. We were established and had deep pockets and a PR machine that guaranteed stories would get their writers attention and lucrative book and film deals. But Harvey had deep pockets too, and Tina was a talented editor. I'm sure Graydon prepared for battle, maybe re-signed some writers and photographers to new contracts so Tina couldn't poach them.

It was no doubt difficult to have the woman whose shadow he'd fought so hard to escape from, who stole his dream job out from under him, get all this attention and praise. And it raises an interesting point about their long-running feud, although I'm not sure that's even the right word for it; perhaps *rivalry* is.

Now, I don't know Tina Brown, I've never met her—and I'm not related to her, although a few people assumed that over the years. But I know Graydon pretty well, so my opinion on the matter is completely one-sided, totally subjective.

Being an editor is a behind-the-scenes job. Your name isn't on the piece or the book; the writer's is. They get all the credit and glory. An editor's job is invisible in the final product. You're not out there onstage in front of the audience; you're backstage, making sure the lighting guy isn't drunk, the caterer sent the right deli tray, the white wine is chilled. Your job is to make sure the performer, whose name is on the marquee and whom everyone came to see, is able to perform without distraction or interference. This is something you have to get used to and accept.

Being an editor in chief of a magazine is a completely different animal. You have to have a foot in both these worlds. You're sort of behind the scenes, but your name is also on the marquee, so you're expected to go out onstage. Now, again, while I lack objectivity, I think Graydon is a better magazine editor than Tina. I can't prove it. It's not a fact. It's just my opinion from knowing both their bodies of work. I think he has a stronger nose for a story, a much better visual aesthetic, and a wicked sense of humor that made his magazines fun to read. But I think Tina is better at being onstage than Graydon.

Graydon once told me that Tina invited him to a cocktail party at her apartment when he was at *Spy*, sometime in the eighties. It was probably a big deal to have been invited. She was one of the most important editors at that time, while he was still coming up. As he spoke to her, he could see her eyes wandering, scanning the room for what he assumed was someone more important than him, ready to move on. And he was probably right. I can understand why that would make someone feel small and create the foundations of resentment. Social climbing is an art form, especially in the magazine world, as social a business as there is. Your location on the masthead rises as you climb your way up to bigger and better rooms, getting noticed by increasingly powerful people. Tina was a tireless self-promoter, which was part of her narrative and a key to her success, and it worked for her. We live in a culture where self-promotion is ultimately rewarded. The squeaky wheel gets the grease. She wanted attention, and she got attention. That was Tina's formula. She behaved like she deserved her success and celebrated it, courting press, writing self-serving pieces, inserting herself into everything. Tina was early on a lot of things, and she understood that a person could be a brand, and brands have value. I'm not saying Tina didn't deserve her success or wasn't a good magazine editor—she did and she was—but she was ahead of her time when it came to cultivating herself as a brand.

In all my years of working for Graydon, he never once took credit for anything, even if it was fully his idea or creation. He just couldn't do it. He was always humble and self-deprecating, deflecting credit for everything. It was always the staff, the writer, or the photographer who had really pulled off the magic. Every great accomplishment of his was someone else's idea, he just helped put it together, made it look nice, or was in the right place at the right time. And this from a man who scaled the heights of one of the most notoriously difficult and cutthroat industries in existence.

Graydon hated doing television interviews or speaking publicly in front of large groups. You could see it in his face when he had to, the anxiety, the way he spoke nervously from a stage while accepting an award or giving a speech. He was so witty and funny in person, but he shut down when he was in the spotlight. It was the part of the job he hated and knew he wasn't very good at. He was more comfortable being the invisible hand and disliked anyone who celebrated their success or sought out publicity. I'm sure he would say it was because he found it tacky, and he wouldn't be wrong, but it was also because he just couldn't do it.

Now, I'm not suggesting that the root of the feud, or rivalry—

whatever you want to call it—was simply envy. I don't think Graydon secretly wished he could be more like Tina. But I do think he struggled with acknowledging his own accomplishments and success, or taking any credit for them, something Tina had no issue with. And her getting attention, like she did when *Talk* launched, just reinforced the idea in his head that whatever he did, it would never be good enough. As someone who has lived with those thoughts rattling around in his head for most of his life, I know how difficult that can be. That those feelings can be triggered by someone's being better than you at something, even if it's something you don't even care about being good at or want to be good at, is an awful thing to carry around.

I remember talking to Graydon's eldest daughter a few years ago (a great kid—and I say "kid" even though she's approaching thirty now, but I held her when she was a baby, so I can still call her that). We were talking about her father, and she made an offhanded comment, a joke about his public profile as a jet-setter, a man who hung out with billionaires and movie stars, and sure, he occasionally would, but not as much as I think the world assumed he did. She laughed as she told me that the truth was he spent most of his time at home, in a robe or shorts, watching movies and reading, hanging out with his family, or at his country house in Connecticut, in a canoe or fishing for trout. And I knew that was true. He rarely traveled without his wife and children, whom he just wanted to be around, and avoided the limelight as much as possible. The Oscar party was his least favorite night of the year. He'd pack his table with friends and family, watch the Oscars, then usually sneak out early. The man behind the curtain wasn't a wizard or a brand, he was just a magazine editor, and that's all he wanted to be. And that was more than enough.

The first issue of Tina's *Talk* eschewed a single portrait of a movie star in favor of a collage of images, more along the lines of a European magazine or an upscale tabloid. Gwyneth Paltrow was on the cover—she had won the Best Actress Oscar earlier that year for Miramax's *Shakespeare in Love* and would be starring in the company's *The Talented Mr. Ripley* later that year. *Synergy!*

Hillary Clinton was on the cover too—there was a long interview with her inside—along with presidential candidate George W. Bush. It was a solid debut, Tina's high/low formula in peak form. The magazine looked sharp and felt modern. From that first issue, it appeared as though *Talk* was going to be competition for not just *Vanity Fair* but *The New Yorker* too, which had been taken over by David Remnick, who had been a writer for the magazine. Tina was coming for not just one but two of her former employer's magazines, both of which had her fingerprints on them.

Around the same time as Tina's abrupt departure from *The New Yorker*, it was announced that Condé Nast was going to be the anchor tenant in a new skyscraper at 4 Times Square, on the corner of Forty-second Street and Broadway, moving in around the century mark. This had sent Tina-to-*Talk*-level shock waves through the building. Times Square was still a dump. An upscale, snobby company like Condé Nast moving from its classy Madison Avenue building to grimy Times Square? It was unconscionable! We would be guinea pigs as the city attempted to turn Times Square into the crossroads of the world, the tourist mecca it would become in the beginning of the next century that would make us all appreciate and miss what had been there before.

The defining characteristic of the new building was Condé Nast's cafeteria, which had been designed by Frank Gehry, the first New York project for the Los Angeles–based architect, and was befitting the Death Star, as 4 Times Square would come to be known. He borrowed forms and shapes from his Guggenheim Museum in Bilbao, Spain—giant panels of curved glass floating in the middle of the room, undulating gunmetal-blue titanium walls, and buttery leather circular banquettes. It reportedly cost $12 million, but rumors persisted that it was closer to $30 million.

"Condé Nast is a major provider of symbolic content, a dream factory of periodic excursions into narcissism's most exquisitely tended gardens," *The New York Times* wrote of the cafeteria. "Gehry has provided an ideal background for those who put out these primers in cultivation."

It was a stunning piece of architecture, as daring and iconic as the Royalton's lobby. Outside lunch dates would want to come eat in the cafeteria. And the food was a notch above cafeteria food—there was even sushi. There was no need to go anywhere else. Even the fashion editors who never ate would eat there—sort of. One morning my assistant, Julian, came back to the office after getting breakfast in the cafeteria and excitedly told this story: He was standing on line behind two fashionable young women, one of whom was holding what appeared to be a cup of ice. She was explaining to her colleague that her diet involved putting a sausage link at the bottom of a cup and filling it with ice. She would nibble on the ice, and when she crunched her way through it all, the sausage was waiting there as her reward. The old sausage-and-ice trick, the breakfast of champions, available only in the Condé Nast cafeteria.

Now that Condé Nast had its own cafeteria, the original Condé Nast cafeteria, 44, would effectively wither away and die.* It had been fading over the previous few years, the power lunch losing out to the working lunch in the late nineties, and now Condé Nast's editors would be eating in most days. This was because Si would be eating in his gleaming new showpiece every day. As Si went, so went everyone else (he even banned garlic from being used in the cafeteria—he hated it, and since he footed the bill for the whole thing, no garlic).

The move to Times Square coincided with a position opening up on the masthead. Vanities editor, which sounded like something to do with bathroom sinks but was the editor of the Vanities section, a "front of the book" section that was right smack in the middle of the magazine, separating the columns and the features (the "well"). I was next in line. I was finally going to be an editor, responsible for anywhere from five to ten pages a month.

The section was anchored by an opening page, an image of an

---

* Brian would abandon 44 before the turn of the century after a falling-out with Ian Schrager, who would sell his Morgans Hotel Group, which included the Royalton, in 2005. Soon after, the Royalton was renovated, including Philippe Starck's iconic lobby.

up-and-coming actor, with a short profile written by our West Coast editor, Krista Smith. This was coveted real estate in Hollywood that, since its inception in the early nineties, had broken a who's who of young Hollywood, including Sandra Bullock, Russell Crowe, Renée Zellweger, Vince Vaughn, Natalie Portman, and Ben Affleck, a success rate that would continue on into the 2000s. It was talent spotting. There was a natural progression in the magazine, from being the Vanities "opener," which was usually an unknown with a breakout role, to getting a Spotlight—a larger featurette in the well shot by a well-known photographer—to landing on a Hollywood cover, to eventually a solo cover when the actor's star had risen to that level. The Vanities page was the gateway to stardom. The competition was fierce. We only had twelve spots a year. The second my name appeared on the masthead, I was inundated by publicists, wined and dined by anxious flacks trying to get their clients into *Vanity Fair*. Young up-and-coming actresses and actors, like Ellen Pompeo and Anthony Anderson, would be brought into my office for meet and greets. I had lunch in the cafeteria with Gerard Butler. It was a strange feeling—I was the buyer; they were the seller. In an instant I was thrown into the deep end of the celebrity-industrial complex.

Krista had it down to a science and ran point on choosing the openers—after all, she was out in L.A., in the belly of the beast, knew all the publicists and agents—but we would go to screenings and film festivals, confer, come to a consensus, and present a list of names with photographs and upcoming credits to Graydon, who usually just signed off on our choices, trusting that we had done our research.

The rest of the section was made up of a collection of short half-page culture pieces, a photograph and a paragraph of text, new authors to read, artists to pay attention to, humor pieces, listicles and charticles,* party pictures, and up-and-coming peo-

---

* I created the "Out & In" list for the magazine and wrote it every month. We had a running joke about the Affleck brothers, alternating each month between Ben's and Casey's being in and out.

ple to watch. In 1990, *Vanity Fair* had done a small front-of-the-book piece on the first Black president of the *Harvard Law Review,* pegging him as a future leader—he was a twenty-eight-year-old Barack Obama. The section was also a dumping ground for favors to advertisers, friends of Graydon and other staff, and contributing editors. Sometimes these favors would turn out well, like when the writer Andrew Cockburn asked me if we could cover his daughter Olivia, a budding actress who was using the stage name Wilde (after Oscar).

In magazines, front-of-the-book sections have busy pages, with lots of information and access points, very visual, an appetizer before the main course of the longer stories and spread after spread of text. The shorter pieces were written by the junior staff and other contributors, and didn't need much editing. Which was great, because I still wasn't exactly sure how to edit, or at least didn't think I was up to the task, and was too afraid to ask for help. If a piece needed cuts, it was easier to send it back to the writer and ask them to handle it. Unlike my previous job as the UK editor, this put me back in the mix, including meetings with Graydon to pitch ideas. I would spend hours of the day research-ing upcoming films and books, store openings, and other cultural events. I would pore over the Books List, the Film List, and the Culture List, the same one Aimee was putting together when I first met her in 1994. There were so many lists to go through, it was exhausting. The trick was to find things Graydon might be interested in. I had to essentially satisfy an audience of one. I wasn't going to go out on a limb and fight for something that I thought was great or worth covering; this was about approval. I just wanted him to say yes. And I had an advantage: I knew him so well, his tastes and interests.

I was now in one of those meetings that I used to listen in on when I sat outside his office, wondering if one of his young as-sistants was now eavesdropping, trying to figure out a game that I was still learning.

But it did get my feet wet, and I started to learn about how to tell a story, which might actually be harder to do in a few hundred words than in a longer piece. You need to find a few key details about this person or place or thing that reveal more than meets the eye, add some depth. A short piece still needs a beginning, middle, and end, it's just that each of these sections needs to be incredibly precise and take up very little space, while letting the reader know why they should be paying attention to this new *thing*.

Most important, on a practical level, the job would begin to teach me about how a magazine piece comes together and the process and collaboration that involves writers, photographers, stylists, designers, fact-checkers, and copy editors. Magazines are incredibly collaborative. A page in a magazine has so many invisible fingerprints on it. An editor's job is to manage that process, and a team of specialists, along the way, almost like a film director, to take an idea and turn it into a finished product. *Vanity Fair* had a big staff, full of extremely bright people who were really good at what they did, many of whom had been there for years. It's easy to find cover when you're surrounded by smart, capable people. I figured I could hide behind their experienced hands, take what I could from each, and did. A common approach for learning on the job.

No longer the bushy-tailed and bright-eyed kid who ran around the office delivering all those notes and newspaper clippings from Graydon with "Let's disc" written on them, at almost thirty, I had pages to fill and was now on the receiving end of these ideas. One such note was a torn-out, half-ripped restaurant review from London's *Sunday Times*, written by A. A. Gill, his name circled by Graydon. I put it in my pile of notes to go over with him the next time we met.

A few days later, when we met, Graydon became animated when I brought up the review.

"Adrian Gill—he's so brilliant. He's the funniest writer I've read in ages. His restaurant reviews are so brutal and so good. Why don't you reach out to him, see if you can get him over to New York. I have an idea."

I did as I was told and called the general number for *The Times*.

I went through the switchboard and was passed around to a few different departments—he was *The Times*'s restaurant and television critic, and wrote travel articles for their Sunday magazine—finally landing on an assistant somewhere, who told me that he didn't work out of the newspaper's offices, but that they would happily pass along a message to Adrian.

Graydon broke down Adrian's writing style to this: He interviewed places. And that's exactly what he did. He usually didn't interview people; he would go somewhere, look around, find the smallest details that most writers would have missed, filter these through his singularly twisted head, and find words to describe what he'd seen that nobody else would have thought of while perfectly capturing and telling the story of that place. His writing somehow managed to be simultaneously autodidactic and educated, the most unique writing I had ever come across, and although I wasn't yet at the stage where I could differentiate between good and great writing, I could tell his was special, because it made me smile and laugh while I read it.

It turns out Adrian was dyslexic. Like, really dyslexic. His brain was just wired differently than other people's. He would type his pieces with one finger, words misspelled so badly that spellcheck couldn't figure them out, then he would dictate the story over the phone to an editor or copy taker, editing as he read his words aloud. What was even more amazing was that he didn't discover this talent until he was in his late thirties.

Adrian was born to English parents in Edinburgh, in 1954. His father was a producer and director, and his mother was an actress. He struggled in school and was shipped off to a progressive boarding school, followed by art school. He also struggled with serious alcoholism throughout an aimless twenties, finally getting sober at twenty-nine, after which he was working in restaurants and teaching cooking classes in London. An editor from *Tatler*, the society magazine that Tina Brown had run before coming to America, was in one of those classes. She suggested Adrian write about his alcoholism and his experience of getting sober at a detox clinic. He did. In 1991, that first piece would appear in *Tatler* under the pseudonym Blair Baillie, launching his career as a writer. Adrian's biography might sound awfully familiar, and I often wonder, if I hadn't had that door opened for me in 1994, if responsibility hadn't been dropped in my lap, would I too have drunkenly stumbled through my twenties and into my thirties, waiting for that spark?

Now christened A. A. Gill, he was hired by *The Times* in 1993 to be their television critic and would soon add restaurants to his beat, where he really shined, becoming one of London's best and most feared restaurant critics. (The character Anton Ego, the critic from Pixar's 2007 film *Ratatouille*, was rumored to be based on Adrian, whose middle name was Anthony, the second *A* in his byline.) He was often accompanied in his restaurant reviews by his girlfriend Nicola Formby, who became a character known as "the Blonde" in his "Table Talk" columns.

He wrote in his 2015 memoir, *Pour Me: A Life*, "I found a corner to work in where I never imagined there would be space for me and I've made a living by watching television, eating in restaurants and travelling."

I was still looking for my corner, and Adrian would help me find it—although our partnership would begin in failure. Fail-*ures*. Two to be exact.

For that first story Adrian and I did together, Graydon wanted to bring him over to "interview" a store, a high-end clothing shop on West Fourteenth Street, in Manhattan's Meatpacking District. It was called Jeffrey and was named after its owner, Jeffrey Kalinsky. He had brought his eponymous boutique to New York in 1999.

Kalinsky made a strange but prescient location choice. The Meatpacking District was nothing in the eighties and nineties. I shouldn't say that, it wasn't *nothing*—it was actually great, full of nightclubs, prostitutes, drug dealers, sex clubs, and bloody animal carcasses. It was the kind of neighborhood you'd find yourself stumbling around at four in the morning and think to yourself, *I better get the fuck out of here* quick. There was an element of danger to it. It was the sort of place we now reminisce about and refer to as "old New York," or "the corner I got mugged on once."

The Meatpacking District had been disinfected and scrubbed by the end of the nineties, as had much of downtown, but it wasn't as full of high-end boutiques, tourists, and brunch—a word I use here as a pejorative—as it would be in later years. Jeffrey opened up the same year Keith McNally opened his bistro Pastis. *Sex and the City*, which had debuted on HBO the year before, in 1998, also played a role in the Meatpacking District's transformation, especially after Samantha (Kim Cattrall) moved to the neighborhood from the Upper East Side in 2001's season three.* Pastis would be priced out of the neighborhood and shut down fifteen years later, before reopening in the summer of 2019. Jeffrey would close in 2020 in the wake of the COVID pandemic.

Jeffrey was as high-end as it got. Men's and women's clothes, and a giant assortment of shoes, for which the store had gained a cult following. It was not only expensive, and so fashion-forward that it was years ahead of everyone else in some chic dystopian future, but pretentious to the point of absurdity, or at least that's what Graydon thought, as did *Saturday Night Live*, which aired a sketch in 2001 starring Will Ferrell, Jimmy Fallon, and guest host Sean Hayes as Jeffrey salesclerks. Graydon must have wandered in there one day, curious; taken a look around; walked out; and thought, *What the fuck was that?* He wanted A. A. Gill to "interview" Jeffrey—the store, not the person.

Adrian called me a few days later. He likely responded to the fact that he would be exposed to a larger audience, and that we paid writers more than anyone. For a foreign journalist, breaking into America was a similar proposition as it was for musicians. It was a *giant* country, with global reach, in contrast to the UK at the time. American culture traveled around the world, our biggest export. Adrian had conquered England, had become one of the most famous critics in the land, was at the top of his game, and like those

* I *promise* I had to look that up.

who came before him, must have wanted to hunt bigger game. And this was an invitation to that hunt. Never mind that the *Vanity Fair* "editor" who called him had virtually no clue what he was doing.

We had a brief and friendly chat as we felt each other out. I explained the assignment. We agreed that he would come to New York in a month to cover the story. He asked me if I'd come along to Jeffrey with him. I agreed, happy to be his co-conspirator.

Adrian came to our offices the day after he arrived in New York. I was nervous to meet him, wearing my best suit. Adrian was going through what we would later refer to as his "Sammy Davis, Jr., period." He was wearing a garish Cosby-like sweater and a gold chain, with his curly brown hair cropped close to his head. The moment we met, Adrian took one look at me, eyed me up and down, and told me I needed a better tailor. I immediately shrunk into that suit. I also knew that he was right. Adrian was one of the most unerring critics around, and he was usually spot-on. I took it as constructive criticism.

He immediately broke into laughter and a wide grin, and I couldn't help but join him.

We took a car to Jeffrey and spent a few hours there. We tried on some clothes, giggling as we did. We ended up chatting with Jeffrey Kalinsky for a few minutes, too, although we didn't tell him we were from *Vanity Fair,* or our ulterior motive. Adrian was deliberate in his movements around the store. I knew he was looking for a detail or two, something he could latch on to. Afterward, we had lunch at Pastis and walked around the West Village before Adrian headed back to London on Sunday night.

A few weeks later, Adrian called to let me know the piece would be coming in the next few days. We stayed on the phone for an hour, talking about what was going on in the world, getting to know each other a little better, and coming up with potential story ideas for after his Jeffrey piece was published.*

---

* Remember earlier, when I said that growing up I didn't know what a magazine editor did? It would turn out that talking on the phone to writers and trying to come up with that next great idea is a big part of it.

The piece arrived. It was around two thousand words long, which would be perhaps three to four pages in the magazine, with photos. It was funny and perceptive and managed to both describe and explain the shop in a couple thousand words. It was firm but fair. I laughed out loud more than a few times. I read it once, then again. Then again. I was an editor now—but I wasn't sure what that meant.

I called Adrian.

"It's *so* so good. Thank you."

"Glad to hear."

I paused. "What do I do now?"

"What do you mean?"

Could I tell him that I had never actually edited a story? That I really wasn't sure what I was supposed to do next? That I had no idea what I was doing? I decided to come clean.

"Look, Adrian, I'm just going to be honest. I've never really edited anything before."

"*What?!* Aren't you an editor?"

"Well, about that . . . I mean, technically, yes. But not really."

"So, you have no idea what you're doing?"

"No. And I don't trust my own judgment on what's good or bad."

"Well, I don't know what I'm doing either."

The call went silent for a few moments before we both broke out in laughter.

"But you think it's good?" he asked me.

"Yeah, I really do."

"So then maybe it is."

And maybe it was? Maybe I had to start trusting my own judgment and point of view.

We agreed to just pretend that I had edited it, give it to Graydon exactly as Adrian had turned it in, and see what happened, which I did. I got the manuscript back a few days later. On it, Graydon had written, "Brilliant!" There were a few minor notes, some details he wanted added. Graydon was big on basic information like dates and ages and specific locations, to give readers context. How old was Kalinsky? What month did his store open? What avenues was it between on Fourteenth Street? Things like that.

All in all, my editing career had gotten off to a stellar start. It was early September 2001, and Graydon scheduled Adrian's piece for the November issue, meaning we would be closing it in the coming weeks and it would hit newsstands in early October. My first feature in the magazine. And Adrian's. We arranged a photo shoot. Kalinsky even agreed to pose in his store for the story. I suddenly had massive pangs of guilt—the poor guy must have been so excited *Vanity Fair* was going to run a feature on his store. He was going to regret cooperating with this one, and I was the one who was going to hear about it and get the blame.

I called Adrian with the good news. It was an anxious and exciting time for me.

I woke up a few mornings later and the world had changed.

I was still asleep at 8:46 A.M. when the North Tower was hit. I was just waking up sixteen minutes later when the South Tower was hit. Word spread quickly. I ran up to the roof of my building. Second Street and Avenue B was about three miles away from the towers. In that moment, it felt a lot closer. The sky that morning was the deepest shade of blue I had ever seen. Thick black smoke was pouring out of gaping wounds in both buildings. I couldn't turn away. Less than an hour after it was hit, the South Tower collapsed. Twenty-nine minutes later, the North Tower followed. As surreal as it was to watch in real time, I couldn't help but think about the implications. We were going to wake up to a new age on the morning of September 12. America hadn't been attacked on its home soil since Pearl Harbor, and an outsized, culture-shifting, and decade-defining response was inevitable.

There was a firehouse across the street from my apartment. Engine 28, Ladder 11. They lost seven men that day. Michael Quilty; Michael Cammarata; Edward James Day; John Heffernan; Richard John Kelly, Jr.; Robert King, Jr.; and Matthew Rogan. I went to the deli, bought a bouquet of flowers, and placed it in front of their door. The next morning there were hundreds of bouquets, and candles burning. That makeshift shrine would stay there for months, the phrase *first responders* entering the lexicon.

Adrian's Jeffrey piece was spiked. It would never run. Graydon didn't want to hurt a small business in New York that would no doubt suffer in the wake of the attacks, and he was right.* Adrian understood. We chatted for a while. There was a lot to talk about. He told me he wanted to go to Pakistan, which was deeply entangled with 9/11 and the global jihadist movement, and in the frenzy and rush to cover what was now the biggest, and only, story, I convinced Graydon to send Adrian with an undefined assignment.

Adrian went off to Pakistan for a week with what seemed like every other journalist in the world. He turned something in a few weeks later about the Western media descending on Karachi en masse. It was brilliant criticism about the sensationalism of Western media and its cynical correspondents, and the state of modern news. "There's precious little journalism being done out here," he wrote. "They couldn't find a story if it were printed on the English-language menu in the coffee shop." He referred to one American reporter as a "dumb bimbo." I was proud of that piece. It was as close to punk rock as journalism got. But it was too satirical and cynical for Graydon's tastes and the pages of *Vanity Fair*.† We were now batting 0 for 2.

Graydon's nixing the article was disappointing, but Adrian and I kept talking, trying to figure out the next perfect subject. And while it took more than a year before we got our first story in the magazine, it was worth the wait, as it landed like a kick to the nuts of New York's restaurant world.

---

* Tina Brown's *Talk* would ultimately be a casualty of 9/11, ceasing publication in January 2002.

† Adrian's piece would appear in *GQ* in the UK, where it ran with the title "Ever Get the Feeling You've Been Jihad?"

Chapter 20

In 2003, the hot new restaurant was a place called 66, in TriBeCa. It had been opened by one of New York's most successful and celebrated restaurateurs and chefs, Jean-Georges Vongerichten. The interior was designed by Richard Meier. It was Jean-Georges's attempt at upscale Chinese food, and it was a hit, packed every night with movie stars, models, and fashion and media figures. Graydon had gone there one night, had a bad experience, and walked out before they took his order. As with Jeffrey a few years earlier, he found it pretentious and absurd. There were rumors he had to wait for his table, felt disrespected, and then was told he couldn't smoke—this was after New York City's restaurant smoking ban—and stormed off in a huff, and maybe that's true, but whatever happened, he called in a hit man to take down 66.

A few weeks later, Adrian arrived in New York, and I took him to 66. Aimee came along, as did a handful of others—there were about ten of us; Adrian liked to fill a big table for his reviews—including the Hong Kong businessman David Tang and the model Lauren Hutton. Aimee sat next to Adrian, and from across the table I could see her giggling as Adrian whispered his thoughts on dishes in her ear, giving her a real-time restaurant review. The piece, titled "Rote 66," which ran over two pages in the September issue, was beyond brutal and laugh-out-loud funny. He described the restaurant's shrimp-and-foie-gras dumplings, one of their signature dishes, as "fishy liver filled condoms. They were properly vile, with a savor that lingered like a lovelorn drunk and tasted as if your mouth had been used as the swab bin in an animal hospital." And that might have been the nicest thing he said about the restaurant. Adrian also went after 66's superstar architect, Richard Meier.*

New York had never seen a restaurant review like this. In fact, *Vanity Fair* had never run a restaurant review before. Everyone was talking about it. Adrian's New York debut was reported on in the press like it was the moon landing. *The New York Observer* wrote a front-page article titled "Grouchy Graydon Sends a Hitman to 66" that was longer than the review itself. "If Mr. Carter did want an assassin, he'd picked the right man for the job—an out-of-towner with no ties to the city's seductive restaurant industry and a lethal pen," Frank DiGiacomo wrote. Richard Meier was pissed. "I thought it was a very odd thing for them to do," he told the *Observer*. "And I wondered what it was all about. . . . Even asking the person to come in and write this article was, I guess, a hostile act. . . . I thought I would invite [Graydon] to dinner there and say something to him."

Tucked into the twelfth paragraph of the story was this line: "Mr. Carter, still fascinated by his experience, instructed the writer's editor, Dana Brown, to send Mr. Gill to 66."

Adrian had introduced himself to New York not with a handshake, but with a slap to the face. And it was now in the public record that I was his editor.

We would spend the next decade and a half working together, whether on the phone just chatting or coming up with absurd story ideas, sometimes off on assignment together, and I was constantly learning from him about life, history, friendship, perseverance, and words. I began to get comfortable as an editor, better recognizing what worked and what didn't, finding the story. Adrian trusted me and my confidence grew. He began dictating his pieces directly to me and I wouldn't hesitate to make suggestions about word choice or punctuation. It was writer and editor in collaboration.

---

* "Why is it that every postmodern, hot-and-cool, less-is-more, minimal, brave, to-die-for dining room looks like every other postmodern, hot-and-cool, less-is-more, minimal, brave, to-die-for dining room you've been in since vinegar went balsamic? When was it that blank emptiness and mild discomfort became a synonym for deep thought?"

I loved watching him work, as he would wander around a place, off in his own head, "interviewing" it, looking for the story. We went to the conservative Christian Creation Museum in Kentucky, spent a day at a wealth conference in Toronto, and attended Trump University at a down-market hotel in the swamplands of New Jersey. We were the only men on a *Sex and the City* bus tour in New York that ended with an uncomfortable visit to an upscale sex-toy shop with a busload of women. We toured apartments with a "real estate agent to the stars" in New York posing as a couple looking for a pied-à-terre in one of Manhattan's new condos. I sent him to Vegas, Brazil, Mumbai, Dubai. Watching his process fascinated me, sometimes just for its sheer ingenuity.

In June 2010, Adrian wrote a cover story about international soccer superstars pegged to that year's World Cup. Excuse me, *football* superstars. Adrian's piece began, "Look, can we get this straight, right from the get-go, from the first whistle: It's football. O.K.? Football, not soccer. It's never been soccer. Nobody but midwestern cougars calls it soccer."

The piece was late, and Adrian was dodging me, which was nothing new. I finally got him on the phone. He was grumpy—he had two weekly columns in *The Sunday Times*, so he was always on a deadline. He sighed loudly.

"Let's just get it over with."

He spent the next hour dictating the story over the phone to me. It was clever, funny, and surprisingly insightful. I was shocked by how much he knew about the history of the sport.

"Wow. That was impressive. You really know your stuff."

He laughed. "No, I don't. I was reading that off the Wikipedia page for soccer."

And he had. He dictated that cover story while looking at a Wikipedia page, and it was perfect, his miswired brain filtering basic facts and in real time turning them into beautifully composed sentences. A few days later, the manuscript came back from Graydon with the word *brilliant* scrawled across it.

Adrian was an avid outdoorsman. He stalked deer in Scotland, shot pheasant, grouse, and partridge in England. He once caused a furor with a restaurant review in 2009 when he wrote about shooting a baboon in Tanzania "to get a sense of what it was like to kill someone." Adrian often went beyond political incorrectness in his writing. Nothing was out-of-bounds for Adrian, or between us.

There was an American company that Adrian liked to order his "hunting kit" and other outdoor equipment from that wouldn't ship to the UK, so I'd place the order for him, have it delivered to my office, then ship it from Condé Nast. When he was heading to the Arctic on an assignment for *The Times*, I ordered extra-heavy-duty boots, gloves, and a parka for him. Before we shipped it off, I had a brilliant idea. I had my assistant, Julian, run out to one of Times Square's dwindling sex shops to buy a dildo that we would hide in one of the boots. The hope was he wouldn't put them on until he got to the Arctic, which we thought was hilarious, the idea of Adrian stranded in the middle of nowhere in the Arctic with a dildo. Julian couldn't decide on one—there was apparently quite a selection—so he came back with two, a realistic-sized one and a giant purple one. We put one in each boot with a note: "Enjoy the pole."

The plan went awry when he tried the boots on in London. He called me immediately. I'd never heard another person laugh as hard as Adrian did that day. He could barely speak. We sat on the phone for half an hour in uncontrollable fits of giggles, neither of us able to form complete words.

Occasionally I'd jump on a plane to spend a few days in London with Adrian. We'd eat breakfast at the Wolseley; go to the Portrait Gallery, the Serpentine, the Tate, and other museums; look at the statues in Trafalgar Square, Adrian giving me lectures on English history and art. I learned so much from him. When he was in New York, I'd return the favor, exploring New York with him, getting out of Manhattan and heading to the immigrant communities and their restaurants and food trucks in the outer boroughs. I took him to Coney Island. We rode the Cyclone. Adrian loved New York, and I loved seeing New York through his eyes.

On the page, Adrian came across to some as a tireless snob, when in fact he was the opposite, gleefully attacking snobbery and all its trappings. In person he was warm and funny, a trusted and loyal friend. He'd been through a lot in life and had gleaned real wisdom along the way. We forged a tight bond over the years, a deep friendship and partnership that not only produced really wonderful pieces of writing but was connected by laughter and joy in each other's company and in life. We would have children around the same time, my first, his third and fourth, his twins, Edith and Isaac, arriving in 2006, a year after my daughter. Adrian was my first writer, a brilliant one at that, and your first is always special.

But he didn't remain my only one for long. Soon after Adrian's 66 piece came out, an editor announced he was leaving. When an editor left, most of the time they weren't replaced, their stable of writers were just sliced and diced and distributed to other editors. After proving myself with Adrian, I had apparently earned the right to inherit some writers.

In 2003, nine years after beginning my career at *Vanity Fair*, I had somehow become a magazine editor.

Chapter 21

Having children changes everything. That's what everybody pulls you aside to tell you when you're about to have your first child. And they're right, but, I mean, no shit—they think they're letting you in on some great secret, but it's not remotely actionable advice. But let me back up here for a moment, because in all the excitement about working my way up, becoming an editor, I forgot to mention that Aimee and I had gotten married amid all of that. It wasn't the most romantic of weddings. In late September 2001, we went down to city hall, signed some papers, and were pronounced man and wife by a public servant. If you know anything about the geography of New York City and significant dates in American history, you might realize that we got married a few blocks away from the still-smoldering ruins of the Twin Towers. And while it might not have been romantic (we celebrated with a small ceremony for family and friends the following month in the Bahamas, which *was* romantic), it was poignant, making a commitment to each other, and to the city where we'd met and were now making a life together.

When you're having your first kid, everyone wants to pass down some wisdom they've learned over the years. Graydon might have given me the best advice, which at the time sounded absurd and had me scratching my head. He called me down to his office one morning when Aimee was approaching her due date, in early March 2005, before he headed off to L.A. for the Oscar party, the first one I would miss since 1995.

"So, the baby's coming, huh?"

"Yeah, next couple of weeks."

He turned serious. "I'm going to give you some parenting advice that I wish someone had given to me."

I didn't know what to expect, but I assumed it would be important. I'd watched him raise four children, and they had all turned out really well, confident and kind, smart and funny. He was a committed father, dedicated to his kids, and it showed. I waited anxiously.

"Under no circumstances"—he paused for dramatic effect— "are you to let your kids eat or drink in the car. Never, ever, ever. Just don't do it. Best advice I can give you."

That's it? He didn't seem to notice the puzzled look on my face, but I thanked him, and he got up and gave me a hug, wished us luck. A few years later, as I looked in the backseat of my car, with fucking Cheerios and Goldfish and rotting pieces of fruit scattered around, juice stains on the floor mats, I wished I'd heeded that advice. It's something I always pass on when given the chance.

Before the baby arrives, it's abstract: *We're having a baby, and it's in that belly right there.* When you're holding your kid for the first time, it becomes real awfully quick. *Holy shit, we have a baby, what do we do now?* You end up wanting to spend more time at home or strolling around with your baby, pushing them in a swing, showing them the city. It is a profound life change. It's also frightening. My first thought when Aimee told me she was pregnant was that we didn't know what we were doing and that we were going to be terrible parents. I think this is a common reaction. But then some innate parenting gene kicks in, starts up like an old engine, some ancient strand of DNA that makes us understand that our only real purpose is to procreate, protect our children, and continue the human race. Procreation, protection, continuity.

My first child was born in March 2005. We named her Isabella. Aimee and I wanted a traditional name at a time when "original" names were the thing, especially in New York, where it was the prevailing name trend, my generation seeming to think we were so clever, setting us apart from our parents, who named everyone Jennifer or David. I'm reassured about this choice at the beginning of every school year when there's some poor kid named Sensei, Rutabaga, Damocles, or Truck. Of course, little did we know that this was the beginning of a countertrend toward traditional baby names—in 2005, Isabella was in the top ten for baby girls' names, along with Emma, Emily, Madison, Abigail, Olivia, Hannah, and Samantha. Cultural shifts don't happen in a bubble. You can't outsmart groupthink and trends.

I was thirty-three, which for my generation in New York City was on the young side to have children, and also the age that Jesus lived to, which I throw in there just so you can say you learned something from this book. With this little bundle of joy, there were the expected life changes, mostly positive, of course, but it takes some adjustment. Not as many book parties, after-work drinks and dinners, or late nights out, and travel is such a pain in the ass for those first few years it's not worth the headache. The drinking and late-night carousing have to be tempered. It forces you to settle down, grow up a little more. That paycheck that was used solely to fund your lifestyle now has to be used for more pressing needs—a bigger apartment, a nanny, an outrageously expensive baby buggy, ironic onesies, and all that other *stuff* that was de rigueur for new Gen X parents in the aughts, as the 2000s became known—half of which you never used.

But professionally, major changes had already been happening to me over the previous two years. After my success with Adrian's first piece in late 2003, I was gifted, or willed, after the departure of an editor, two writers, Nancy Jo Sales and Rich Cohen.

Nancy Jo and Rich had both been somewhere between rising stars and established names in the magazine business when they arrived at *Vanity Fair* a few years earlier. They were immensely talented writers, keen cultural observers, and general pros. Nancy Jo had made her name at *New York* magazine in the nineties, where she covered, among other things, youth culture and the burgeoning world of hip-hop, and occasionally the intersection of both of those things. *Vanity Fair* had poached her at the turn of the century—her first piece for *VF*, in September 2000, had introduced the world to Paris and Nicky Hilton—and she was a fearless reporter and stylish writer, taking an almost cinematic approach to her pieces, like one of those auteur directors from the sixties and seventies. She could turn black type on a white page into Technicolor, scenes popping off the page. Rich had been at *Rolling Stone* in the nineties, a natural writer and story-teller whose skill with a turn of phrase was unparalleled, like he had made a deal with the devil. They were both a few years older than me but much more seasoned than I was. I was instantly in-timidated, even with a new title: articles editor. Which means I did exactly that: I edited articles. I still had serious bouts of self-doubt, but I knew what the job entailed and how to do it. I might not have been great at it just yet and still had a lot to learn, but I knew enough that I could appear competent. Little did Nancy Jo and Rich know they were going to be my gateway drug to being an editor and teach me the first rule of being an editor: Work with really good writers.

About that time, I started dressing better, spending a little more money on suits and shoes. I liked talking about ideas with colleagues and others, and had absorbed enough through my job and had lived enough life by then that I could talk about anything competently. I was a generalist, in the best sense of the word. My career—and it really was now a career, not just a job—was an im-portant part of my life, giving me an identity and a purpose. And I liked being a *Vanity Fair* editor, liked going in to the office every day, the lunches and dinners with writers, the invitations to par-ties and premieres, the cultural capital it gave me. People found me interesting and were nice to me based solely on my job title, which was completely fraudulent and transactional but was better than their finding me dull and dismissing me.

I started getting better tables at restaurants, where I now used my new corporate American Express card, another perk of the job, which would turn out to be life-changing. It was like discover-ing the petty cash economy when I was an assistant; this was that but on fucking steroids. As I sat there looking at that green card with my name embossed in silver, right below the words *Condé Nast*, I made a decision: I would spend until they told me I couldn't anymore.* It was a one-sided abusive relationship from the beginning. Having come of age at Condé Nast during its mythologized expense account heyday, when nothing seemed off-limits or too outrageous, it was all I knew. And I'd learned from the best. Our expense accounts were seen as a right, a lifestyle tax on the company for salaries that paled in comparison to those of other industries, especially in the 2000s as the financial sector and its army of overpaid douchebags took over New York to a level not seen since the 1980s.

When budgets were finally instituted, in the late 2000s, we would get an envelope on our desks, placed there in the middle of the night at the beginning of each year by some mysterious expense account fairy, with a single piece of paper inside, containing a figure indicating what you were allowed to spend in the coming year. A colleague once came into my office, looking forlorn, holding his envelope, and closed the door. He had been cautious, spent well under his allotted figure by a third, and the company had lowered it from the previous year by that amount. He asked me if mine had been cut too. I had gone *wildly* over-budget the year before, as I had in most years, and my figure had been *upped*, and quite substantially. If you didn't spend what you were allotted, they assumed you didn't need it. If you went over-budget, they assumed they hadn't allotted enough. (I don't think this approach to corporate expense accounts is taught in business schools, or at least the decent ones.) I lied that day and told him that yes, mine had been cut too, and made a sad face in solidarity.

That endless expense account and corporate card would turn out to be a necessity in 2006, when Graydon added restaurateur to his résumé and bought the Waverly Inn, the fabled and faded lit-

---

* In 2018 I received an email from a journalist working on a story about the good old days of Condé Nast editors' legendary expense accounts and profligate spending, which had, by then, waned. She wanted to write an obituary. "Everyone I talked to told me to call you," she wrote, "*everyone*." I thought about it for a moment, my synapses tingling briefly in bright nostalgic flashes, then politely declined. *Too soon.*

tle gem of a restaurant on the corner of Waverly Place and Bank Street, a few doors from his town house (in the late nineties he had sold the Dakota apartment and moved downtown to the West Village). He turned the Waverly into his fantasy of a supper club from an earlier age, a highly curated, nostalgic facsimile, no detail overlooked, commissioning the illustrator Ed Sorel to paint a mural along the restaurant's western wall with a century's worth of iconic artists and writers and putting midcentury classics on the menu like oysters Rockefeller and a McCarthy salad. Overnight, the Waverly became the hottest and most exclusive restaurant in New York, impossible to get into for mortals, half full of A-list celebrities every night, the other half filled by Condé Nast editors and writers. This was the place to see and be seen. Dinner at the Waverly was the closest thing to those lunches at 44 from what now felt like a bygone era.

Like Brian before him, Graydon had hit on a brilliant business plan at the expense—and on the expense accounts—of Condé Nast, but with a twist. So many diners on a typical night were dropping an American Express card with the words *Condé Nast* embossed on it. He would open two more restaurants in the coming years, the Monkey Bar, on Fifty-fourth Street, and the Beatrice Inn, just around the corner from the Waverly, on West Twelfth Street, which would also fill up with Condé Nasties. Most of *Vanity Fair*'s events were held at one of them, all those book and holiday parties. The company paying his salary was also lining his pockets outside of the office, the purest definition of a side hustle if ever there was one.

The Waverly quickly became a clubhouse for *Vanity Fair* staff. We could always get a reservation and one of the best tables. Aimee and I became friendly with the English actor Paul Bettany and his wife, Jennifer Connelly, around the time the Waverly opened, and invited them for dinner one night along with a few other friends. Like 44 back in the day, this was the place to be seen, so having dinner with a couple of movie stars was going to bring me attention and glory.

We went out for a few drinks beforehand, arriving for our

eight P.M. reservation well lubricated. While we were in the packed front room, by the bar, waiting for our table, Paul over-heard a man say something untoward about Jennifer, who was across the room, and Paul went after him, pinning him to the wall by his throat before starting a brawl that quickly spilled outside onto the sidewalk. In an instant it was chaos. No punches were thrown, eventually cooler heads prevailed, and things didn't esca-late. The other man ran off, and we went inside and had a lovely, if a little tense, dinner. But word got around. Paparazzi swarmed the place, waiting for the shot. After dinner we had to sneak Paul out the back into a waiting car. Leave it to me to have an act of public starfucking backfire so badly.

I figured the next day I would tell Graydon the story, which I was sure would have gotten back to him by then, and apologize. But a few hours later I got a call from a number I didn't recog-nize. I didn't pick up, letting it go to voicemail. It was a reporter from the *New York Post* who had somehow found out Paul was a guest of mine that evening. She was writing a story for the next day's paper. I immediately called Graydon to tell him what had happened, apologize, and get ahead of the *Post* story.

He picked up after a few rings.

"DB."

"I'm sorry it's so late, but I need to tell you something."

"That's never a good start to a conversation."

"You're correct."

I told him the whole story and how sorry I was, how embar-rassed Paul was. I waited for the expected upbraiding.

"Why are you apologizing? This is amazing. A celebrity getting in a fistfight is great publicity for the restaurant. Just another quarter in the legend meter. Tell Paul not to worry."

The next day the *Post* ran a full-page story. When I brought Paul back to the Waverly for dinner a few months later, there was a pair of boxing gloves sitting in the middle of the table with a note: "Paul. Thanks for building the legend. Best, Graydon."

Aside from getting into drunken fights at restaurants and

smoking pot with movie stars, what else did I do as an articles editor? What were the days like? The actual job? Every editor at the magazine had a stable of writers they worked with, many of them contributing editors who were on a yearly contract and a monthly salary. Their contract might call for four stories a year, or it might be as many as six. If they didn't hit their target in a year, the outstanding piece—or pieces—would be carried over to the next year, and on and on, until they might find themselves owing the magazine ten stories a few years down the line, which was a virtually impossible task. It was a heavy responsibility, getting those assignments for my writers. A lot of the ideas came directly from Graydon, with a note landing on my desk—"Let's discuss Nancy Jo on Kimora Lee Simmons"; "Let's discuss Rich Cohen on Jerry Weintraub"—but it also meant coming up with story ideas on my own that Graydon would spark to.

The process of finding story ideas became an obsession, all-consuming. You never know how or when they're going to appear to you. It might be something you see on television or read in a newspaper—and you're watching and reading *everything* on this quest—or an idea might arrive in a dream, like how the riff for "Satisfaction" came to Keith Richards in the middle of the night, and you wake up in a sweat and scribble it down, hoping to make sense of it in the morning. It might be something you overhear at a dinner or in a restaurant bathroom. One night at a party in the West Village I went outside to have a cigarette with a famous actress who told me that she had discovered the owner of a high-end Beverly Hills spa had been stealing hundreds of thousands of dollars from her and a number of other major celebrities for years. She thought it would make a great *Vanity Fair* story and told me she would be a source.* I now understood how those little scraps of paper or ideas scrawled on cocktail napkins I was handed as an assistant came to be.

* This happened all the time, although that particular story broke in the tabloids before we were able to do it.

The writers themselves came up with ideas, too. On phone calls and over lunch or drinks or dinner, or sometimes all three right in a row, you'd discuss potential stories, weigh the pros and cons, eventually settling on one or two, shelving the others for a later date or dismissing them outright. You'd have to then put on your salesman hat and pitch this idea to Graydon, who with one word could send an editor back to the drawing board or set the wheels of a story in motion. If you walked out of his office with two or three green lights from a stack of ten, that was considered a success. He might say no but have another idea for the writer, or assign them a cover story, which was easy money and great for filling out contracts.

Most of these meetings were one-on-one. There weren't weekly editorial meetings full of editors throwing out ideas, like I assume a lot of publications had, or like you see in films and television shows about magazines. We occasionally had them, and over the years Graydon tried to institute them, but they were more political than constructive and were usually abandoned. It was blood sport, an exercise in self-preservation, as you fought to get your own writers assignments and worked to keep your best ideas from being stolen by other editors for their writers. After some tough lessons, I ended up saving my best ideas for when I was alone with Graydon.

For a number of years, these editorial meetings were complicated by the presence of Fran Lebowitz. Fran was a legendary, if a bit cultish, figure in New York's literary and social circles, mostly because she had a famous case of writer's block dating back to the early eighties after the publication of her second book. In lieu of writing, she somehow crafted a career out of just being caustic and grumpy, and always around, like a scene-chewing supporting character in a sitcom. She became the unofficial spokeswoman for pre-gentrified, lost New York, turning that into a career, with speaking engagements and a recurring role as a judge on *Law & Order*.

Graydon had hired Fran as a contributing editor, with the idea of getting her writing again. When this didn't quite pan out, she was set up with various editors or assistants who would interview her about a topic, then turn the transcript into a piece with Fran's name on it. She did a few of these over the years.

Fran would hang around the office often enough, spending her days at Graydon's side chain-smoking, saying witty things, and would occasionally sit in on these senior staff meetings. If you walked in and saw her, it took every ounce of your energy not to audibly groan. She would balk at every idea and say it was stupid, every writer terrible. Her unhappiness and misery were contagious. It got to the point where you just wouldn't say a word if she was there. She might have been fun to read, or watch onstage or on-screen, but being part of the Fran show definitely was not.

That said, turning her into a show wasn't a terrible idea, so Graydon did exactly that—he got Wes Anderson on board to direct a documentary about Fran. Production stopped and started a number of times over the course of a few years. Wes Anderson walked away at some point. With a dwindling production budget, Graydon somehow persuaded Martin Scorsese to come on board. They set up a few cameras around a Waverly Inn banquette one day; blacked out the windows; brought in all the *Vanity Fair* assistants to sit at the other tables and pretend to eat, like it was just another night at the Waverly; and filmed Scorsese and Fran having a conversation for a few hours. And that was essentially the movie, the cheapest, most expensive documentary ever made, called *Public Speaking*. But it was a hit and would lead Fran to a wider audience. She and Scorsese (they had ditched Graydon somewhere along the way) premiered the docuseries *Pretend It's a City* on Netflix in 2021, which was a direct descendant of *Public Speaking*.

But back to those story ideas, the lifeblood of the magazine.

With an approved story idea in hand, I would send the writer off on their own, out into the world. Sometimes I wouldn't speak to them for weeks or a month or *months* as they reported their story, traveling to far-flung locations, interviewing sources; other times we would talk every day, going over the twists and turns, or they just *had* to tell me about their latest interview or major breakthrough on the story. Eventually, they would return home to write, alone in front of a computer for weeks, occasionally calling me if they were stuck, or wanted to bounce some ideas off of me, or were frustrated and going crazy. Writing is a solitary and difficult endeavor, and even the best writers occasionally second-guess themselves. Often this is when an editor has to put on their therapist hat, trying to fix whatever dark thoughts are getting in the way of the writing. This process always ended with their turning something in, confident they'd delivered a strong first draft or racked with anxiety that they hadn't.

I would print that piece out, take it to a bar after work, settle in on a stool, and start reading, digging in, making notes in the margins. I didn't always know what I was looking for, especially at the beginning, but in time, things began to reveal themselves. I'd stay up until three or four in the morning with that piece, reading it over and over, getting to know it, word by word, line by line, paragraph by paragraph. I was teaching myself as I went along. I'd eventually open the document on my computer, transferring all my notes into it. I would wake up the next morning, bleary-eyed, and read through the document, sometimes amazed at the skill and care I had managed to apply to the piece while half-asleep, like I had been possessed by some editing demon that had actually done the heavy lifting.

The more stories I edited, the more I understood storytelling. As with anything, repetition makes you sharper. As I added writers to my stable, I got to know writing better, began to distinguish the good from the bad, what was missing and what was too much. There's a rhythm to good writing, the way words and punctuation work together, the way sentences are structured. Those words you see on the page, as you're reading them, you're saying them in your head. When the right words hit the right notes, when there's just enough *but not too much* punctuation, occasionally slowing things down, it creates a beat, or a rhythm, in your head. Good writing has a beat. Great writing sounds like jazz.*

I would turn the annotated story over to the writer, and we'd have a long discussion. They would sit with the piece for a few days, address any notes they felt were worth addressing, push back on some and ignore the others, and send it back to me. I'd read it again, three or four times, make sure it was polished and perfect, print it out in twelve-point Times New Roman with justified margins, turn it in to Graydon, and wait, usually convinced he was going to hate it.

When I was an assistant, delivering all those manuscripts to editors every morning, I never considered the potential chain of events after I dropped each one into its inbox; I just moved down the line to the next office. For a writer, a piece in *Vanity Fair* could launch a career, with the potential for book and movie deals that could come as a result. Failure might set that writer back years. For an editor, the more stories you got into the magazine, the safer your job was. And it all hinged on the opinion of one person.

Manuscripts would be returned with Graydon's penciled notes throughout, oftentimes with a few words written on the front page next to his initials. You were hoping for "Brilliant" or "Terrific" or "Love it," which meant it would probably see the light of day in print. You'd immediately call the writer and tell them the good news. If it was just initialed, he didn't hate it, but its future was a little less clear, and you might not call the writer immediately. If he wrote "Let's discuss" on it, you were fucked, dreading that conversation about what had gone wrong and why he didn't like it while avoiding the writer or telling them you hadn't gotten it back yet. "Let's discuss" on a manuscript was coded language for failure, and everyone knew it. And there were failures, for every editor and writer. Pieces were killed all the time. Occasionally one

---

* This is the paragraph a reviewer trashing this book will quote to point out that my own writing has none of that rhythm I describe, so I might as well get in front of it.

was worth fighting for, but most of the time it wasn't. Once Graydon had gone cold on a story, it was hard to come back. Writers were usually still paid in full—especially our contributing editors, as it counted against their contract. If it was an outside writer, they might ask to take the story elsewhere, get half their fee, able to take the piece to another publication. But this was a tricky proposal, peddling tainted wares, sloppy seconds. The first question would usually be *What's wrong with it and why didn't* Vanity Fair *run it?*

But let's focus on the positive, and one of those stories that were "Brilliant" or "Terrific," and scheduled for the upcoming issue.

You would first turn the text over to the production department. They would look at the length, to see how well it was fitting in its allotted space in the issue. Maybe they'd ask you to cut it by five hundred or a thousand words, maybe more—a feature story around that time was around five thousand words, which is one thousand two hundred and seventy-two words less than this chapter because I overwrote—and depending on the writer, you'd do it yourself or they'd want to do it, or you'd have an endless phone call cutting it with the writer in real time, then resubmit it.

Once it was the right length, it would be put into the editorial computer system, where it would be available for everyone to read. That would mean a designer, who would start working on a layout; the photo department, to see what photographs were needed; a copy editor, who would begin copyediting the text; and the research department, where a fact-checker would be assigned to the piece. Earlier I compared an editor's role in the process of closing a piece to that of a film director, who oversees a group of specialists while making sure the creative vision of the endeavor remains intact.

Then it would come hard and fast, and in waves and stages. A first galley would arrive at your desk, followed closely by a copy editor and then a fact-checker, both of whom would sit with you and go through the piece. We were an old-school operation, working on paper with colored pencils even as much of the industry began to transition to fully digital editorial systems. Those changes would be input by some poor soul in the production department, at which point a second galley would arrive, again followed by the copy editor and fact-checker for round two. Meanwhile, the art and photo departments gathered all the art for the story, whether pulled from an original shoot or researched photographs, or a combination of the two, and lined the walls of the planning room for Graydon to make his choices. Once that was done, they would create a layout, and the editor would write the captions and find pull quotes, at which point the text, display type, and layout would be merged into one document and the process continued with the copy editor and fact-checker—who by then would have had the piece reviewed by legal, to make sure there was nothing libelous in the story—for a few more rounds until the piece was finished and the issue shipped off to the printer. A week later, the issue would land on your desk, just as you were beginning the whole thing all over again.

I've obviously condensed this process into a few paragraphs here, as this part of the job doesn't sound exciting, but it was. I loved being the conductor of this orchestra each month. It was the moment when everything came together—the writing, the photographs, the layout—the moment when that initial idea began to take its final form. To use a well-worn cliché, this was where the magic happened. If it was your own original idea, a story you had championed and succeeded in pushing through, seeing the end result had a little more meaning. The whole process took two to three weeks from when the story came in, was exhausting and stressful, and often involved a number of late nights making last-minute cuts and changes amid thoughts of a permanent career change. In some way, the more difficult a piece was to close, the more satisfying it was to hold in your hands a few weeks later.

That process, the chain of events I just described, was almost constant, with a week in between to catch your breath. You might be closing one or two stories—sometimes even three or four, in a busy month—oftentimes about completely different subjects, while talking with a fact-checker about whether to describe Emma Stone's eyes as green or hazel, the correct spelling of an Iraqi Shia warlord's name, or the year of a specific Max Beckmann painting that was plundered by the Nazis. Meanwhile, your other writers were in various stages of reporting or writing or rewriting. A new story or rewrite might arrive every few days. And you were always searching for story ideas, on the phone constantly, having lunch or drinks or dinner with writers. That was the life of a magazine editor. And that was what I had become; I had somehow cracked the code, figured it out in my own way and learned how to tell a story, or at least help writers tell theirs. And not just a magazine editor, but an established editor at one of the most successful magazines in the world. I'd managed to pull the wool over the eyes of such brilliant writers and my colleagues for so long.

Even when a story of mine would get recognized, I couldn't accept that I'd had anything to do with its success. One, "Pat Dollard's War on Hollywood," an epic story about madness, addiction, celebrity, and the war in Iraq, written by Evan Wright, won an ASME in 2007 for Best Profile, one of the highest honors a story could receive—at the time it was the longest piece in the history of the magazine, at twenty thousand words, and one of the most talked-about *Vanity Fair* stories ever. After the awards ceremony, a dozen of us celebrated at the Waverly Inn. I was clutching the award, the Ellie, a copper elephant sculpture based on Alexander Calder's *Elephant Walking,* in one hand, a glass of champagne in the other. As Graydon made a toast and I was offered congratulations all around, I couldn't help but think back to that piece's landing on my desk almost perfect, one of the best first drafts I'd ever read. I might have worked hard getting it across the finish line, but I did so little editing on it. I felt immense guilt for getting any credit for it, let alone an award *for editing.* And yet I craved that validation. Was desperate for it.

Another piece, Charlie LeDuff's poetic profile of the photographer Robert Frank, was nominated two years later in the same category. While I was able to convince myself that I was a worthless hack, on the verge of being found out, I had somehow created a little niche for myself at the magazine, bringing in younger writers and some of the more outlandish and wild stories. Graydon trusted me, trusted my ideas and point of view, my nose for a story, and my ability to see those ideas through the editorial gauntlet and turn them into finished products. "He is now a senior articles editor and makes it his mission to bring in some of the more unusual and outrageous stories in the lineup every month," according to the text that ran with my picture on the Contributors page around this time. I wasn't just on a roll, I was now a senior articles editor. I'd gotten a promotion along the way.

Like Adrian before me, I'd found a corner to work in where I never imagined there would be space for me. And it felt good. I had a happy marriage; both Aimee and I had flourishing careers, a beautiful daughter. As the decade marched on toward the next, I just assumed this was what I would do for the rest of my life, maybe one day getting the top job somewhere, a better paycheck, retiring with a gold watch and a healthy pension. I was only in my midthirties, making a name for myself; the industry was stable, vibrant; *Vanity Fair* was still full of those luxury ads. I had my whole life ahead of me.

That first decade of the new millennium would turn out to be a pivotal one culturally, and an exciting one to be in the thick of as an editor. The frothy scandals of the nineties had faded after 9/11, as the culture shifted its focus to war and politics, and journalism was a vital component of the national conversation. It was also a decade with once-in-a-century technological advancements and major pop-cultural shifts, most prominently the rise of social media and reality television, which would both quickly become ingrained in modern life. Although those two would come back to haunt us in the following decade.

Decades aren't measured in ten-year intervals, don't begin or end according to the Gregorian calendar, at least in a cultural sense. The math is fuzzy, the dates a moving target, and the shifts are usually tied to a defining event or moment. The 2000s didn't begin until 9/11. The nineties didn't get going until January 11, 1992, when Nirvana's *Nevermind* knocked Michael Jackson's

Dangerous out of the top spot on the Billboard 200. The eighties—and the Cold War—were put out of their misery almost on time when the Berlin Wall fell in November 1989. The sixties ended in 1968, when Martin Luther King, Jr., and Robert Kennedy were assassinated two months apart. Of course, these beginnings and endings are never clear in the moment—there needs to be some distance, some time before you can look back and say, "Yep, that was it."

We didn't know it at the time, but on the morning of September 15, 2008, the aughts came to a crashing halt. On that day, dark clouds began to form over the magazine world.

Chapter 22

As the 2000s came to a close and the new decade began to come into focus, I was on the cusp of turning forty. Middle age, a scary time, especially for someone with two kids under ten—Oliver arrived in 2009—and a hefty mortgage, as Aimee and I bought our first apartment, a loft in Chelsea.* New York had gotten increasingly expensive over the previous decade, as Wall Street exploded during the Bush years. It was awash in banker and hedge-fund cash, and the cost of living was adjusting to this new reality. The creative class was on a downward trajectory, our salaries no match for a city catering more and more to the wealthy and superrich.

By then Aimee and I were two veterans of New York's film and publishing businesses, and doing better than most. For many of those in creative fields, it was becoming a struggle, as layoffs were beginning to hit both industries in the wake of the 2008 financial crisis. In fact, Aimee had been let go in 2009 by Paramount when they shut their New York office, which she had been running, although it was a welcome change for her as she had been thinking about starting her own production company anyway. And I suddenly had an under-siege expense account, as budget cuts at Condé Nast put increased scrutiny on them. I don't expect any sympathy over this, I just thought I'd mention it.

It was a scary time in the magazine business. We had been going through what was kindly being referred to as a "correction" since the 2008 crash, but it was becoming clear there was something more going on. Newsstand sales had been falling, and advertisers

---

* Okay, technically *Flatiron*, but I still prefer to call it Chelsea.

were fleeing print. We were always on the verge of turning a corner, or so we were being told, but in reality, we had been bleeding out slowly. We were living through the industry's descent into a dark age.

Obviously, the financial crisis, the worst since the Great Depression, which began with the collapse of Lehman Brothers on September 15, 2008, took its toll. Suddenly spending a few dollars on a magazine seemed like an unnecessary expense. Advertisers got cautious, shut off the spigot. But economic downturns and recessions happen; industries and businesses take a hit, make some adjustments, cut some costs, ride it out until the next boom. This was different. And it was becoming clear why. A year before the economic collapse, in 2007, the iPhone had been introduced, instantly accelerating the explosion of mobile technology and the rise of social media. Twitter had arrived the year before that. Facebook's users grew from one hundred million to two hundred forty million in 2008. It was a perfect storm. The financial crisis, the iPhone, Facebook, Twitter: the four horsemen of the magazine apocalypse.* Suddenly everyone was on their phones and social media, instantly connecting with the world, posting and tweeting and tagging and sharing, creating their own little social ecosystems, curating their own little magazines and stories, some even turning themselves into celebrities.

Along with the rest of the industry, *Vanity Fair*'s newsstand sales were in free fall. We were averaging under 200,000 copies a month. When I began in 1994, and throughout much of the 2000s, our average monthly newsstand sales were somewhere in the 350,000 to 400,000 range. Sales under 200,000 would have been cause for alarm. Hollywood Issues would regularly edge into the 500,000 or even 600,000 territory, and a blockbuster issue could get into the 700,000s. September 2005's cover of Jennifer Aniston, the issue in which she broke down during the interview about her split from Brad Pitt, sold 738,929 copies. Tom Cruise,

---

* Instagram and Snapchat would launch in 2010 and 2011, respectively. Two more horsemen in what would soon become a marauding cavalry.

Katie Holmes, and Suri's October 2006 cover sold 713,776.* But beginning in 2008, newsstand sales began to tank. For the next decade, they would fall by at least 10 percent a year industry-wide. By 2018, they had fallen by 60 percent.

And digital advertising and print advertising weren't just on two different tracks, they were on two different kinds of trains, one modern, sleek, and high-speed, the other an old steam engine grinding down the tracks. In 2012, Google collected more advertising revenue than the whole print industry—magazines and newspapers—*combined*. Just a few years later, advertisers would spend more on digital advertising than on print and *television* combined, and the digital market was on pace to capture two-thirds of all advertising dollars by 2023. The shift was quick and profound.

Facebook, which began selling ads in 2007, and Google were able to target advertising at *very* specific demographics and then show advertisers actual figures of who saw the ad, who clicked on it, and who made a purchase. They were data-driven businesses. We would sell you a page of advertising for $100,000, tell you it was going to reach a lot of influential and wealthy people, take you out to dinner, dangle an invite to the Oscar party, order expensive wine, get you drunk, and hope you forgot to ask any questions.

Magazine editors weren't data people. There was never anything scientific about how we made editorial decisions. An established actor had a big movie coming out, they'd sold well in the past, so we'd put them on a cover, or an up-and-coming actor had such a breakout performance that we knew it would be talked about, so we would take a chance and give them a cover. When it came to stories, for the most part, it was a meritocracy—the best stories won and made it into the issue. Maybe there'd be some office politics involved, internal discussions, but there were never

---

* Rounding out the top five: Carolyn Bessette Kennedy, September 1999, 640,816; Hollywood Issue, April 1995, 606,894; John F. Kennedy, Jr., and Carolyn Bessette Kennedy, August 2003, 598,744.

any focus groups or anything like that. Magazine editors didn't need focus groups—we were above that, we were our own focus group, cultural curators. Decisions were made on instinct and gut feeling alone, maybe some history. We'd put the issue on the stands and let the market dictate what happened. Then we'd move on to the next issue. Sometimes we guessed right, sometimes we guessed wrong. Sometimes we'd experiment, like when we put a fresh-faced Justin Bieber on the cover in 2011 in a desperate and transparently cynical attempt to appeal to younger readers.*

Suddenly, you could look at web traffic, actual numbers and analytics, and you could see what people clicked on, where they spent the most time—*engagement*—where they were. And worse, advertisers were able to see that information. Overnight, there was science available to what we did. Content and distribution quickly meant something different from simply putting a magazine on the newsstands every month and hoping for the best.

As a result of the tectonic shift in advertising from print to digital, there was a bloodletting going on in the industry. Magazines were downsizing, jobs were being eliminated, and there was nowhere to go—it was a game of musical chairs, and the music was stopping more often and the chairs were disappearing quicker. The booming digital media platforms with their inflated valuations and stock prices and—fleeting, it turns out—"success," or optics of success, weren't looking to hire an overpaid middle-aged print magazine editor who drank at lunch, bristled at open office plans, and thought CMS had something to do with country music.† They were beginning to hire kids who spoke this new digital language.

By 2011, three years after the financial meltdown, it had become clear that this was more than just a correction. Our business was going through fundamental changes, or worse, an end-of-days comeuppance for our excess and arrogance. After the 2008 economic collapse, Condé Nast brought in McKinsey, the corporate

---

* It bombed. Young people weren't buying magazines anymore.

† "Content management system," by the way.

consulting firm, to "study" how to transform the company from a print-based dinosaur into one that could compete in the digital media age. That transformation led to massive cost cutting and layoffs and very few solutions, if any. Every few years after that, Condé Nast would bring in another consulting firm or excitedly announce some great company-wide realignment, which had the same outcome.

We were living in a moment of profound technological disruption and a revolution in communication that may be unparalleled in human history. The Techpocalypse was upon us. In what seemed like a quick montage sequence in a film to show the passage of time, suddenly everything had changed. We were becoming slaves to the whims, wants, and needs of Facebook, Google, Amazon, Apple, and the other tech giants that were gobbling up or destroying everything in their path, collecting data, creating algorithms, growing exponentially, getting more and more powerful, like a monster in those old Godzilla movies. The number crunchers and MBAs began to replace the creative class in New York's media hierarchy, business-school acronyms taking the place of actual words in meetings with our corporate overlords. The bland catchall *content* was affixed to the end result of any creative endeavor—there were no longer writers and photographers and editors, just *content creators*. Pixels replaced words. Pitch decks, Excel spreadsheets, and PowerPoint presentations replaced casual meetings, conversations, and boozy lunches about what was going on in the world and how to cover it—those of us who created the content suddenly became less important than those whose job it was to find an audience for that content.

In the wake of this tectonic shift, a new generation of content creators was being hired, bought in bulk straight from the factory. Younger, prettier, with perfect teeth and great hair, raised in the digital age, savvier—*cheaper*. Open office plans would begin to replace traditional offices, rubber balls replacing desk chairs under the SoulCycle-toned asses of this new millennial and then Gen Z workforce. Vegan cupcakes slowly replaced the buttercreamfrosted birthday cakes at office birthday parties; juice replaced solid food for lunch; piccolos and cortados replaced matcha, which had replaced the flat whites, which had replaced the green tea that had replaced the chai lattes that had replaced the cappuccinos that had replaced the plain old coffee; oat milk replaced the cashew milk that had replaced the almond milk that had replaced the soy milk that had replaced the regular old milk from cows; kale and avocados took over lunch menus until everything was suddenly blended together and served in recyclable bowls like baby food. Phones stopped ringing, conversation stopped. The office was being overrun by rows and rows of silent, headphoned, Invisaligned, and Warby Parkered twentysomethings on bouncy balls slurping slop in tiny cubicles, tapping away at their keyboards. The modern workplace was turning into a dystopian, Dickensian, Gilliam-esque adult nursery school.

The good old days weren't just behind us, they were reaching out of the grave, strangling us one by one. Print, at least of the daily, weekly, and monthly variety, was dying. Two decades into that information age that *Vanity Fair* had helped define and was so closely tied to, this journey that I was on was faltering. The magazine business, at least what it had been for more than a century, a print-based, subscription-and-sales, ad-selling business, was becoming less and less of a viable industry. Newsstand sales continued to tank, advertisers continued to flee, revenue was dropping. Condé Nast stopped calling its titles magazines; we were now brands, "multi-platform brands with numerous revenue streams and paths to monetization"—mostly phantom streams and paths that never quite seemed to appear. We were chasing something that was always out of reach. Everything was increasingly digital, especially advertising, our reason for existing.

Digital advertising, and specifically digital video advertising, was rising at such a rapid rate that it couldn't be ignored. Social media was becoming a powerful marketing and distribution tool for brands, and video wound up being shared at a rate that's more than one thousand times greater than that of a written piece of content.* Consumers had short attention spans and audiences were getting younger, so advertisers, and therefore media brands, were beginning to chase millennials and Gen Z. They weren't reading long-form stories on their phones, if at all, and digital really began to mean a phone, thanks to the iPhone, with most online traffic coming from mobile devices and shared via social media and other links. This led to a move into video, creating short videos, and lots of them, and building a distribution network while hoping something would go viral.

In 2011, in an effort to find some of those new sources of digital revenue, Condé Nast hired a woman named Dawn Ostroff to head up a new division of the company, called Condé Nast Entertainment. The company was losing money at this point. Well, *apparently*; according to some press reports, it was estimated that Condé Nast was losing more than $100 million a year. And there was no end in sight.

Condé Nast Entertainment was created to try to capitalize on the power of Condé Nast's brands and the gold rush into digital video advertising. The idea was simple: To create shareable† video for Condé Nast's brands and reap the rewards of some of those ad dollars. To diversify, continue moving away from print. Which from a business standpoint makes total sense and is something we should have begun to do much earlier. But we were a magazine company—we wrote stories and took pictures. Making video wasn't what we did. We were writers, and photographers, and text editors. This was a completely different skill set. So, we needed help, needed someone to come in and do it for us. But of course we didn't want help, were reluctant to give up any control, were being dragged kicking and screaming into this new era. Enter Condé Nast Entertainment.

Dawn had had a long career in television, most recently as head

---

* This is worth mentioning: A 2018 MIT study looking at news on Twitter found that "false news stories are 70 percent more likely to be retweeted than true stories are."

† The word *snackable* was thrown around a lot.

of the CW, a successful run that saw the network launch hit shows like *Gossip Girl* and *The Vampire Diaries*. Her mandate was two-fold: to leverage and monetize Condé Nast's feature stories by turning them into film and television series, something Tina Brown had tried to do with *Talk*, and to create an in-house production company for Condé Nast's magazines to produce short-form branded digital video.

The most successful of these videos at Condé Nast would be *Vogue*'s series *73 Questions*, in which celebrities answered seventy-three rapid-fire questions, all in one take. It launched in 2014 with Sarah Jessica Parker, and they rode that horse as far as it would take them.

No matter how much I protested and pointed out how absurd it was, Graydon put me in charge of *Vanity Fair*'s move into digital video. Even though I was forty by now, Graydon still perceived me as a "kid," and therefore up on all of this new technology. I'd also had some experience with screenwriting, had written a few movies and television pilots over the years that had gotten me some meetings in Hollywood, although nothing much came of them.

Our relationship with Dawn Ostroff and her senior executives got off on the wrong foot—*literally*. We were still in 4 Times Square, a few years away from moving downtown to One World Trade Center, and were meeting with Dawn and her two senior executives for the first time. After introductions, we sat on the couches in Graydon's office, and as we sat, I could see Graydon's eyes drifting down to the floor, to the feet of one of Dawn's executives, his face recoiling in visible disgust. He was wearing some sort of leather clog, the kind you might see on a chef or a nineteenth-century Dutch fruit peddler. And Graydon had a *thing* about bad shoes. He was already mistrustful of these interlopers, who had been hired to help translate the magazine to the digital video age, in which he would have to give up some level of control. And now they had offended him sartorially and aesthetically, sullied the highly curated midcentury motif of his office. As Dawn and her team went through their vision for our move into digital video, Graydon barely paid attention, his gaze rarely leaving the shoes for half an hour.

After the meeting was over and I was back in my office, I got a call to come back and see Graydon. Before I could sit down across from him, he immediately got into it.

"Did you see those shoes?"

"Yeah. I know. They were really bad, like a faux-leather Croc."

"It was a . . . dirty clog."

"Can we talk about this video stuff—"

He cut me off and we talked about the shoes for a few minutes, trying to come up with new ways to describe them.

Now, I know this makes us sound like dreadful snobs, even judgmental and cruel. But they were really bad shoes, and we had a standard to uphold. It was *Vanity Fair* and Condé Nast after all; we were selling a fantasy, a lifestyle, and that crossed over into the real world and our appearances. We were expected to be walking billboards for the fantasy we were selling. (Why do you think editors in chief got clothing allowances?) If I was bringing someone into Graydon's office whom he'd never met before, I would always do a shoe check. If they didn't pass muster, I'd make sure we sat at his desk, passing up a more casual chat on his couches, where the offending loafer or moccasin or dirt-caked work boot would be on full display. If this Condé Nast Entertainment executive was someone who was going to be making aesthetic decisions for us, and he had made the decision that morning to wear those cartoon shoes, well, this might be a problem.

I finally got him to focus on video, and I got my marching orders: Work with Dawn and her team, don't embarrass the magazine, and "don't fuck it up."

The two executives wouldn't last, but Dawn did, and we grew to really like her and trust her. We put her through her paces, as did most of the other titles, but she was clever, began to understand the politics of the company, was patient, persistent, and figured it out, building a successful new division* from scratch,

---

* Again, since Condé Nast is a private company, the real financial picture is unknown to all except a few. So when I call CNE a successful new division, that was at least the story that was put out there, the optics. It might have been a total money pit for all I know.

eventually getting hired away to be the head of content for Spotify. I'm proud of the early work we produced, which was upscale, smart, and on brand, short documentaries and a few satirical series.

I wrote an animated series called *The Vanity Code*, an animated spoof of online "How to . . ." videos ("How to Feign Interest in Your Boss's Children," "How to Deal with Millennials in the Workplace," "How to Behave at a Swingers Party") that won a Webby, or was nominated for a Webby—something to do with the Webbys; honestly I wasn't really paying attention. They were even picked up by Italian *Vanity Fair* and translated into Italian ("Come Superare un Test Antidroga").* Another series, *The Snob's Dictionary*, which both poked fun at and celebrated cultural snobbery, created by *Vanity Fair* writer David Kamp, was nominated for an ASME—even ASME had added a video category to their annual awards. Of course, upscale and smart doesn't really work on the internet, as we discovered—they were judged failures. Over the years *Vanity Fair*'s videos would have to be adjusted, get even shorter—more "snackable"—and more celebrity driven, silly, and superficial. Give the people what they want. Scale or die.

The Condé Nast Entertainment work would begin to take up more and more of my time. With ads on a steep decline in the magazine—and in the industry as a whole—for a number of years, that meant fewer editorial pages, meaning fewer stories, and they were getting shorter. It was harder to get your writers assignments. We began to pay them less; their contracts began to disappear. This was industry-wide. Editors and writers were being pushed out of their jobs at an alarming pace. Print wasn't just losing the war against digital, it was beginning to look like a one-sided rout. Dawn sold a show to the Investigation Discovery network called *Vanity Fair Confidential*, which was an hour-long true-crime docuseries based on the magazine's library of crime stories, which I helped get off the ground and was a producer on.

---

* Perhaps my greatest achievement.

It was down-market for *Vanity Fair,* and not something we would have done in the past, but we were being forced to bathe in the middlebrow swamp to "extend the brand," a phrase that by necessity had become an ethos in the magazine business. *Vanity Fair Confidential* ran for four seasons and was considered a success.

A few years after CNE came into existence, I had a meeting on my calendar, along with Graydon, in our conference room on the twenty-second floor of One World Trade soon after we had moved there, with Dawn and her team, which had grown exponentially. It popped up one morning in my Google calendar—which I barely knew how to use, and things would just appear, like magic—as a "CNE/KPI meeting." There were so many of these meetings that I rarely paid attention to their titles or what they were about, my eyes glazing over at the thought of the endless and confusing PowerPoint presentation that awaited me. I stopped by Graydon's office, and he saw me outside, nodded with something not even close to approaching enthusiasm, and got up, and we started walking down the hall.

"What's this meeting about?" he asked.

"I have no idea. Just nod and smile. And don't ask *any* questions. We won't understand the answers and we'll never get out of there."

He nodded. That was our approach to most of these meetings.

We walked into the conference room and said hello to Dawn. She had a team of maybe six or seven with her, sitting around the big conference table, most of them at least a decade younger than me. They all had laptops. I had a pad of paper and a pen. Graydon and I sat across from them as Dawn suggested they introduce themselves. The first one told us her name and her title, which was something like "VP of social activation," or maybe "director of social outreach." We nodded politely and smiled as they went around the table, saying their names and titles that meant nothing to either of us.

With the introductions now over, someone got up and dimmed the lights: It was time for the dreaded deck. This deck was no different from the last one, or the next one, slide after slide of charts, and graphs, and numbers and logos and acronyms. This one had references to KPIs on every slide. It was a KPI meeting, after all.

About halfway through the presentation, Graydon grabbed my notepad, then my pen, wrote something down, and slid the pad back to me.

I looked down.

What does KPI stand for?

I was running digital video for *Vanity Fair,* had been tasked with building this new initiative, was one of Graydon's trusted deputies, still the one he turned to when he wanted to know what was happening with *the young folks.* Never mind that I was now older than he had been when he took over *Vanity Fair* and had no idea what any of this shit meant or how it actually worked. I stared at that piece of paper for a few moments and in that instant knew how much the world had changed, and knew that it had left me behind. The new technology and changes to the industry were coming so fast, it was impossible to keep up. This PowerPoint, these terms and acronyms, the job titles, the business model, this new millennial and now Gen Z workforce and audience. While we were making fun of them, the joke was on us. They had been raised with this stuff; the internet and social media and new technology were intertwined with their DNA. It was part of the very fiber of their being. The cutting-edge new technologies that emerged when I was growing up were things like cordless phones, microwave ovens, and VCRs. If something stopped working properly, we just hit it really hard and hoped for the best. My generation was past our sell-by date before we'd even gotten a chance to be put on the shelf. Cassettes in a streaming world.

I scribbled three words on that notepad and slid it back.

No fucking idea.

He smiled and laughed quietly to himself. I couldn't help but join in. What else is there to do but laugh in the face of your own obsolescence?

The deck came to an end. We smiled, told them it looked great and we were ready to move forward with whatever it was they had just pitched, even though we had no idea what had actually been pitched. But we were on board with this KPI thing! Dawn asked us if we had any questions. I shook my head and smiled. But then Graydon spoke up.

"Yeah, I have one question."

My directive had gone unheeded. It was a pointless exercise. And worse, now we were never getting out of there.

"What does *KPI* stand for?"*

The other side of the table just stared at us with blank looks.

That just about sums up where the industry was by the mid-2010s and the generational shift that was skipping right past mine. We were supposed to be the translators between the generation in front of us and the ones behind us before taking over—that was the way it had always worked in the past—but we didn't understand this new language.

While we didn't know how to read spreadsheets, use Google Docs, or understand any of these dreadful marketing and business acronyms, we still knew how to tell a story with words and images, still knew how to occasionally break news the old-fashioned way, and, once in a while, still knew how to drive the cultural conversation. And what we did next might have been the last great moment for the monthly magazine.

* According to kpi.org, "Key Performance Indicators (KPIs) are the critical (key) indicators of progress toward an intended result. KPIs provide a focus for strategic and operational improvement, create an analytical basis for decision making and help focus attention on what matters most." In plain English, benchmarks, goals. I think.

Chapter 23

*V*anity Fair broke a number of major stories over the years, maybe none bigger than Deep Throat in July 2005. Revealing the identity of Bob Woodward and Carl Bernstein's secret government source who led to the end of the Nixon presidency was maybe our crowning achievement of that decade. It had been one of the great mysteries of journalism and American pop culture over the previous half century. We had been approached a few years earlier by a man named Mark Felt, the number two at the FBI during Watergate, who wanted to come clean before he died. That we beat Woodward and Bernstein and *The Washington Post* to the scoop—they were waiting until Felt was dead before revealing his identity—was seen as a major coup. On the other end of the cultural spectrum was the cover with Tom Cruise and Katie Holmes and their newborn daughter ("Yes, Suri, she's our baby!") in the fall of 2006—it was one of our bestselling issues ever. The key to these kinds of stories and covers, these reveals, is keeping them a secret until the issue is released, so they were done with a limited amount of staff involvement in their creation and closing. This got more complicated as the internet and social media took hold. If a cover image or story leaked early, it would travel around the world in minutes. We'd be left exposed.

But breaking news and getting access to the powerful and famous is important for a magazine's survival, especially a monthly culture and news magazine like *Vanity Fair*. It goosed sales, kept you relevant, in the conversation. But it was becoming harder to do consistently with the internet and social media. We moved at a glacial pace, couldn't keep up with the online sites that were breaking stories twenty-four hours a day, gathering and disseminating information while we were oblivious, out to lunch or at a fancy dinner party. The news cycle began to speed up.

We had a website, but it was underfunded and mostly a dumping ground for pieces that didn't make it into the print magazine. We treated it like our junior varsity—*VF* JV. And with social media, celebrities began to own their own narratives, were suddenly able to reach the world in an instant with 140 characters or a simple photograph, announce divorces, births, come out of the closet or apologize, and promise they were seeking treatment or heading off to rehab. Why not break your own news without having to put your story in somebody else's hands?

Followers were becoming more important to studios and brands than magazine covers, so why leave the house? This was a major shift in celebrity culture. The stars we relied on to sell magazines didn't need us anymore.* That tacit agreement that had benefited both sides for so many years was coming to an end. Social media was a disruption to the celebrity-industrial complex's food chain, and we were the odd man out, no longer an essential link between the apex predators and the minnows.

In late 2014, Graydon was meeting with features editor Jane Sarkin and had a thought, although the kind of thought one usually keeps to oneself. It had been reported over the years in down-market tabloids that Bruce Jenner, the gold-medal-winning Olympian and late-seventies icon, was secretly a cross-dresser. Of course, to a new generation, Jenner was the sad-sack husband of Kris Jenner, father to Kendall and Kylie, stepfather to Kim, Kourtney, and Khloe,† patriarch and bit player on *Keeping Up with the Kardashians*. There's always a kernel of truth to these kinds of tabloid rumors—although Richard Gere might beg to differ—or if not truth, some past indiscretion or misunderstanding that got twisted into some whispered narrative that follows someone forever. Jenner had been spotted leaving the Beverly

---

* Meanwhile the new celebrities who the internet and social media were creating—YouTubers, influencers—were of a different breed and considered well beneath us.

† And apparently someone named Rob?

Hills Surgical Center earlier that year with a bandage around his neck, after reportedly undergoing a laryngeal shave, a process to minimize the size of a man's Adam's apple. It couldn't be denied that Jenner had begun looking more and more like a woman. Other paparazzi shots of Jenner began popping up with his appearing to have what looked like budding breasts, a sign of estrogen hormone therapy common among those making a male-to-female transition.

So Graydon said to Jane, "Why don't we reach out to Bruce Jenner and offer him a cover." Was Jenner ready to come out, and publicly, on the cover of *Vanity Fair*?

Jane was mortified. I don't think this was a call she wanted to make. It seemed not only like a long shot but potentially offensive, or at the very least uncomfortable. It felt a little down-market and tabloid-y, and beneath *Vanity Fair*. But she did as she was told; found the only contact for Jenner she could find, his speaking engagement agent; and left a message. I don't think she was expecting to hear back, and it was no surprise she didn't. It was assumed that was the end of that.

A few months later, Jane called and asked me to come down to her office. By this point she was my work wife, and I spent almost as much time in her office as I did my own. The look on her face told me something was afoot.

"Close the door."

I did. She paused for a few moments, trying to find the words.

"I just got a call from Alan Nierob"—Alan was a longtime publicist, part of the deep state of the celebrity-industrial complex, representing a number of big stars over the years, like Mel Gibson, Denzel Washington, Liam Neeson, and others—"about Bruce Jenner."

While Alan represented movie stars, he also knew how to deal with a crisis—I did mention he represented Mel "Sugar Tits" Gibson—and I assumed that Jenner had called him in to make all the cross-dressing stories go away, triggered by a call from *Vanity Fair*. Maybe we were being dangled that story? Bruce Jenner denying he was a cross-dresser. But I was wrong. Jane took a deep breath.

"Bruce Jenner . . . has begun the transition to becoming a woman," she whispered.

"What the fuck!? Really?"

"Shhhh. And *she* wants to debut on the cover of *Vanity Fair.*"

"Are you fucking kidding me?"

"No!"

"That's huge, Jane."

"I know. You can't tell anyone."

"Okay."

"Annie's going to shoot it. We need a writer—what about Buzz?"

I immediately nodded. Buzz was Buzz Bissinger, one of my writers. He made perfect sense. Born Harry Gerard Bissinger III in New York, Buzz had a pedigreed biography and top-notch education, like so many others at Condé Nast and *Vanity Fair.* His father was a Wall Street big shot, and he'd attended Phillips Academy in Andover, Massachusetts—where his roommate was future Patriots coach Bill Belichick—then the University of Pennsylvania. He went on to a sparkling career in journalism, for many years using the byline H. G. Bissinger, and wrote about sports as well as anyone. But Buzz could write about anything, and did, and is considered one of the best journalists of his generation, and for good reason. He was a joy to work with, needed very little editing. (My kind of writer.) In his early thirties, in 1987, he had won a Pulitzer Prize for investigative reporting while at *The Philadelphia Inquirer* for a series on the Philadelphia court system. His 1990 book *Friday Night Lights,* which has sold more than two million copies, was turned into the 2004 film and the successful NBC television series, which ran from 2006 through 2011. It's considered one of the best sports books ever written.

When Graydon hired Buzz in the midnineties, you would have described him as a typical preppy, in button-down shirts, blazers, and khaki pants or bland suits. A family man, he appeared to be like any other commuter or office drone. You wouldn't have given him a second look. But in the 2000s, something started to change with Buzz. He began showing up at the office, book parties, and other magazine events in head-to-toe leather, wearing mesh shirts, steel-tipped high-heeled boots, and eye shadow, with chunky chains around his neck. It wasn't a slow transformation; it was all of a sudden. Overnight, he'd gone from Gene Siskel to Gene Simmons. People would talk, whisper, "What's going on with Buzz?" But Buzz didn't seem to give a shit. Whatever this was that he was going through, it was his, he owned it, and he seemed happier and more confident. Call it a midlife crisis or identity crisis, but he came out the other end exactly who he wanted to be. Harry Gerard Bissinger III was gone. Buzz had been reborn.

In 2013, Buzz wrote a story for *GQ* about his shopping addiction, cross-dressing, and lust for leather, and the process of claiming his life back from conformity. He was embracing his authentic self, which is what these personality crises are always about. The *GQ* story was one that he first offered to *Vanity Fair*, but we stupidly passed because it felt off-brand, a little too edgy for us. But Buzz, and his story, tapped into an ongoing discussion about gender identity, something that was bubbling up to the surface of the American cultural conversation, that would ultimately lead to a litany of new self-identification pronouns beyond *he* and *she*. Buzz's *GQ* story would go viral and turn him into a counterculture icon. In 2019, HBO made a documentary about him and his transformation and awakening, called, well, *Buzz*, obviously.

As he wrote in *GQ:* "The self-expression feels glorious, an indispensable part of me. As a stranger said after admiring my look in a Gucci burgundy jacquard velvet jacket and a Burberry black patent leather trench, 'You don't give a fuck.' I don't. I finally don't."

And: "Some of the clothing is men's. Some is women's. I make no distinction. . . . If the clothing you wear makes you feel the way you want to feel, liberated and alive, then fucking wear it. The opposite, to repress yourself as I did for the first fifty-five years of my life, is the worst price of all to pay."

Buzz didn't give a fuck anymore. Unshackled and unrepentant, freed from judgment and judging, Buzz wasn't just the best man for the job, he was the *only* man for the job. It was simple math: Gender Identity + Sports = Buzz. Interviewing Bruce Jenner was tailor-made for him.

I called Buzz and explained what was going on, that he would have exclusive and unfettered access to Jenner as he began his transition to—well, we didn't know to whom, as Jenner hadn't picked out a name yet. I told him that he could tell *no one* what he was up to. The success of this mission was going to hinge on its remaining a secret until the very last moment. Immediately, Buzz was in.

I knew from the beginning that this had all the makings of something special, something that could really land. First of all, Bruce Jenner crossed generational lines. To baby boomers and Gen Xers, Jenner was a sports star, an all-American hero. He had gone to the Montreal Olympics in 1976 representing his country, at the height of the Cold War; kicked some commie ass; and come home with gold in the most difficult competition there is, the decathlon. He was "the World's Greatest Athlete," made it onto the Wheaties box. He was even a guest star on *The Love Boat*! To younger generations, Jenner was a Kardashian—husband, father, and stepfather to that pack of pampered prima donnas, the man of the house, another foil on a show full of nothing but foils. Then, throw in gender and identity politics—not to mention Jenner was a Republican!—two air masses that had been swirling for years, and you had the makings of a perfect storm, a cultural tornado. If we could pull it off.

Buzz spent the next three months with Jenner in her Malibu home as *he* slowly made the difficult transition to *she*. And her name was Caitlyn. Caitlyn Jenner. As Buzz later wrote in the story on Jenner's transformation, "This is the most remarkable story I have ever worked on in 38 years as a journalist, the only writer in the world with unlimited access to Jenner for a story of global interest, witness to the final months of one of the most iconic male athletes before he disappears and a woman appears in his place. I spent hundreds of hours with the man. . . . Then I spent countless hours with the woman." And it really *was* a remarkable story. Just as journalists had been embedded with units in Iraq a decade earlier, Buzz was embedded with a celebrity on the verge of doing something that had never been done so publicly before. He and I would talk often, his end of the conversation punctuated by long pauses as he processed what he had witnessed on his most recent stay. Jenner was incredibly open with Buzz in a way that many subjects aren't, trusted Buzz with his, and then *her*, narrative. They grew close.

From an operational standpoint, this would turn out to be the easy part. Even though Jenner was hounded by the paparazzi in Los Angeles, Buzz could come and go with relative anonymity without its being connected to Jenner's transformation and to a *Vanity Fair* project. Even if they made Buzz—and he was a well-known writer, recognizable to some—it would have been unlikely anyone would have been able to figure out it had anything to do with *Vanity Fair*. Buzz was a well-known sportswriter, Jenner a famous former athlete—they could have been together for a number of different reasons. Even simply friends. But the photo shoot was another story. How do you do a secret photo shoot with Annie Leibovitz, arguably the most famous photographer in the world, and Bruce Jenner, whose every move was watched, in a dress and heels, without someone telling someone, or *something* leaking? Or worse, a paparazzi photograph of the shoot? Protecting the secrecy and sanctity of the photo shoot was going to be the first major hurdle of a number of increasingly difficult hurdles.

The photo shoot was scheduled for May 6, 2015. A one-day shoot at Jenner's home on top of a ridge in Malibu overlooking the Pacific. On a typical cover shoot there might be upward of twenty or thirty people, even more if it was for a Hollywood Issue and multiple subjects. This was a stripped-down operation. Annie had a much smaller team than usual, just a few assistants. Our fashion and photo teams were four or five people. There was no DJ playing music, no catering team, just a few sad trays of sandwiches and crudités on Jenner's kitchen counter. Security was tight. We had flown in our own security team from New York, headed by Keith Duvall, a former NYPD cop who looks like a movie star or the best-looking Kennedy you've ever seen. He had a number of his men stationed around the perimeter of the house, with walkie-talkies and binoculars, scanning for paparazzi hidden in the brush and scrub of the Santa Monica Mountains, or an incoming drone.

I'd flown out the day before with Jeremy Elkin, *Vanity Fair*'s one-man video department, who brought a camera—we were going to try to get Jenner to sit for an interview once the shoot was over. I'd talked to Alan Nierob, who told me he'd do his best to get Caitlyn to sit and talk to Buzz on camera, but there were no guarantees. We *had* to get video. It was critical to what would be a digital rollout, and we knew how important video of this historic day was.

Buzz, Jeremy, and I were staying at the Viceroy in Santa Monica. We were given instructions to drive to Zuma Beach, in Malibu, at two P.M. and wait in the parking lot for someone from Keith's team to come get us and drive us up the hill to Caitlyn's house. We did as we were told, and ended up waiting for more than an hour.

We were finally collected and driven up the winding road to Caitlyn's modern concrete-slab house, which looked like a World War II bunker. There was a small tent set up outside, and our cell phones were taken from us. There would be no phones allowed in the house during the shoot. Jeremy waited outside while Buzz and I went in.

Jenner is six foot two, and in heels she towered over everyone. She looked *stunning*. It was a jaw-dropping transformation. To paraphrase Buzz, Bruce Jenner had disappeared and a woman had appeared in his place. You have never seen a subject as excited to be part of a photo shoot, her first as a woman, getting made up by a professional makeup artist, having one of the most famous hairstylists in the world, Oribe, do her hair. Caitlyn browsed through the racks and racks of clothing, all in her size, that Jessica Diehl, our fashion director, had pulled for the shoot.

Annie was moving from room to room so the photos had different backgrounds. She would shoot Caitlyn in one room, then Caitlyn would change outfits and they'd move to another: There was Caitlyn in a gold Badgley Mischka gown staring out at the Pacific in her living room; in Zac Posen in her bedroom; leaning against a mirror in an Agent Provocateur corset; reclining on her living room sofa in Hervé Léger.* They were cautious about taking her outside but did for one shot, in her Porsche—a gift from Kris Jenner from when they were married—parked in front of Caitlyn's garage and blocked by a truck. What would turn out to be the iconic cover image was shot in front of a painted gold wall, with Jenner in a custom-made satin corseted bodysuit.

Buzz had spent hundreds of hours in this house when it was just the two of them, so it was jarring for him to see the house full of people. Yet it was a quiet shoot. We stayed out of Annie's way—the first rule on an Annie shoot is to stay out of her way—and sat around the kitchen counter, catching up with Alan and Jane. We knew what a historic photo shoot and story this was. It was a major moment, and we were in the middle of it.

At one point we saw the security guys outside stir—something was going on. They gathered together and focused their binoculars on the same location, down the hill toward the Pacific. A few moments later, Keith came in and approached us, looking concerned.

"There's a Bentley coming up the hill." He paused for a moment. "Kim."

And by "Kim," he meant Kim Kardashian. This was a problem, a potential security breach. She can't make a move without paparazzi on her tail. What if she was followed? This put the whole carefully planned operation in jeopardy. It was an unexpected visit but not one that was a surprise. The most famous photographer in the world was here photographing her stepfather for what would surely be an iconic cover of one of the world's most famous magazines, and she wanted in.

---

* I know I'm underplaying it, but the whole thing was surreal and dreamlike.

Kim pulled up to the house in her Bentley. She went through the same security checkpoint we had. Her cell phone was confiscated. And just like that, Kim Kardashian was in the house.

Kim is not tall, a few inches over five feet, and is curvier than the winding mountain road she drove in on. She has what can best be described as an hourglass figure, but an hourglass that counts a significantly longer period of time than a single hour. An oval line traced her face, where the thick coating of makeup began and ended. Kim was camera ready.

Vanity Fair and the Kardashians didn't have a relationship. In fact, we had an unofficial ban on any Kardashians appearing in the magazine. We took a stand. None of them had ever been invited to the Oscar party. It was a cultural cold war. And no one was happy to see her on this day—she was a distraction, could throw off the energy and connection between photographer and subject that makes for great photographs. Buzz and I were tasked with running interference, keeping her out of frame and occupied while Annie snapped away.

We introduced ourselves, led Kim to the kitchen, and sat on stools around Caitlyn's kitchen counter. She was perfectly nice. With no reality-TV cameras around, she seemed relaxed; she was just Kim, a normal human being, albeit one of the most famous women in the world whose equally famous stepfather was in the next room in heels and a wig, not to mention with new breasts, being photographed by the world's most famous photographer. Kim said she was proud of her stepfather, excited for the world to meet Caitlyn. But she was less interested in us than she was in getting into one of Annie's photographs. She would turn her head often, toward the voices and popping of strobes coming from the other room. She occasionally got distracted by the sad-looking tray of crudités surrounding a bowl of gooey dip that sat in front of her. You could see that she wanted to grab a carrot or celery stalk but held back. If she did make it into a photograph, she didn't want to mess up her perfectly lined lips, let alone have a piece of celery stuck in her teeth.

After half an hour, we had run out of things to say to one another. And without phones to look at, to distract us, it got awkward. I should have asked her how Kanye was doing, but it didn't occur to me in the moment. By then it had become clear Kim wasn't going to be photographed that afternoon, Annie wasn't taking the bait, so she decided to leave. On her way out, she grabbed a carrot and a stalk of celery.

As the photo shoot was wrapping up, I needed to try to get video of Caitlyn. Poor Jeremy had been standing outside for three or four hours and was relieved when I finally waved him in. He only had a few minutes to set up his camera in the living room, facing the long sofa, where Caitlyn would be framed by large sliding glass doors behind her and the Pacific in the distance.

We had one shot at this. I looked at Jeremy.

"Don't fuck it up."

He looked terrified.

Annie's shoot came to a close and I got Alan and Buzz to help corral Caitlyn, ask her if she would sit for a few minutes on camera. She agreed. Caitlyn was wearing a black Hervé Léger skirt and top, with a long zipper down the front, her final outfit of the photo shoot. As she sat on the couch, Jeremy hit record, and Buzz began peppering her with questions for more than half an hour. She was comfortable with Buzz, easygoing and funny, understanding the scale of what she was embarking on while not taking herself too seriously.

Once the interview wrapped, we sat around Caitlyn's kitchen counter and opened a bottle of white wine, then another, catching our breath, celebrating what had been a historic day. We clinked glasses. While the coming-out party was a few weeks away, I looked at Caitlyn, marveling at the transformation, then at Buzz, who had been a witness to it all, in his black leather jacket and tight black jeans, thick silver necklaces and maybe a touch of eyeliner. They made an odd couple, but I'm glad they connected. These were two people who had gone through major life changes, transformations, embraced who they were and how they wanted to fit into the world. They were beyond judgment. I envied them. Not everyone gets that opportunity.

A few days later, now back in New York, Buzz emailed me his story using some fancy encryption application to protect it. It was more than eleven thousand words, which is long for a magazine piece, especially in 2015. I was blown away. It was perfect. I had some notes, a few issues about clarity here and there, which I emailed back to him, ending my email with this: "You know what, man, I can't imagine anyone else having handled this story as well and with an absolute perfect tone from start to finish. This wasn't an easy one. My hat's off to you. You fucking did it." And he had.

The photographs came in soon after. They were astounding. Annie had triumphed. Caitlyn was completely transformed and looked as stunning in the photographs as she had the day of the shoot. Graydon hadn't seen any Polaroids or stills, which were forbidden in case one leaked, so he had no idea what to expect. His jaw hit the floor. The pictures defied expectations. I thought back to that moment when he told Jane to "reach out to Bruce Jenner and offer him a cover." Unbelievably, it happened, but more so as documentation of one person's journey to finding, revealing, and embracing their true self.

With story and photographs in hand, the next challenge was putting them together while keeping it a secret from the staff, although by this point it was a pretty open secret—most of them knew what was going on, what we had. But we couldn't take any chances. We papered over the window of an interior office and created a base of operations to which I had the only key. We put two computers in there that weren't hooked up to the internet or the internal editorial system. This was the only room where the story and the photos would be, and only eight of us would have access to it. I spent the better part of two weeks in there. Chris Dixon, our creative director, would come in to work on the twenty-two-page layout and the cover. Graydon and Jane would sit with Chris to review everything. I had a dedicated copy editor and fact-checker for the piece. Any changes or questions I had for Buzz were done over the phone. Nothing was to be emailed.

When it came time to put the cover together, we went back and forth on the image, settling on the shot in the satin bodysuit in front of the gold wall, the *Vanity Fair* logo in a simple and elegant black. Next up were the cover lines. Did we need Bruce Jenner's name on there? Would anyone know who this was? In the end we decided to leave the name off. Bruce Jenner was gone for good. She was now Caitlyn Jenner. We landed on three words, in quotes: "Call me Caitlyn." Below that, on one line, "By Buzz Bissinger" and "Photos by Annie Leibovitz."

Ellen Kiell, our assistant managing editor, flew to the printer in Lexington, Kentucky, with the file containing the cover and story. We sent our own security team to the printer to safeguard our precious cargo. And then we waited anxiously.

There was a brief security breach. The daughter of an employee at the printer tweeted something about her father's telling her that he saw a *Vanity Fair* cover of Bruce Jenner dressed as a woman. We called the printer, who got the tweet deleted, and thankfully it had gone unnoticed.

On June 1, 2015, we were ready to hit the button. We were rolling out the cover, a few images, and the first few paragraphs of the story online—if you wanted to read the whole story and see all of the pictures, you had to pay for a subscription. The complete issue was also for sale in the app store, though the magazine wouldn't be on newsstands for a week. We hoped that an issue like this would be seen as a historic document and collector's item, and that people might actually want to buy a physical copy, even after seeing the photographs and reading the story online.

A few of us, including Graydon, Jane, Jessica Diehl, digital director Michael Hogan, and our PR director, Beth Kseniak, gathered in the conference room a little after noon. We were going to post everything on our website at twelve-thirty, including a one-minute teaser video that Jeremy had put together, then tweet out the cover, with a link back to the site, and see what happened. We had the website's traffic numbers projected onto the conference room's big screen, so we could see the results in real time.

As twelve-thirty rolled around, Mike hit the button. It took a few minutes for the numbers to start moving up. They went slowly at first, then started ticking up a little faster, then, like an avalanche, they began to increase rapidly. At the fifteen-minute mark, the numbers began moving up so fast we thought the machine might break, if such a thing were possible. Twenty minutes later, we had more than a million people on our website, and the numbers weren't slowing down.

The Caitlyn story brought nine million unique visitors to our website in the first twenty-four hours, a company-wide traffic record. It had 3.9 billion social media impressions, whatever the hell that actually means. The video generated more than 20.9 million views, also a Condé Nast record. That day, and for the rest of the week, if not longer, Caitlyn Jenner was the only news that mattered. It was all anyone could talk about, not just in America, but around the world. The White House even issued a statement from President Obama, saying Caitlyn Jenner had shown "tremendous courage." The day we released her cover, Caitlyn joined Twitter. She hit one million followers in four hours and three minutes, breaking the record set by Obama himself two weeks earlier. It's a record that still stands. The issue went on to sell 432,000 copies, more than double what we'd been averaging.

"What we saw with this cover is that the Internet is now another newsstand for us," Graydon told *The Wall Street Journal*. "The social, video and digital content was compelling in a way that piqued people's interest in owning a physical copy of the magazine. It created a digital moment, as it were, that made people want to hold the story in their hands."

But the internet wasn't a new newsstand, it was *the* newsstand. The Caitlyn issue would turn out to be an anomaly, one final victory for print in an increasingly pixelated world.

Chapter 24

I got a phone call from Henry Porter, *Vanity Fair*'s London editor, in late September 2016. Henry was one of Graydon's first hires when he took over *Vanity Fair* in 1992, a rakish, good-looking English journalist and a novelist who wrote John le Carré–like spy thrillers. He didn't write for the magazine that often but was our well-connected fixer and eyes and ears in the UK.

"Henry. How are you? How was your summer?"

Henry wasn't in the mood for small talk. "I heard your friend is sick," he said mysteriously.

"What friend?"

"A. A. Gill. It doesn't sound good."

I'd spoken to Adrian a few weeks earlier, caught up with him as the summer was winding down. I hadn't seen him in person in almost a year, and we hadn't talked that much over the previous few months, as we were both traveling quite a bit. He had mentioned that his neck hurt, which he thought was a pinched nerve from sleeping in a funny position on a flight. He was going to get a massage, hoping that would take care of it. I didn't think much of it, made fun of him for getting old, had in fact jokingly started calling him Gramps. But to get a call like that from Henry, who was deeply connected among London's writers and editors, made me concerned. I texted Adrian and left a message. After a few more calls and texts went unanswered, I grew anxious. He didn't get back to me for about a week or two. In the meantime, I heard from a number of people that something was seriously wrong, without any specifics. When Adrian finally called, I shut my office door and picked up.

"Hi, Duckie."

"What's going on? Are you all right?"

"Not really."

Adrian told me that he had finally gone to see a doctor about his neck, and they'd found a tumor—then, tumors. It, or they, had traveled, metastasized, to his lungs, his brain. They were everywhere. He was going to begin chemotherapy. He was upbeat for someone staring death in the face. He told me he missed New York, a city he loved, and if this was the end, he'd like to see New York with the twins and Nicola before he died. Hearing that broke my heart, with tears following close behind. This city that was so important to me, my home that I had grown to resent, dismiss, in middle age. I wanted to see him in New York. I wanted to see New York through his eyes again. Be reminded of its magic, which I had forgotten. I asked him if I could try to make that happen.

"I'm not sure I can get on a plane. My immune system is too weak."

"Maybe there's a way. Let me work on it."

I tried to make him laugh and told him how much he meant to me, and we talked about all the stories we hadn't gotten to yet. Adrian and I stayed on the phone for almost an hour, like we had so often over the previous fifteen years. We talked about Brexit, which had passed in June. He had written one of the strongest pieces I thought he had ever written a few months earlier, in *The Times*, a passionate pro-Europe, anti-Brexit argument. We talked about the upcoming American election and the rise of Trump. As our conversation wound down, I pleaded with him.

"Please don't die. Okay?"

"I'll try, Duckie."

I hung up. I kept my door closed for half an hour until my tears dried. My first writer, one of my dearest friends, was dying.

I collected myself and walked down to Graydon's office, shared the news. He was as distraught as I was. We sat in silence for a few minutes.

I told him about Adrian's wish to come to New York, to see it for what could be the last time, and to bring his young children. Graydon had an idea. He picked up the phone and called Diane von Furstenberg, who was married to Barry Diller—my career flashed before my eyes, my whole narrative arc, back to that dinner, Diane's not showing up, getting a seat at that table. Diane and Barry were also friends of Adrian and Nicola's. Graydon explained the situation to Diane, who said she would call Barry and see if he would send his private jet to London to take Adrian, Nicola, and the twins to New York for a weekend. I was hopeful.

I immediately texted Adrian:

> If I get a private jet for you, can you come to New York?

Depends what's on Teresa
Tetevision
Television

> Bad Showtime softcore porn.

You had me at softcore

At least his sense of humor was intact.

Adrian told me that he'd ask his doctor if it was safe to fly private. I started to plan a dinner in New York, to get a group together. A celebration of Adrian. I reached out to Anthony Bourdain, another friend of Adrian's, for help planning something great. I didn't want it to be a goodbye—I wanted to give Adrian something to live for, to look forward to, to help him keep going. A few years earlier another friend of Adrian's, Eric Fellner, the film producer and co-founder of Working Title Films, had had a similar bout with cancer. It looked dire for Fellner, but Adrian and a group of Eric's friends had convinced him to book an expensive holiday, a boat trip in Vietnam for him and his friends, for his next birthday. Fellner pulled through. I wanted to do the same for Adrian.

Adrian called me a few days later. He sounded scared. His doctor told him he couldn't fly. Even private. The risk was too great. I was crushed. For once, the other end of the line went quiet. We had nothing to say to each other. Neither of us could find the words.

I talked to Adrian as often as I could over the next month, as he went back and forth between home and the hospital, trying to encourage him to live. He was weak and exhausted, but he wanted to live. And I wanted him to live. He had so much to live for. Nicola, his kids. His *words*. We, *I*, needed them.

I remembered something Adrian had said to me at the Hotel du Cap in the spring of 2005. *Vanity Fair* was throwing its yearly Cannes party, which didn't have the star power and high profile of the Oscar party but was everyone's favorite; we'd jet off to the South of France for a week, spend a few days closing down the bar at the du Cap every night with a bunch of hammered movie stars. The party was a little more fun, a little wilder, than the Oscar party, in one of the most stunning settings, with a touch of wealthy Eurotrash, which is additive in small doses and destructive in larger ones. As with the Oscar party, there was a dinner, then the tables were cleared away, and the party opened up to a larger crowd as the sun went down. Adrian and I were sitting at the same table, with Nicola. Tom Ford and his longtime boyfriend, Richard Buckley, were also at our table, as was the Russian model Natalia Vodianova and her then husband, Justin Portman, an aristocratic Brit. Gazing at the crowd, a glamorous group of celebrities, supermodels, and billionaires, and our tablemates, then out at the Mediterranean, full of enormous yachts, Adrian turned introspective. He looked at me.

"This is all make-believe. A fantasy. This is not our lives. It's a job. Don't ever forget that."

I didn't pay much attention to what he said in that moment, just nodded in agreement. But for some reason, it stuck with me.

Adrian announced his cancer publicly on November 20, 2016, in, of course, a restaurant review, and in food terms no less. "I've got cancer," he began. "Sorry to drop that onto the breakfast table apropos of nothing at all. Apropos and cancer are rarely found in the same sentence. I wasn't going to mention it, the way you don't. In truth, I've got an embarrassment of cancer, the full English." It was a review of a restaurant in Whitby, North Yorkshire, called the Magpie Café, which he gave five stars. He called their fish and chips the "best in the world." I'd like to get there one day. It was the last restaurant he would ever review.

In early December, I got a call from the English writer James Fox, a friend of Adrian's and mine. He told me it wasn't looking good. Adrian had been hospitalized, perhaps for the last time. James prepared me for the worst. I debated flying over, but it was too late.

On December 10, 2016, Adrian died. He was sixty-two, the same age that Christopher Hitchens was when he passed away. They died five years and five days apart. Adrian always looked up to Christopher. I don't believe in the afterlife or heaven, but I hope there is one, if only so those two could have gotten to know each other over these past few years, talk, about politics and art, poetry and culture and history. They'd agree on as much as they'd disagree on. They would debate, argue. They would giggle with laughter. It would be an eternal conversation that would no doubt attract a crowd, becoming the longest-running show in heaven. Maybe Adrian would have gotten Christopher to stop drinking. Or maybe Christopher would have gotten Adrian to start drinking again.* I'm still sad that Adrian didn't get to see New York once more before he died. And that he didn't live to celebrate his young twins' tenth birthday.

I think about Adrian a lot. Occasionally I'll stumble on one of those old recordings of him dictating a story over the phone. Sometimes it's my voice on the other end, other times it's one of my assistants' from over the years. There is always laughter and joy on these recordings, real wisdom hidden among wickedly offensive jokes. Recently, one of my old assistants found an audio file from 2012 I'd never heard. She was interviewing Adrian about modern parenting, a subject he had written about for the magazine and one that Adrian and I had talked about often now that he had young children, along with two adult children, Flora and Ali. It was going to run online as a Q & A companion piece to the

---

* If there is a heaven, there better be booze.

story. At one point he was talking about schooling and his children's school marks. I love this: "As Kipling tells us, treat our triumphs and disasters just the same. I never really cared or even read their school reports. I have no idea what their exam results were and I made sure that they both knew right at the very beginning that I would never be prouder of them than I was the day they were born. I didn't care if they scored one hundred percent or one percent. It didn't make any difference to me. I was just thrilled to have children and I was thrilled it was them."

Unconditional love. The most beautiful thing there is. It's in short supply in most of our lives, hard to come by, and even harder to recognize, and something that, especially as a parent, you need to deeply understand. It's the key to life, really.

Chapter 25

It was the first day of school for many of New York City's kids, Thursday, September 7, 2017, a few days after Labor Day, that yearly shift from the summer back to real life that the beginning of September brings. The evenings were turning cool, getting darker a little earlier. Late that morning, the senior staff was called to the conference room for an unscheduled meeting. While these impromptu meetings weren't that uncommon, my first thought was always *Is this it?* And by "this," I mean the moment we had been anticipating for a few years: Graydon's retirement. And while it had yet to come to pass, this felt different.

We filed into the conference room overlooking the 9/11 Memorial, about twenty of us, most of us having worked together for more than two decades, and sat around the long table, waiting for Graydon to arrive. When he did, a few moments later, his face told the story, all we needed to know. He looked wistful, vulnerable, maybe even relieved. He sat down, looked around the room, and told us that at that very moment—he looked at his watch—*The New York Times* would be posting a story announcing his retirement, one that he'd arranged with the reporter a few days earlier in secrecy and would run on the front page of the *Times*. *Vanity Fair*'s website, too, would be posting a story, written by David Kamp. It was emotional. Graydon spoke softly. He had just told Condé Nast's CEO, Bob Sauerberg, and Anna Wintour, who as artistic director would be involved in finding his replacement, that he would be stepping down at the end of the year. He would assemble and close the next Hollywood Issue, which would be his last. A fitting tribute and end. He had caught the company by surprise—by design. He had thought it out, choreographed the whole thing. He wanted it to be clear that he wasn't being pushed out, that he was going out on his own terms.

It had been almost exactly twenty-five years since he'd taken over *Vanity Fair*. A nice round number. After some summer reflection, during which he'd turned sixty-eight, maybe he'd finally decided the time was right. I'm pretty sure he had been considering it for longer. Six months earlier, at that year's Oscar party, he'd had the photographer Mark Seliger take a portrait of the senior staff. It felt Last Supper–ish, Graydon with his disciples surrounding him.

"Graydon Carter, the editor of *Vanity Fair*, plans to step down from the magazine in December after a 25-year tenure, leaving the role that established him as a ringmaster of the Hollywood, Washington and Manhattan power elite.

"Mr. Carter's influence stretched from the magazine and entertainment worlds into finance, literature and politics, where President Trump, a target of Mr. Carter's poison pen for decades, still bristles at the mention of his name. One of the few remaining celebrity editors in an industry whose fortunes have faded, Mr. Carter—famous for double-breasted suits, white flowing hair and a seven-figure salary—is a party host, literary patron, film producer and restaurateur whose cheeky-yet-rigorous brand of reporting influenced a generation of journalists."

These were the first two paragraphs of the *Times* story, which was not only a celebration of his run and his accomplishments, but in many ways an obituary for the superstar editor and an industry that had once glowed so brightly that its power and energy lit up the whole city. It was the end of an era.

I think one of the reasons Graydon stayed on as long as he did is that he wanted to protect his staff from what was sure to be a bloodletting the moment he left. Condé Nast had been suffering financially for almost a decade, which had been accompanied by layoffs and other cost-cutting measures. Yet he had always managed to protect us. But he had to think about himself. He must have been exhausted, watching the only business he had ever known and dedicated his life to changing so drastically, and now in free fall. Ultimately, he had to do what was best for him. And whoever took over next was going to clean house.

Unless, of course, that person was me.

Looking back, it seems far-fetched, that a barback from the Royalton Hotel could one day become editor in chief of *Vanity Fair*, but I was Graydon's mentee, an experiment that had panned out, one of his trusted lieutenants—in 2012, I had become a deputy editor—who knew the place inside and out and had memorized the secret formula. I had learned from him everything that I needed to learn. I had turned myself into a magazine editor. There had been whispers over the previous few years that I was the logical choice, that if there was one person who could carry on his legacy, it would be me. I had broad support from the staff, and many writers and contributing editors, if not out of a belief that I would be good at it, then purely for survival or out of familial obligation.

I'd had the conversation with Graydon a number of times over the years, and he'd agreed I'd be a perfect fit. But then, did Condé Nast really want to carry on his legacy? The world had changed so dramatically over the previous twenty-five years. Print was limping along, the future was digital, and I was still considered a print guy, and a Graydon guy. Deep down I knew I'd never get the job, and was resigned to that eventuality, but I owed it to myself, and the institution that had given me so much, to give it a shot.

I walked into his office that afternoon. A steady stream of well-wishers had been going in and out all day. To pay their respects, reminisce, thank him, let him know we'd be okay and that his decision was the right one. This was a man who single-handedly changed the course of my life, believed in me like no one had before. As I walked in, he looked up.

"DB."

"Hey, boss. Are you okay?"

"Yeah. You?"

"I am. It's been a good run, you know?" I sat down across from him as I had so many times before.

"It has."

"You know how grateful I am for all you've done for me, right? I still don't know why you took a chance on me all those years ago, but I'm glad you did. It's given me everything."

"I knew it would work out." He smiled.

"No you didn't. But I just wanted to say thank you."

I took a deep breath.

"I'm going to throw my hat in the ring."

He looked at me. "You should. You'd be a great editor of *Vanity Fair*."

"I have to. It's a long shot—more than a long shot—but fuck it, I owe it to myself. And I owe it to you, and this place that's given me so much. I've got to try."

"I'll do what I can, although I'm not sure how helpful that's going to be. It's going to be an uphill battle. You'll need to throw me under the bus a bit."

I knew he was right. They wanted to move on from the Graydon Carter era. "I know."

He paused for a few moments.

"I'm here if you need me."

He got up from his desk and walked over and hugged me. "Good luck."

As I was walking out, he called out: "One more thing."

I turned back.

"Don't fuck it up."

Those immortal words from my first day all those years ago at that little desk outside his office, and here they were again, bookending a twenty-three-year arc of my life. We both couldn't help but laugh, thinking back to that same moment.

I emailed Anna Wintour. She knew who I was, but I didn't know her that well. I'd been in meetings with her over the years, occasionally at the same social events. She was always cordial. But Anna is impossible to read, even without her dark glasses on. She responded almost immediately. She thanked me for my interest and told me she was heading off to Europe for the fashion shows and would schedule time with me when she returned in a few weeks.

This quixotic endeavor of mine was complicated by Anna and Graydon's relationship. They were contemporaries, the last remaining superstar editors at the company, vestiges from the golden age. They had always gotten along, were even friendly, but things had turned frosty between them after Anna was named Condé Nast's creative director, in 2013. Her new title meant that she oversaw all of the company's editorial, although there was apparently an understanding, a tacit agreement, that Anna wouldn't be that involved with *Vanity Fair*. Over lunch one day soon after, Anna asked Graydon if she could offer him some advice on the fashion styling in *Vanity Fair*'s pages. Graydon snapped back, "Can I offer you some advice on *Vogue*'s writing?" It had gone downhill from there.

Over the next week I sat down and wrote a twenty-page document titled "*Vanity Fair:* The Path Forward," with my vision for the future of the magazine, or brand, as we now had to call it. It would be waiting for her upon her return from Europe. I decided the only chance I had was to stand out and try to make her laugh. I littered it with jokes. I broke it down into sections. One of the sections was titled "Random biographical information, more blatant self aggrandizing, some slight starfuckery, and a photo of one of my kids for good measure."* But I also laid out what I thought was a coherent plan for the future of *Vanity Fair*, although it wasn't rocket science: Print was fading as a viable business, digital was the future, costs would need to be cut, there would have to be more integration between the print and digital staffs and writers, and new sources of revenue would have to be found. I must have used the word *diversity* in every other sentence. As instructed, I threw Graydon under the bus—the magazine had lost touch culturally, the readership was aging, we needed to get younger, more digitally savvy—if only to show her that I was my own man. I ended with a line that kissed her ass while tugging on her heartstrings, an attempt to make her nostalgic for a

---

* I recently dug out this document. It was kind of funny. I did actually include a picture of my son, and I can't believe I sent it to Anna. I'm such an idiot.

bygone era: "I still believe there's magic in what we do. And I'd do a great job harnessing that magic, and taking *VF* deeper into the 21st century. I'd work hard. I know I'd learn a lot from you, and I think you'd like working with me."

In the ensuing weeks, the media rumor mill would go into hyperspeed. As *The New York Times* put it, "The coming departure of Graydon Carter, *Vanity Fair*'s editor for 25 years, has set off a race to inherit his throne. Rarely does such a coveted editorship come up for grabs, even in an industry undergoing an unusual amount of churn."

The New York Times went on to list a number of potential high-profile candidates, including the *Hollywood Reporter* editor Janice Min, *New York* magazine's Adam Moss, *GQ*'s Jim Nelson, *Esquire*'s Jay Fielden, and *Marie Claire*'s Anne Fulenwider, an old friend who had spent a decade or so at *Vanity Fair*.

While I wasn't one of those high-profile editors, a few days later I was mentioned in Keith Kelly's "Media Ink" column in the *New York Post:* "On the inside list is Dana Brown, one of three deputy editors on the magazine."

But then, in early October, a cultural bomb exploded. And it came from within the building. Ronan Farrow, the twenty-nine-year-old wunderkind son of Mia Farrow and Woody Allen, published a story in *The New Yorker* that exposed years of alleged sexual assault and rape by Harvey Weinstein. It was a piece of journalism that would topple one of the most powerful men in American media and shift the cultural conversation instantly.

A few years earlier, *Vanity Fair* had published a big profile of Ronan's mother written by Maureen Orth. It coincided with Ronan's emergence as a semi-public figure, out of the shadow of his famous parents, at least in New York's social and media world. It was also when the rumors that Frank Sinatra was his father, and not Woody Allen, hit a fever pitch in the gossipy halls of New York media and beyond. (Sinatra and Farrow were married for a year and a half in the late sixties and had apparently remained on good terms until Sinatra's death in 1998. Ronan was born in 1987.) In the planning room, among the photos of Mia Farrow throughout the decades, there were photos of Ronan and Frank Sinatra, at roughly the same age, hanging on the wall side by side, and the resemblance was more than striking. When Maureen asked Farrow point-blank if Sinatra was Ronan's father, Farrow replied, "Possibly."

Around the time that the Mia Farrow piece hit, I was introduced to Ronan over email by Matt Ullian, a friend of Ronan's, who was *Vanity Fair*'s deputy director of special projects—his nickname was "Party Boy," for his boyishness, energy, and job description—with the idea that Ronan could write for the magazine, as he wanted to embark on a career in journalism. I ran the idea by Graydon, who said sure, so I sent Ronan an email.

While Ronan and I were going back and forth about story ideas, Graydon invited him to a dinner party in honor of Antoine Arnault, the son of Bernard Arnault, the French billionaire who assembled the powerhouse luxury goods conglomerate LVMH, which began in 1987 with the merger of Louis Vuitton and Moët Hennessy. LVMH was one of Condé Nast's most important advertisers, if not *the* most—not just in America but globally. Graydon had decided to give Ronan a prime seat at his table, in between Graydon's wife, Anna, and Natalia Vodianova, who was dating Antoine Arnault. But Ronan was a no-show. Matt had to take his place. (Remember, *no empty seats*.)

I decided Ronan's act of social aggression might be a sore spot with Graydon, so I let our email chain fade away.

Soon after Ronan and I stopped corresponding, he got a job hosting a show on MSNBC, the short-lived *Ronan Farrow Daily*, which ran for a year, from February 2014 to February 2015, at which point he took a role at NBC News, where he began to work on the Weinstein story. I often wonder: If Ronan had shown up to that dinner, been charming and witty, made an impression on Graydon, maybe that earth-shattering Harvey piece would have ended up in the pages of *Vanity Fair* instead of *The New Yorker* in the fall of 2017, and I would have gotten a contact high from having brought it in, gotten it over the finish line, a career boost that would have helped me in the horse race for Graydon's job.

It was nothing new that Harvey was a monster and a bully. The stories were legendary. Rumors had persisted for years of atrocities committed against women—especially actresses—by Harvey, but no one had managed to nail down the story, or they had been scared off by threats from Harvey or his team of high-priced lawyers. Ronan found a number of brave women, many of them famous, who went on the record, which was no easy feat. Like David before him, Ronan Farrow—and, to his credit, *The New Yorker*'s David Remnick—had taken down Goliath, and sparked a revolution.

In the wake of Farrow's piece, the culture shifted overnight. As *The Guardian* put it, "The selection of a new *Vanity Fair* editor has become a prism through which to read a changing landscape." According to *The Guardian*, Ronan's name was now in the mix to take over *Vanity Fair*.

By then, Anna had come back from Europe, and I was summoned. I spent hours that morning trying on different outfits. I had to get it just right. In maybe a subconscious nod to *The Devil Wears Prada*, I landed on a double-breasted blue Prada suit paired with a dark gray cashmere sweater. No tie. I finished the outfit off with a pair of outrageously expensive brown Balenciaga wingtips that I had bought at Jeffrey, the same store I had gone to for the first time with Adrian all those years ago.

Anna had two offices in the World Trade Center, one at *Vogue*, which was on a lower floor, and one on the corporate floor, the forty-second, right above *Vanity Fair*'s. She was doing the interviews on forty-two, to keep prying eyes away from the process. I was nervous. Anna makes me nervous. I think Anna makes everyone nervous. I was greeted by her stunning, statuesque assistant and led-in. Anna smiled and greeted me. She was friendly. She wasn't wearing her signature dark glasses. I sat down across from her at a little round table. She smiled.

"I liked your memo."

She liked my memo! She smiled!

It was a casual conversation. I mentioned that I'd had dinner with her future son-in-law, Francesco Carrozzini, an Italian photographer and director, in Los Angeles a month earlier.* Francesco was marrying Anna's daughter, Bee Shaffer, the next summer, and I figured it was a good name to drop. I had instantly connected with Francesco, whose mother, Franca Sozzani, had been the longtime editor of Italian *Vogue* and had died a year earlier. Francesco had a reputation as a playboy—I mean, he's handsome, charming fashion royalty and drove a Ferrari—but he was down-to-earth, funny, smart, and had an emotional intelligence well beyond his years. I told Anna how much I adored him and that I gave the union my blessing, which made her giggle.

I wish I could give some *Devil Wears Prada*–like anecdotes, to continue the Anna-as-monster narrative, but I don't have any. She was thoughtful and engaged. Anna was under a lot of pressure to make the right choice, as it would be part of her legacy. And the changes to the business, and generational and cultural shifts, must have been just as jarring for her as they were for the rest of us, maybe more so. We talked about the business, all the changes. I mentioned Brian McNally and my 44 days, the Agnès B suit, and my climb up the masthead of *Vanity Fair*.

But she and I both knew this wasn't going anywhere. This was perfunctory, just a courtesy. She had no intention of giving me the job. In fact, I think she had already made her mind up on who was going to replace Graydon.

Around the time that Farrow's piece landed, one of the names that had emerged in the *Vanity Fair* sweepstakes was Radhika Jones, a books editor at *The New York Times*. She wasn't as high-profile as some of the other candidates, had never run a magazine before, and in fact none of us had ever heard of her. She was pedigreed—Columbia, Harvard, *The Paris Review, Time* magazine—but unknown. David Remnick was also involved in the search along with Anna and had apparently gotten behind Radhika. "It was Remnick who championed her and brought

---

* I asked Francesco if he had any advice for when I met with Anna. "Just be yourself," he told me. Spoiler alert: That turned out to be terrible advice.

her to the attention of Anna Wintour," Keith Kelly wrote in the *Post*.

A month later, the competition to take over *Vanity Fair* came to an unofficial close. On November 11, *The New York Times* broke the story that a decision had been made. "In a dramatic changing of the guard, Radhika Jones, the editorial director of the books department at *The New York Times* and a former top editor at *Time* magazine, is expected to be named the next editor of *Vanity Fair*, according to two people with knowledge of the decision." Two days later, Condé Nast made it official.

I wasn't surprised or disappointed. I never expected to be seriously considered, and deep down I knew my days at *Vanity Fair* were numbered no matter who came in. In fact, out of all the names that had been thrown around, I was happy Radhika got it. She wasn't a big-name editor like the others, had started the process as a long shot, and I can't help but root for the underdog. I know the feeling.

Radhika was introduced to the staff a few days after the announcement. Everyone began to assemble in the wide hallway between Graydon's office and the planning room—which happened to be right outside my office—waiting for Anna and Bob Sauerberg to show up with their new quarry. As the trio arrived, they stood right in front of my office, almost in its doorway. I was trapped, awkwardly, stuck watching Anna and Bob introduce Radhika from behind, like I was a stagehand.

Radhika was clearly nervous, staring out at a sea of new faces, including that of her soon-to-be predecessor and his many loyal subjects. She was wearing a dark blue dress with an array of zippers, and matching blue tights with little cartoon foxes on them. This would lead to a scandal when *Women's Wear Daily* reported on her introduction to the *Vanity Fair* staff the next day, including an anonymous critique of her style from someone in our fashion department: " 'The outfit was *interesting*,' the staffer noted. According to the fashion editor . . . the incoming editor wore a navy shiftdress strewn with zippers, a garment deemed as 'iffy' at best. Jones' choice of hosiery proved most offensive, according to the editor. For the occasion, Jones had chosen a pair of tights— not in a neutral black or gray as is common in the halls of *Vogue*— but rather a pair covered with illustrated, cartoon foxes."

The internet jumped to Radhika's defense. She became a fox- tighted fashion martyr and cause célèbre. It did make us look petty to the outside world and probably didn't buy us any good- will with her, but I'll admit it was sort of refreshing to see some of that old-school bitchy Condé Nast snobbery and fashion sham- ing, which, frankly, the company's mythology, and Anna Wintour's career, had been built on. I thought back to the embarrassment of Adrian's pointing out the poor tailoring of my suit all those years ago when we first met, and how in the long run, it was con- structive, if for no other reason than it got me to care about how I presented myself.

Although many of us were looking forward to something dif- ferent after careers spent at *Vanity Fair*, and already on the hunt for new jobs, change is scary. Especially in an industry whose sands had shifted so dramatically under our feet. We weren't in demand. There weren't other magazine jobs to jump to anymore. But we all had mortgages to pay, kids to feed; some had college tuitions. Maybe Radhika would keep a few of us around?

Over the next month, we had a chance to meet with her one-on- one, to make an impression, make our case. She was soft-spoken and friendly. As I talked to her, I couldn't help but think how difficult it was going to be for her, having to follow and constantly be compared to her legendary predecessor. Graydon had gone through the same thing, and it took him a few years for things to fall into place. Would they give her that much time? She would have to tear it down and reassemble it in the midst of so many changes, like rebuilding a car while driving sixty miles an hour downhill. Her budget would be slashed; she'd have to do every- thing with less. And *Vanity Fair*, as constructed, wouldn't work for her. Graydon had kept it together through sheer force of will and personality, the man behind the curtain. But the culture was going through an unprecedented transition. Like Graydon before her, she would have to figure out *Vanity Fair* for a new era, a new age, a new moment. Fulfill that mandate and make it her own at a time when the business was going through such major upheaval. No easy task.

In the middle of December, after a tearful goodbye, Graydon walked out of his office and into the elevator for the last time, and headed off to the South of France. We closed the Hollywood Issue throughout January, like we had for so many years, though this time with Graydon four thousand miles away. Radhika sat in his old office, plotting a future that didn't include most of us. She stopped responding to our emails, there was no communication, there were no meetings. Once we shipped off the last pages of the issue, we had nothing to do but wait. We thought the end was imminent, but it took a few weeks.

There was something freeing about the thought of not coming in to an office every day, being chained to a desk. I could be out in the world, moving at my own speed and doing my own thing, like all those writers I'd worked with over the years. I'd never thought I'd end up shimmying up the slippery pole of corporate America in the first place, and while *Vanity Fair* and Condé Nast didn't feel corporate when I began, and neither was, there was no denying they had become exactly that over the previous decade. Maybe this was the fresh start I needed.

I put on a brave face for Aimee, Izzy, and Ollie, prepared them for my firing, spinning it as ultimately a good thing, even though I was understandably scared of the unknown fate that awaited me afterward. They bought it, and I think I did too in some way, convincing myself that I was scrappy and would figure out the next phase of my career somehow, and we'd be okay.

On Wednesday, February 14, and Thursday the fifteenth, it all went down. More than twenty of us were fired. It was almost everyone in that Last Supper photograph from the Oscar party a year earlier. The St. Valentine's Day massacre. One by one, editors were called down to Radhika's office.

I didn't get the ax on that first day. But I knew it was coming the next. I had a reservation at the Odeon at twelve-thirty for lunch with the longtime *Vanity Fair* columnist James Wolcott, who went all the way back to *Vanity Fair* in the eighties, under Tina Brown, and Lili Anolik, who had been writing for the magazine for a few years and was one of my writers. I hoped to get it over with in the morning so I could make it in time for lunch. As I got the call late that morning, I looked at my assistant, Louisa, and smiled.

"I'm up."

Dead man walking.

As I sat across from Radhika at Graydon's old desk, she read quietly from a prepared script under the watchful gaze of a dour Human Resources representative. My services were "no longer required." I was handed a folder by the woman from HR, who told me how to deal with my health insurance and pension. I received the standard six months' severance for longtime employees. A few people were asked to stay on for a month or two, but most of us were given until the end of the week to clean out our offices. A quarter of a century after walking into that place, I was no longer required, pitched onto the Gen X scrap heap. The never-ending party, that movable feast, came to an abrupt end.

As I walked back to my office, the looks on the faces of my colleagues must have been the same one I had all those years ago on that day Graydon had fired a handful of staff. Now the shoe was on the other foot.

I headed to the Odeon soon after. It was warm for February, still chilly but sunny, a beautiful winter afternoon in New York. I'd been having lunch at the Odeon at least a few times a week since the magazine moved into the World Trade Center, on most days attempting to save the liquid lunch from extinction, especially over the previous few months as I grappled with a cloudy future. I headed to my usual table, the second banquette in the back on the right, against the wall. Table 36. It has the best view of the room. Jim and Lili were already there, looking sullen. Jim's longtime editor, Aimée Bell, had been fired the day before. Our family was being ripped apart. As I slid into the booth, the wait-ress approached.

"Nice to see you. Glass of Sancerre?"

I smiled and nodded.

"That'd be great. Thanks."

Postscript

While I knew it was coming, I wasn't at all prepared for when I actually lost my job. A job I had spent more than half my life at. In an instant, everything changed. The routine of waking up, showering, walking the dog, taking the kids to school, grabbing a coffee and the paper, jumping on the subway, and heading in to the office—now abruptly ending halfway through the sentence. Now what?

I looked for a job, went on a few interviews. At forty-five, I wrote my first résumé. I had to google how to format it. Under SKILLS, I didn't know what to list. "Somewhat proficient in Microsoft Word 98" didn't seem like a major selling point. A pampered middle-aged magazine editor with no digital skills was not exactly in demand. You would think that staying at one place for your whole career would be a positive, make you appear loyal and a model employee, but it doesn't. It scares off prospective employers, as they wonder if you could actually function in the more rigid corporate culture that the media world had become. And they were probably right.

With my confidence shattered and what little savings I had beginning to dwindle, I didn't know where to turn. Adrian's words from that Cannes dinner more than a decade earlier began to haunt me. *This is all make-believe. A fantasy. This is not our lives. It's a job. Don't ever forget that.* Over the years, did I get too caught up in the fantasy? The fancy clothes, the expense account, the parties, the meals, the obsession with status, the transactional relationships. The world we created in the pages of *Vanity Fair* was make-believe—did I live in them for too long? Lose myself in it all? From the age of twenty-one, my identity was so tied into my job, and my career, and the magazine. Then suddenly it was gone. And what was left? A closet full of expensive suits and shoes and a crippling insecurity and paralyzing fear that I'd managed to mask for so many years. That key I was given in 1994 no longer worked, couldn't open any doors.

I began to isolate myself, withdraw, question my identity and my own life's narrative. I fell into a deep depression. Joy became elusive. I couldn't find answers. At one point I quit drinking for six months, and following in Adrian's footsteps, attended AA meetings daily, but sobriety and the twelve steps didn't seem to be the answer. The questions still lingered. Did those twenty-five years mean anything? Who was I? *What* was I? And what am I now?

Almost two and a half years after I was fired from *Vanity Fair*, as I was writing this book, alone in an abandoned, pandemic-stricken New York City, after months of lockdown—and no small amount of therapy—I began to reassess, no doubt helped by sitting down and telling my story. I could look back at my twenty-five years at *Vanity Fair*, all I learned, all that I accomplished, all the friendships, and all the fun, and realize how valuable it was to me. And while Adrian was right—your sense of self, and self-worth, should have nothing to do with your career—what he didn't understand was that *Vanity Fair* was more than a job and a career for me. I walked in there a confused and empty kid looking for answers. It ended up giving me confidence, hope, a voice, an education, a sense of purpose, lasting friendships, and everything else my life never had before I got there. It taught me everything I needed to know. Not about a vocation but about life.

I did live in a fantasy for twenty-five years, a gilded bubble, and it was great. Is that so bad? I was lucky. And who wants to live in the real world anyway? Everything I experienced over that quarter of a century was part of turning me into who I am, and in the end, that's all we're left with.

As the months passed, I began to venture out into the city as it slowly came back to life. I went to museums when they reopened and started running along the Hudson River every evening as the sun set. And I hate running. I noticed things that I hadn't in years, looking up and admiring details on buildings I'd walked by for decades but had stopped seeing. Memories began flooding back as I'd pass a restaurant, or bar, or building I once lived in, or walk through a park where something significant in my life had occurred. I felt a deep connection to New York for the first time in a long while, my middle-aged disdain for the city and my own aging transforming into gratitude.

Even though one chapter ends, our past is always part of us, even as we move on to the next one. Take from it what you can. Don't dwell on it or overthink it, but cherish it, learn from it, and move forward. The only things guaranteed in life are birth and death, and everything in between should be a celebration. Honor your past, live in the present, and don't be afraid of the future. And for fuck's sake, have fun along the way.

Acknowledgments

The seed of this book was planted almost a decade ago as a television pilot I wrote called *Disappearing Ink*, a comedy set at a monthly magazine with a character not unlike myself at the center of it. I sold it to one of the streaming services, but when it failed to get made, a number of people suggested I do it as a memoir. I thought that was a terrible idea. And it sounded like a lot of work.

Flash-forward a few years, after my time at *Vanity Fair* had come to an end, and I warmed to the idea, no doubt because that chapter of my life had come to a close. On a whim I called my friend Christy Fletcher, one of the best literary agents around, and asked her if she thought I had a book in me. Whether she was humoring me or just wanted to get me off the phone, she said yes, and I wrote a proposal with her guidance. So thank you, Christy, and your Fletcher & Company colleagues Melissa Chinchillo and Sarah Fuentes.

I owe a huge debt of gratitude to Gina Centrello, Kara Welsh, Jennifer Hershey, and Pamela Cannon at Random House and Ballantine for taking a chance on this book. Especially Pam, the poor soul who had to edit it. She was patient when she needed to be, tough when I needed her to be, and a brilliant collaborator and editor. This book wouldn't have happened without her. Sydney Shiffman, too, and Aja Pollock, for copyediting this beast.

To my *Vanity Fair* family, now scattered around the country and the world, we had a hell of a run: Graydon Carter, Anna Carter, Cynthia Carter, Chris Garrett, Jane Sarkin, Aimée Bell, David Kamp, Krista Smith, Matt Ullian, Sara Marks, Susan White, Jonathan Becker, Riza Cruz, Pat Kinder, Evgenia Peretz,

Anne Fulenwider, Punch Hutton, Reinaldo Herrera, Patricia Herrera, Cullen Murphy, Craig Offman, Elizabeth Saltzman, Andy Tepper, Dafydd Jones, Annabelle Dunne, Beth Kseniak, Matt Tyrnauer, Michael Carl, Doug Stumpf, James Wolcott, Heather Watts, Carol Blue Hitchens, Hamilton South, Liz Welch, Sara Switzer, Henry Alford, Wayne Lawson, David Harris, Greg Mastrianni, Chris Dixon, Lisa Berman, Bob Colacello, Richard Young, Larry Fink, Lisa Robinson, Henry Porter, Annie Holcroft, Bruce Handy, Michael Hogan, Ellen Kiell, Chris Mitchell, Edward Menicheschi, Wendy Stark, George Wayne, Anne McNally, Lisa Eisner, Lizzie Wolff, Jon Kelly, Nathan King, Jessica Diehl, Robert Walsh, Peter Devine, John Banta, David Friend, Jeremy Elkin, Julia Wachtel, Ari Bergen, Dana Matthews, Britt Hennemuth, Sharon Suh, Ron Beinner, Mark Seliger, Ann Schneider, Jeannie Rhodes, Dan Gilmore, Patrick McMullan, Mike Sacks, Justin Bishop, Ben Kalin, SunHee Grinnell, Lauren Tabach-Bank, Anthony Rotunno, David Foxley, Matt Trainor, Beth Altschull, Victoria Bonomo, Adam Nadler, Claire Howorth, Chris George, Rachel Williams, Kathryn McLeod, Andrea Cuttler, Josh Duboff, Caitlin Morley, Elien Becque, Rebecca Sacks, and Louisa Strauss.

To those we lost along the way: Adrian Gill, Christopher Hitchens, Dominick Dunne, Bernice Ellis, Darryl Brantley, John Falk, George Hodgman, William Prochnau, Hannah Thompson, Marjorie Williams, Tim Hetherington, Herb Ritts, Helmut Newton, David Halberstam, and Si Newhouse.

I spent my career working with writers, and I was always in awe of them. Many became, and remain, some of my dearest friends. I tried to be there for them when they needed me, back off when they didn't, but I'd never really been on the other side until now. Writing is hard, a lonely and solitary endeavor, and oftentimes terrifying. I learned so much from them and they made me look awfully good over the years, and I owe them a debt of gratitude, a few in particular: Adrian Gill, Nancy Jo Sales, Rich Cohen, Lili Anolik, Buzz Bissinger, Scott Anderson, Evan Wright, Charlie LeDuff, Suzanna Andrews, Bruce Feirstein, Alex Shoumatoff,

Max Potter, Ben Wallace, Steven Daly, Derek Blasberg, Jim Windolf, Howard Blum, Edward Helmore, Laura Holson, Craig Unger, John Connolly, and James Ellroy.

Graydon occasionally referred to me as the "fifth Carter child"—then the sixth, when his youngest daughter came along—and it meant so much to me to be included in such an extraordinary group: Ash, Max, Spike, Bronwen, and Isabella. It was like having younger siblings for the first time in my life, and watching them grow up and flourish was a gift.

A big thank-you to Paul Bettany, one of my favorite people in the world, for his support, friendship, and (mostly) picking up the phone when I called, and the Wine Gallery at 576 Sixth Avenue for when he didn't. Both have great attributes for best friends and liquor stores: They're open late, they deliver, and they're natural problem solvers.

Very special thanks to the Last Lights Gang (you know who you are), my ASP/Like Minded crew—Mark Kassen, Kaylin Minton, Chris Evans, Simone Lapidus, Sal Alvarez, Iliana Nikolic, and everyone up in Montreal—my *Harvest Moon* family, Jonathan Morr, Brian McNally, Julian Sancton, Benjamin Hardiman, Rebecca Chaiklin and Anthony Nicolich, Judd Apatow, James Fox, Jeremy Barber, Hunter Hill, Oberon Sinclair, Susie Lopez, Lisa Dwan, Nicola Formby, Marcia Miller, and Tina Chai, a veteran of Condé Nast in the nineties whose memory is much better than mine and was an invaluable resource.

Thank you to my actual family: Carol; Neal; Judy; my brothers, Nathaniel and Eric; and my sister and brother-in-law, Courtney and Paul, and their offspring, Jonas and Maia.

And finally, I wouldn't have been able to write this book, or do much of anything really, without the love and support of Oliver, Isabella, and especially Aimee, who somehow put up with my shit for so long.

About the Author

DANA BROWN is the former deputy editor of *Vanity Fair*, where he was responsible for hundreds of feature stories on topics ranging from geopolitics to business, pop culture to crime, and high-society scandal to the art world, a number of which were recognized by the National Magazine Awards. He has also written and developed films and television pilots for Miramax, Hulu, AMC, Imagine Entertainment, and CBS. He lives in New York City.

@mrdanabrown

About the Type

This book was set in Bodoni Book, a typeface named after Giambattista Bodoni (1740–1813), an Italian printer and type designer. It is not actually one of Bodoni's fonts but a modern version based on his style and manner and is distinguished by a marked contrast between the thick and thin elements of the letters.